Cross-Border Services and Choice of Law

Internationalrechtliche Studien

Beiträge zum Internationalen Privatrecht, zum Einheitsrecht und zur Rechtsvergleichung

Herausgegeben von Ulrich Magnus

Band 45

PETER LANG

Frankfurt am Main · Berlin · Bern · Bruxelles · New York · Oxford · Wien

Ulla Liukkunen

Cross-Border Services and Choice of Law

A Comparative Study of the European Approach

PETER LANG
Europäischer Verlag der Wissenschaften

Bibliographic Information published by the Deutsche Nationalbibliothek

The Deutsche Nationalbibliothek lists this publication in the Deutsche Nationalbibliografie; detailed bibliographic data is available in the internet at <http://www.d-nb.de>.

ISSN 0947-0395
ISBN-10: 3-631-55964-X
ISBN-13: 978-3-631-55964-2
US-ISBN 0-8204-8746-5

Printed in Germany 1 2 3 4 5 7

www.peterlang.de

Acknowledgments

Studies on cross-border service provision in Europe have often focused on EC law and various obstacles to trade. With globalisation, private international law issues are coming to the fore where they belong. When carrying out this 'intercontinental' study I have benefited immensely from the support of a large number of colleagues around the world, and only a few of my most precious contacts can be mentioned here. First of all, Professor *Ulrich Magnus*, University of Hamburg, has shared with me his deep knowledge of conflicts law and comparative law. He has given valuable advice and invited me to publish this book in his series of Peter Lang GmbH.

Many Scandinavian colleagues have not spared any effort in helping me with this research project. These scholars have, first and foremost, shown what seems to lie at the heart of Scandinavian cooperation: a constant commitment to kind and professional interaction. Also Professor *Larry E. Ribstein*, University of Illinois College of Law, should be mentioned here with special thanks.

The Max Planck Institute for Foreign Private and International Private Law in Hamburg has become a very important place for me – as it is for many other private international law and comparative law scholars. On the basis of my Ph.D. study I was very honoured to be invited by Director *Jürgen Basedow* to give a presentation on my research results at the first European PostDoc Conference organized by the Institute. The stimulating dialogue we had there on the theoretical aspects of private international law and comparative law was also much due to the Conference participants from various EU Member States, Turkey and Russia. The encouragement I received from Director *Basedow,* Director *Hopt* and Director *Zimmermann* has inspired me in this research project.

I am also indebted to Director *Pia Letto-Vanamo*, the Institute of International Economic Law (KATTI) in the University of Helsinki, for her support for this project. The funding from the Finnish Ministry of Labour has made the underlying research work possible. Director *Matti Salmenperä*, who is also a Member of the Governing Body of the ILO, has been generous in his support for the research project.

Once again no effort has been spared by my friends in the Finnish Ministry of Justice in putting valuable information at my disposal.

M.Sc. *Leena Huovinen*, the Library of the Faculty of Law in Helsinki University, has been capable of almost miracles when gathering research material for me from libraries around the world. *Christopher Goddard* has done the revision of the language; I would also like to thank *Reg Kennedy* and *Minna Hjort* and research assistant *Marja Paavilainen* for all their assistance during the various stages of my research project. The publishing procedure has been in the expert hands of *Ute Winkelkoetter*, Peter Lang GmbH.

The debt of gratitude I owe to my loved ones remains beyond words.

Porthania, Helsinki 25 September 2006

Ulla Liukkunen

Table of Contents

Table of Abbreviations

BAG	Bundesarbeitsgericht (the Federal Labour Court of Germany)
BAGE	Amtliche Sammlung der Entscheidungen des Bundesarbeitsgerichts (Collection of the Decisions of the Federal Labour Court in Germany)
CISG	United Nations Convention on Contracts for the International Sale of Goods
CMLR	Common Market Law Review
Colum. L. Rev.	Columbia Law Review
COM	Commission documents
Cornell Int'l L.J.	Cornell International Law Journal
DG	Directorate-General
DL	Defensor Legis
Duke J. of Comp. & Int'l L.	Duke Journal of Comparative and International Law
EC	European Communities
ECHR	European Convention of Human Rights
ECJ	Court of Justice of the European Communities
EEA	European Economic Area
EEC	European Economic Community
EGBGB	Einführungsgesetz zum Bürgerlichen Gesetzbuche
EU	European Union
EUI	European University Institute
FSU	Finnish Seamen's Union
ICLQ	International and Comparative Law Quarterly
ILO	International Labour Organisation

Ind. L. J.	Indiana Law Journal
IntJCompLLIR	The International Journal of Comparative Labour Law and Industrial Relations
IPRax	Praxis des internationalen Privat- und Verfahrensrechts
ITF	International Transport Workers' Federation
JHA	Justice and Home Affairs
JT	Juridisk Tidskrift
JUSTCIV	Judicial Cooperation in Civil Matters
JZ	Juristenzeitung
LM	Lakimies
LQR	The Law Quarterly Review
MJ	Maastricht Journal of European and Comparative Law
NGPIL	Nordic Group for Private International Law
NZG	Neue Zeitschrift für Gesellschaftsrecht
Ohio St. L. J.	Ohio State Law Journal
OJ	Official Journal of the European Communities
PECL	Principles of European Contract Law
Prop.	Regeringens proposition (Sweden)
RabelsZ	Rabels Zeitschrift für ausländisches und internationales Privatrecht
Rec. des Cours	Recueil des Cours de l'Académie de droit international de La Haye
RIW	Recht der Internationalen Wirtschaft
SAE	Sammlung arbeitsrechtlicher Entscheidungen (Collection of Labour Law Decisions)
SCE	European Cooperative Society

SE	European Company
SOU	Statens offentliga utredningar (Sweden)
SvJT	Svensk Juristtidning
TfR	Tidsskrift for Rettsvitenskap
U. Chi. L. Rev	University of Chicago Law Review
UNIDROIT	Institut International pour l'Unification du Droit Privé
Vol.	Volume(s)
ZEup	Zeitschrift für Europäisches Privatrecht
ZfA	Zeitschrift für Arbeitsrecht
ZVglRW	Zeitschrift für Vergleichende Rechtswissenschaft

Chapter I Introduction

1 The Basic Premises of the Study

In the past few years, as globalisation has proceeded faster than ever, cross-border trade in services has gained considerable momentum. In open markets, business contracts are increasingly made between parties from different legal systems. One of the most central issues for the contracting parties is how the law applicable to the contract is to be determined, because the substantive rules that apply differ from legal system to legal system.

The cornerstone of the law of obligations is the principle of freedom of contract. The freedom to select the applicable law corresponds to this principle in conflicts law. In an international sales contract, a choice of law clause is useful, and can also be found in several standard contract terms. The contracting parties are often recommended to make a choice of the applicable law because it is in the interests of both parties to clarify choice of law questions and remove the related uncertainties beforehand. This is also a question of minimising transaction costs because uncertainties in choice of law may cause considerable expense.

Sometimes the parties cannot agree on the applicable law, or they forget or ignore the question. Cases also arise where it is very difficult to determine whether the parties have made a tacit choice of law. In practice, if a choice of law clause is missing and the parties want to know whether they have made an enforceable contract, they first need to carry out a choice of law analysis to determine the applicable law. [1] This also means that the parties have to ascertain the applicable substantive legal rules, which may derive from a foreign legal system. To be able to do this, they may need to turn to a legal expert, which may make the process a costly one.

---

1 See Winship, "Private International Law and the U.N. Sales Convention", p. 532.

Even when a choice of law clause has been made, it does not always succeed in the way one expects. It may happen that according to the law chosen by the parties the choice is considered invalid. This is also possible when the parties have attempted to make a choice by following standard terms of contracts.[2] When making a choice of law clause, the parties should be aware of the relevant content of the law they are choosing. Furthermore, the parties should be fully aware of the limits of the freedom of contract, and also of the status of various multinational rule and principle collections, such as the Principles of European Contract Law (later: PECL) and the UNIDROIT Principles on International Commercial Contracts (later: UNIDROIT Principles), that are commonly used in international business contracts.

International sale contracts are often more multiform than national sale contracts. Several legal questions are involved in international contracts that cannot be answered without knowing conflicts rules in other respects as well as just with regard to determination of the applicable law. The rules that apply to the right to choose the court that will handle a possible dispute arising from the contract are vital with respect to the rights of the parties. Cross-border proceedings often give rise to problems that are unknown to wholly national proceedings. This explains why it is common to use arbitration clauses in international business contracts. For many practical reasons, such as the avoidance of delays and extra costs, arbitration is often considered preferable to court proceedings.[3] If the parties have not chosen the applicable law, then the arbitral tribunal determines it.

In private international law, the state to whose law an international legal relationship is subject is resolved on the basis of the conflicts rules. Efforts to unify conflicts rules aim at levelling the adverse effects that international trade suffers because of the lack of unanimity between states over which law should be applied to disputes. Work has long been under way to remove the underlying reason for inconsistencies, i.e. the differences between the substantive trade norms of

---

2 Magnus, "Action Plan for a European Contract Law. European Contract Law and CISG", p. 3.

3 See Ramberg, International Commercial Transactions, pp. 76–77 and Juenger, "The Recognition of Money Judgments", p. 300.

different countries.[4] In determining both the competent court and the choice of law, consideration often needs to be given not only to national legal sources but also to an increasing amount of unified or harmonised rules of international origin.

Traditionally, private international law has been considered to be pronounced in its formality. However, with legal developments during the past few decades, an approach that keeps to neutral conflicts rules has proved to be inadequate. In Europe, the rules of private international law have become a significant part of the EC legal order.[5] The coming into force of the Amsterdam Treaty has made Europe admit that the view according to which private international law is part of national law which governs international legal relations has become relative.[6]

From the standpoint of conflicts law, the present legal framework of cross-border service provision in Europe can be characterised as a complicated mixture of various rules governing contractual relationships of different private law areas. At first sight, though, the picture might appear quite clear: the basic approach in the field of international law of obligations is based on the rules in the Rome Convention[7], and in the future most likely on the forthcoming Rome I and Rome II Regulations. However, along with the creation of general conflicts rules on contractual, and soon also on non-contractual, obligations, specific conflicts rules have been set out for purposes of boosting European integration. These rules need to be paid heed to in order to fully understand the European legal framework of cross-border service provision from the standpoint of private international law.

A considerable part of the general law of obligations is typically non-mandatory by nature. In private law areas where mandatory rules also play a highly significant role, the conflicts law approach is differ-

---

4 See Jokela, Irtaimen kaupasta kansainvälisen yksityisoikeuden kannalta, pp. 43–44.

5 See Liukkunen, "Kansainvälinen yksityisoikeus ja Euroopan integraatio", p. 339.

6 See Jayme, "Internationales Privatrecht und postmoderne Kultur", p. 236.

7 Convention on the law applicable to contractual obligations opened for signature in Rome on 19 June 1980 (80/934/EEC).

entiated to an increasing extent from the main approach of the EC, which is based on unification work under Title IV EC Treaty. In activities falling within the scope of EC law on free movement, the main conflicts law approach is facing constant tensions caused by specific rules closely linked to advancing internal market objectives. Recently, developments have occurred where tendencies towards internal market-oriented legal instruments have even threatened the basic approach adopted in European private international law.

2 The growing Trade in Services

Trade in services has become the fastest-growing field of international trade. During the past few decades, it has grown significantly faster than goods trade. For companies, the effects of the growing field of trade in services are multiple. Among other things, the growth of the service sector involves an increasing amount of subcontracting. The internationalisation of service companies often takes place through foreign investments, mergers and acquisitions. In a global market, cross-border restructuring has become a constant phenomenon.[8]

The potential benefits of a harmonised EU service market are enormous because services dominate the EU economy.[9] The EU report on the impact of the proposed Services Directive emphasises the huge economic and employment-increasing effects of the service sector in Europe. Trade in services, service exports, and the internationalisation of service companies have significant growth potential. This is why development of the rules of cross-border service provision is considered to be essential for European competitiveness. According to the European Commission's estimate, freeing trade in services would boost the European service sector immensely.[10]

---

8 See, for example, Blanpain – Colucci, The Globalization of Labour Standards. The Soft Law Track, p.47.

9 Communication from the Commission to the Council, the European Parliament, the European Economic and Social committee and the Committee of the Regions: Second Implementation Report of the Internal Market Strategy (2003–2006). COM(2005) 11 final, p. 8.

10 Ibid.

Initially, the purpose of European economic integration was to create a strong internal market in which, for example, production could be transferred across borders to whatever area within the Union was the most competitive at any given time. The development towards free movement of production factors is typical of the global market as well. On a global scale, barriers for the movement of goods, services, and capital have been removed, which has enabled globally-operating companies to transfer their production to countries and continents where they can do business at the lowest possible cost.[11] Generally speaking, it can be said that the features that European integration has aimed at by means of creating the internal market have become characteristics of the global market.[12]

At the same time as the competition environment of companies has undergone drastic changes due to globalisation, the Union has enlarged. In 2004 the EU expanded significantly when ten new members joined it. This enlargement substantially increased the population of the EU and the size of the internal market. For companies, the expansion of the market was a positive development. However, great economic and social differences exist between the old and the new Member States which are not completely unproblematic in terms of the internal market. Several of the new Member States lack the normative framework that provided the legal orders of the old Member States with a basis for adopting the *acquis communautaire*.

The EU's eastward expansion meant that some types of threat associated with globalisation, such as transfers of production to low-cost countries, became intra-EU problems as well. The new Member States attract production because they can provide faster growth and lower production costs. It has been estimated that the eastward expansion will make EU countries compete increasingly for companies and their locations. The new Member States have implemented several changes that have accelerated productivity

---

11 See also Held – McGrew – Goldblatt – Perraton, Global Transformations. Politics, Economics and Culture, p. 260.

12 See Liukkunen, Globalisaatio, EU ja henkilöstön osallistuminen. Tutkimus globalisaatiojuridiikasta ja eurooppaoikeudesta erityisesti rajat ylittävissä yritysjärjestelyissä, p. 37.

growth and improved the standard of living. According to some economists, however, the differences between the GNP per capita in the old and the new Member States will take a long time to level out.

It is not unproblematic, at least not yet, to complete the internal market of the Union in its current size.[13] This is illustrated, for example, by the fact that several old Member States introduced a transitional period for the free movement of labour from the new eastern Member States. The transitional periods have been of different lengths, so countries adopt free movement of labour at different times. To some extent, this is also the case with services, because Austria and Germany even adopted a transitional period for the posting of workers under the free movement of services.

The transitional periods can be seen as a concrete demonstration that when it expanded for the fifth time, the EU gained a new type of member: not welcomed without reservations. Many hasty estimates of the high amount of cross-border movement of workers have proved wrong. Although the movement of labour has somewhat increased within the EU, significant growth has not yet been seen. This has been explained in geographical, historical, and cultural terms.

3 Cross-Border Services in the Context of EC Law

In the global economy, services abound. However, a precise definition of the term 'service' cannot be given. Services are often seen as a non-material counterpart to goods. Still, it is increasingly often emphasised that the supply of various goods necessarily requires service inputs and that, similarly, contracts for the sale of goods may include provision of services.

---

13 It has been estimated that so far the expansion of the internal market to the ten new Member States has gone relatively smoothly. See Communication from the Commission to the Council, the European Parliament, the European Economic and Social committee and the Committee of the Regions: Second Implementation Report of the Internal Market Strategy (2003–2006). COM(2005) 11 final, p. 10.

The EC law concept of service is extensive, and has been constantly extended by the ECJ.[14] According to the Court, the concept covers any economic activity normally provided for remuneration, without the service having to be paid for by those benefiting from it and regardless of the financing arrangements for the remuneration received in return, by way of consideration.[15] Thus, any service whereby a provider participates in the economy, irrespective of the provider's legal status or aims, or the field of action concerned, constitutes a service.

In the EU, the spotlight is on freedom of services and the related concept of service. In a conflicts law study, we need to go further. A service-provider seeking to enter a cross-border market, whether through establishment or cross-border service provision, often faces questions of choice of law that relate to contractual obligations. Contractual obligations are still governed by the conflicts rules of the Rome Convention, and *business to business* contracts fall within the scope of Articles 3 and 4 of the Convention. Since the Convention is not part of EC law, the application of the EC law concept of service does not extend to it. However, many EC law instruments which contain specific conflicts rules belong to the sphere of the particular EC law concept of the provision of services.

Hindrances to cross-border trade within the EU hamper the economic growth of the Union. A common view is that legal uncertainty over-complicates cross-border trade in services within the EU.[16] In recent times, emphasis has been increasingly placed on creating enough flexibility for business operations by tackling legal barriers to

---

14 For recent development, see, for example, Case C-384/93, Alpine Investments BV v. Minister van Financiën, [1995] ECR I-1141; Case C-36/02, Omega Spielhallen- und Automatenaufstellungs-GmbH v. Oberbürgermeisterin der Bundesstadt Bonn, [2004] ECR I-9609 and Case C-215/01, Bruno Schnitzer, [2003] ECR I-14847.

15 See, for example, Case C-263/86, Belgium v. René Humbel and Marie Thérèse Humbel née Edel, [1988] ECR I-5365.

16 Communication from the Commission to the Council, the European Parliament, the European Economic and Social committee and the Committee of the Regions: Second Implementation Report of the Internal Market Strategy (2003–2006). COM(2005) 11 final, p. 8.

service provision. The four economic freedoms constitute a broad legal framework for cross-border service provision within the Union. It is not only the rules of freedom to provide services that form a highly relevant part of the legal environment of cross-border trade in services, but also the rules of freedom of establishment.

However, harmonisation of Member State national legislation governs only a limited area of the legal framework for cross-border service provision. The fragmentary nature of the harmonised parts of private law has received much criticism, as has the reluctance to admit that international commercial contract practice has followed its own path. To a large extent, international commercial law is self-regulatory. Self-regulatory rules allow the contracting parties themselves to resolve any problems concerning national legal diversity that may arise, without the need to pay heed to public policy concerns. The interaction between trade usages, contractual practice, and rules of various organisations, as well as arbitral practice brings a degree of uniformity to international contract adjudication.[17] It is usual that international commercial contracts include an arbitration clause, which ensures that various trade practices are followed in the case of a dispute. However, from the standpoint of conflicts law, it should be noted that these practices are not comprehensive enough to replace the applicable law of a state.

Legal rules affecting cross-border services constitute a large and complex entity. Because international harmonisation of these rules has been slow, choice of law rules and the efforts to unify them continue to be of central importance. From the standpoint of business parties, one of the fields where legal uncertainty needs to be removed to the largest possible extent is the conflict of laws. It has been claimed that unnecessary uncertainty exists about the outcome of choice of law in the field of the law of obligations in Europe, since the main legal source of law applicable to contractual obligations, the Rome Convention, is still in the form of an international convention. It is well

---

[17] In more detail see, for example, López Rodríguez, Lex Mercatoria and Harmonisation of Contract Law in the EU, p. 84.

known that conflicts rules that originate from an international convention may be applied in different ways in different countries.[18]

From the standpoint of regional unification of conflicts rules, until the entry into force of the Treaty of Amsterdam in 1999, judicial co-operation in civil matters remained completely a matter for governmental co-operation between Member States. Even at present, the unification work based on the EC Treaty is incomplete since the Articles of Title IV EC Treaty do not apply to all Member States.[19]

In the field of choice of law, the most significant European outcome of governmental co-operation has been the Rome Convention, which was signed in 1980 and came into force internationally eleven years later. It has often been claimed that the conflicts rules on contractual obligations in the Convention do not in all respects fit today's requirements. During recent decades, the environment in which businesses operate has gone through significant changes. It is claimed that new types of transactions require new kinds of legal solutions from the EU if the Union wants to maintain its competitiveness under conditions of hardening global competition. In this respect, one of the key questions is often said to be whether business parties should be allowed to make a choice of international principles or rules applicable to their contract instead of the law of a state.

One of the well known problems with the Rome Convention has been that it was only in August 2004 that the ECJ finally received the jurisdiction to interpret it. By virtue of the Protocols of the Convention, this competence is a limited one.[20] Hence, the Court cannot ensure uniform interpretation of the Convention. Another matter to be

---

18 See Jänterä-Jareborg, "Foreign Law in National Courts – A Comparative Perspective", p. 253. She remarks that the order of priority between different rules depends on whether the state follows a monistic or dualistic tradition concerning the effects of an international convention.

19 Title IV EC Treaty does not apply to Denmark by virtue of the Protocol concerning it. Nor does it apply to the United Kingdom or Ireland, unless these countries exercise their option of joining the initiative (opt-in clause) on the conditions set out in the Protocol annexed to the Treaty.

20 The two Protocols on interpretation of the Convention by the ECJ were signed in 1988.

noted is that the ten Member States that joined the Union in 2004 were not able to implement the Convention immediately. By virtue of their accession to the Union, they committed themselves to adhering to the Convention and the Protocols regarding its interpretation by the ECJ. The Member States signed the accession Convention in April 2005. So the conflicts rules on contractual obligations are not yet uniform in the enlarged EU.

A third matter that has prompted discussion is that the Convention has been criticised for lack of legal certainty because it does not contain rules on some questions that are particularly relevant for application of foreign law. *Maarit Jänterä-Jareborg* has pointed out that Article 1(2) of the Convention has been interpreted to mean that pleading and proof of foreign law are excluded from the scope of the Convention. She argues that the Convention fails to achieve its main aim, which was to ensure that the same solution on the applicable law will be reached regardless of the Member State where the proceedings take place.[21] Therefore, in order to promote true European integration, she argues for the conflicts rules to be supplemented with necessary procedural rules.[22]

Fourthly, the question of characterisation deserves attention. In conflicts law, problems of characterisation are typical and their minimalisation is considered difficult but desirable.[23] Legal literature has presented serious doubts as to whether the question of characterisa-

---

21 See Jänterä-Jareborg, "Foreign Law in National Courts – A Comparative Perspective", p. 369, where she writes that the *van Schijndel* case (C-430/93) of the ECJ confirms the decisive role of national procedural rules in the Member States.

22 See ibid., p. 376. It should also be noted that forum shoppers also shop for procedural advantages. *Friedrich K. Juenger* has presented an illustrative example of this: victims injured in Europe by defective products are in general advised to sue in the United States because they can more easily afford to litigate there. This is enabled by the fact that American attorneys are prepared to take personal injury cases on a contingency fee basis. Moreover, the amounts that can be recovered in the States greatly exceed those that are awarded in Europe. See Juenger, "The Problem with Private International Law", p. 294.

23 See, for example, O'Hara – Ribstein, "From Politics to Efficiency in Choice of Law, p. 1189-1190.

tion, which lies at the heart of conflicts law, could be solved by means of legislation.[24] The European approach reflects this view. The Rome Convention does not address the question of characterisation, nor do the Rome I or Rome II Proposals. When attempting to achieve decisional harmony among the EU Member States, approaches to characterisation should become as unified as possible. This provides a future challenge for an EU of 25 Member States. So far, characterisation by the *lex fori* has often gained support in Europe, for example by *Kahnd-Freund*'s famous model of characterisation by 'an enlightened *lex fori*'.[25] However, when discussing the question in the framework of the Rome Convention, many have also supported characterisation by the *lex causae* or a third approach, where characterising would occur by means of the method of autonomous and comparative interpretation.[26] The question whether it is desirable that each forum applies its own characterisation rules will need to be tackled. The uniform interpretation of forthcoming Rome I and Rome II, being part of EC law, in this respect is likely to be advanced by the ECJ. It is also to be expected that the Court will build its interpretations on the guidance which derives from the case law concerning the Brussels Convention[27], followed by the Brussels I Regulation[28].

In some significant areas that affect cross-border service provision, such as international company law, conflicts rules are still mostly in national hands in Europe. However, EC law has increasingly diminished the margin of discretion left to Member States when formulating these rules. In recent years, new cross-border rules have been created in the field of EC company law to facilitate freedom of establishment and development of the internal market. At the same time, many EU Member States have reformed their national company law,

---

24 See Hernández-Breton, "An attempt to regulate the problem of 'characterisation' in private international law", p. 338.

25 See Kahn-Freund, General problems of private international law, p. 227 ff.

26 See, for example, Magnus in Staudingers Kommentar, EGBGB 30, para. 35.

27 Convention on Jurisdiction and the Enforcement of Judgments in Civil and Commercial Matters (the Brussels Convention) concluded in Brussels on 27 September 1968, OJ L 299, 31/12/1972, p. 32.

28 Council Regulation (EC) No 44/2001 on jurisdiction and the recognition and enforcement of judgements in civil and commercial matters.

not least because they want to attract companies and investments from other countries.

Regulatory competition between Member States has been encouraged by the development of EC law. Recent company law directives have created more flexibility in cross-border restructuring. Moreover, by extending the scope of freedom of establishment, the ECJ has weighed in on the competitiveness of European companies. From the viewpoint of private international law, the case law of the Court starting from the 1990s has *de facto* considerably influenced Member State conflicts rules in international company law. At the same time, the regulatory approach in the EU has been increasingly influenced by the fact that the legal rules set out by EC law should not create competitive disadvantages for EU companies when compared with non-EU companies.

For a long time now, the Member States have faced increasing pressure to harmonise rules on cross-border trade in services. This is one of the reasons why the proposed Services Directive has been considered the core legislative project of the EU single market and for the Internal Market Strategy for Services.[29] The need for such a legal instrument has been emphasised by many as enabling the opportunities provided by the service sector to be better taken advantage of and at

---

29 The aim of the Internal Market Strategy for Services set out by the Commission is to enable services to move across national borders within the European Union just as easily as within a single Member State. The strategy is based on a horizontal approach across all economic sectors involving services and on a two-stage process. The first stage concerns identifying the difficulties which hamper the smooth functioning of the internal market. The second concerns developing appropriate solutions to the problems identified. See Communication from the Commission to the Council and the European Parliament: An Internal Market Strategy for Services. COM(2000) 888 final. In July 2002, the Commission presented a report on 'The State of the Internal Market for Services', thus, completing the first phase in the strategy. See Report from the Commission to the Council and the European Parliament on the State of Internal Market for Services presented under the first stage of the Internal Market Strategy for Services, COM(2002) 441 final. In 2004, a Proposal for a Services Directive was adopted. See Proposal for a Directive of the European Parliament and of the Council on services in the internal market. COM(2004) 2 final/3.

the same time facilitating the realisation of freedom of establishment.[30] The original Proposal for the Services Directive, adopted by the Commission in 2004, had wide scope and extensive effects. The most controversial element of the Proposal was the country of origin principle. This principle emerged in EC secondary legislation some years ago and has proved to be particularly complex from the viewpoint of choice of law.

From the standpoint of social protection, one of the most debated issues concerning the original Services Directive Proposal was the status of employees in cross-border service provision. The importance of the distinction in EC law between migrant workers and posted workers should here be underlined. Free movement of workers is laid down in Article 39 EC Treaty, whereas free movement of services is laid down in its Article 49.

For example, when an Estonian cleaning or building company sells services to Finland, the employees doing the cleaning or building work in Finland are temporarily posted to the country but do not enter the Finnish labour market in the sense of the EU rules on free movement of labour. They remain in the service of the Estonian company and return to the home state after the posting period. In such a situation, the provisions of the Directive on Posted Workers are crucial for the protection of posted employees, as they ensure observance of the mandatory rules of the state of destination of the services, i.e. the host state.[31] The Directive does not interfere with the substantive content of EEA Member State labour legislation. Instead, it defines the minimum terms of employment, which are determined on the basis of the law of the temporary Member State of employment.[32] Besides its aim to pre-

---

30 Communication from the Commission to the Council, the European Parliament, the European Economic and Social Committee and the Committee of the Regions: Report on the implementation of the Internal Market Strategy (2003–2006). COM(2004) 22 final, p. 8.

31 Directive 96/71/EC of the European Parliament and of the Council concerning the posting of workers in the framework of the provision of services.

32 The hard core list of Article 3(1) of the Directive governs (a) maximum work periods and minimum rest periods; (b) minimum paid annual holidays; (c) the minimum rates of pay, including overtime rates; this point does not apply to supplementary occupational retirement pension schemes; (d) the conditions

vent social dumping, the EC legislation on free movement of services strives towards a single market by trying to create a level playing field for all companies and by promoting free competition.

Growth of the trade in services has led to an increase in the number of posted workers but a trend is also growing to transfer service production from industrialised countries to countries with cheaper labour. In general, mergers and acquisitions have become characteristics of economic integration and globalisation. For cross-border restructuring, rules on international company law need to be flexible enough to fit the fast-changing needs of companies. At the same time, social aspects of restructuring deserve attention. It is sometimes claimed that the social consequences of globalisation have been offloaded onto national states. In order to cure social problems, employee protection has been improved in EC law through sets of rules that assure information and consultation of employees in cross-border restructuring processes. This has meant intertwining company law and labour law by means of conflicts law.

Finally, when facilitating the cross-border trade in services it is important to take into account the role of legal rules that affect the decision-making of the demand side. Service users can nowadays consume services in other countries more easily than before. Consumer confidence is increased by conflicts rules that provide predictability and legal certainty about the applicable law. In the EU, this has meant a regulatory approach that places emphasis on ensuring application of mandatory rules in EC legislation that protect consumers. It has been underlined that consumers, as weaker parties, should be better protected in a consumer trade environment that has become global because of e-commerce. The growing field of e-commerce has also received increasing attention in terms of choice of law, as it has its own characteristic features. These developments have led to specific EC

---

of hiring-out of workers, in particular the supply of workers by temporary employment undertakings; (e) health, safety and hygiene at work; (f) protective measures with regard to the terms and conditions of employment of pregnant women or women who have recently given birth, of children and of young people; and (g) equality of treatment between men and women and other provisions on non-discrimination.

legislation, which has proved especially complicated for private international law.

4 Globalisation, Regionalisation, and the Conflicts Law Approach

The international norm-setting regime has undergone far-reaching changes due to globalisation. International business law, international company law and international labour law in its broad sense share the common feature that actors other than the traditional ones of international or national law are increasingly taking part in their norm-setting. One of the reasons for this is that traditional legislation is inadequate to guide societal processes.[33]

Globalisation has been gaining pace alongside regional regulatory activity and led to the emergence of new rule-making and legislative areas and thereby several scattered norm-setting processes. Many private norm-setting processes have developed independently of national legislators, for example, through business contracts, arbitration, and several forms of *lex mercatoria*. Recently, the normative development has led to entirely new areas of private rule-making whose development is out of reach of national legislators. It is ever-frequently emphasised that a strict distinction can no longer be made between private and general or national and international law.

The role of law has changed with the growing importance of *soft law*. The law is increasingly often expected to create an ethical discourse, which leads to a large amount of various sets of norms.[34] Arguably, the abundant use of various norm sources, in the shape of sets of both binding and non-binding rules, has become an important way of seeking a counterforce to the increasing dynamics of the global economy. From the viewpoint of global law, sets of binding rules and non-binding rules can no longer be categorically separated from each

33 See Wilhelmsson, "Vastuu ja yksityisoikeuden systeemi", p. 1194.
34 See ibid., p. 1193.

other if the idea is accepted that the *de facto* applicability of various sets of norms is crucial to their importance.[35]

It is well known that attempts to promote international trade liberalisation are linked to new demands concerning the manner in which cross-border legal rules should be drafted. These demands often arise from the need to pay more attention to the activities of multinational enterprises and the fact that these activities do not follow the borders of any regional integration. In addition to economic integration, the market operations of multinational enterprises bring national and local economies together in global and regional production networks.[36] In the current world economy, no single economic centre could dictate the rules of world trade. Multinational enterprises cover all sectors of world trade and reorganise economic activities within and between the most important economic zones of the world.[37] Hence, for their part, the activities of multinational enterprises also shape the EU legal environment into one that is expected to promote more flexibility in cross-border business operations.

Regionalisation of conflicts rules has become one of the characteristics of private international law. However, although we have been witnessing this increasingly in conflicts law in Europe, it has to be remembered that economic operations have not regionalised at the expense of globalisation. On the contrary, regionalisation has enabled globalisation and even encouraged it, because regionalisation is nowadays mostly open and emphasises the liberalisation of national economies instead of a protected market.[38] For regional legislators, this means that regional rules should more often be considered in a global framework.

---

35 Liukkunen, Globalisaatio, EU ja henkilöstön osallistuminen. Tutkimus globalisaatiojuridiikasta ja eurooppaoikeudesta erityisesti rajat ylittävissä yritysjärjestelyissä, p. 340.

36 See Held – McGrew, Globalization/Anti-Globalization, p. 50.

37 See ibid., p. 53. Multinational enterprises are already responsible for approximately 10 per cent of total worldwide production and approximately one third of world exports. The top international producers comprise about 61,000 multinational enterprises with over 900,000 foreign subsidiaries. See Finland's Trade Policy Programme.

38 See Held – McGrew, Globalization/Anti-Globalization, pp. 50–51.

It can be said that global competition requires constant consideration from multinational enterprises as to whether to relocate their operations. Ongoing economic development has proved to be a true challenge not only for regional but also for national legislators, since countries now need to attract companies and investments more actively. The global nature of markets also provides a challenge for regional rule-makers such as the EC: rules designated for the single market should promote the competitiveness of companies on a global scale.

It is clear that when developing EC conflicts rules the need is increasing to pay heed to cases that have connections to both EU and non-EU States. European courts face increasingly frequent conflicts cases where a legal relationship has connections to both EU and non-EU States. In such areas of private law that are characterised by a considerable amount of mandatory regulation, the EC has been focusing on ensuring the application of mandatory EC rules, even if the case in question has connections to both EU and non-EU States.

Increasing regionalisation with an emphasis on openness beyond regional borders also provides a challenge for comparative law. In the present era of globalisation, an urgent need exists to explore the dynamic Asian legal systems instead of focusing only on the western perspective. However, for western comparativists, even the borders between Europe and the US sometimes seem too difficult to cross.

In the ongoing debate within the field of comparative law, the basic question of how deeply anyone can really understand a foreign law arises more frequently. A strong emphasis on the diversity of legal systems can be recognised in statements that have weighed whether it is actually possible to gain a profound knowledge of a culturally different foreign law. Moreover, fresh demand has arisen for a more open attitude towards culturally different laws. When emphasising the cultural dimension of law, mainstream comparative law also calls for an approach where differences are allowed to emerge and are not instinctively explained away.[39]

---

39 See also Frankenberg, "Critical Comparisons: Re-thinking Comparative Law", pp. 442–443.

5 On the Discourse concerning Method of Legal Comparison

Fields of research such as law, which study human beings as intentional subjects, can be characterised as fields that understand the phenomena at hand, while natural sciences explain them. I have stressed elsewhere that this distinction, which is commonly used in the theory of science, can be seen to relate to the increasingly frequent demand nowadays that legal comparativists should use the method of understanding.[40] There are, however, views in the contemporary theory of comparative law that may give cause for criticism. The following analyses certain fundamental methodological questions, specifically in the light of theories by *Örücü* and *Kennedy*.

A basic question which any researcher who is serious about legal comparison has to face is what method to use in comparative studies. Despite the abundance of discussion, the discourse on the method of comparative research is plagued by a certain lack of structure. As *Örücü* also points out, this is partly explained by the fact that comparison itself is a method, so that a single standard method which all scholars should follow cannot be suggested. Like *Örücü,* among others, *Husa* stresses that current comparative law lacks such a methodological paradigm, and so it should be. One of the central methodological points of departure is to take into account the diversity of normative systems.

Mainstream comparative law has often been regarded as methodologically modest and pragmatic. Comparativists are cautious in their interpretations and explanations. *Örücü* suggests that this might be because a methodology that would fully explain legal phenomena is unattainable by lawyers.[41] In her view, in order to be genuine, comparative research should extend beyond the boundaries and limits of traditional comparative methodology. The subject of genuine comparison would be law in action and law in interaction with social and

---

40 This methodological distinction has been analysed in my forthcoming Article "The Method of Understanding and Internal Viewpoint – on the Interface between Comparative Law and Private International Law" (to be published in ZVglRW 2/2007).

41 Örücü, The Enigma of Comparative Law. Variations on a Theme for the Twenty-First Century, p. 59.

cultural systems. *Örücü* seems to present ambitious demands for real comparative law. In her classification, traditional comparative law is a secondary and far more modest alternative, which is normative, institutional, and positivistic (called 'variation II').[42]

In mainstream comparative law, the comparativist does not apply, as *Örücü* presents it, the method of explaining: start from hypotheses, formulate theories and test them and make inductive generalisations (called 'variation I'). It is worth noticing that *Örücü* seems to present here the 'monistic' scientific method as a model of legal comparison.[43] In this respect, the methodology differs from that often suggested in the theory of science according to which the methods of natural sciences and humanities should be kept separate.

However, an important starting point for locating the method of legal thinking is being committed to the view that law, as a field of research, belongs to the humanities, and not to those sciences which explain phenomena instead of interpreting and understanding them.[44] Epistemologically, the use of the method of understanding in the study of law means that the subject is examined from an internal viewpoint. It is clear that much research in sociology and anthropology is also based on the method of understanding.

Örücü is somewhat severe on comparativists who wonder how much they should know of a foreign law in order to engage in legal comparison. She stresses that legal comparison requires a wide historical, political, socio-economic and psychological context. [45] *Husa* has, in fact, encapsulated *Örücü*'s core message to be an appeal for

---

42 Ibid., p. 56.

43 "Whether a comparative lawyer starts with hypotheses or with facts, when she goes to explanation, as she must do if the intention is to use *the universal method of science* and extract ultimate legal knowledge, she must make sure that the hypotheses are consistent with the facts", Örücü writes in The Enigma of Comparative Law. Variations on a Theme for the Twenty-First Century, on p. 54. [My emphasis.]

44 See further my forthcoming Article "The Method of Understanding and Internal Viewpoint – on the Interface between Comparative Law and Private International Law" (to be published in ZVglRW 2/2007).

45 Örücü, The Enigma of Comparative Law. Variations on a Theme for the Twenty-First Century, p. 43.

methodologically and theoretically pluralistic and ambitious comparative law. According to *Husa*, the science of law concentrates too much on the legal system in the analysis of its subject, while legal sociology focuses on the external elements of law, and legal history, obviously, on the past. In his view, comparative law should operate somewhere in between these extremes.[46] In this respect, both authors seek support for legal comparison from beyond the methods of the science of law.

It should be stressed that legal comparison has its special methodological characteristics.[47] Comparison requires the comparativist to go beyond the surface level of law. Historical, cultural, and social differences are reflected in legal thinking, legal practice, and the application of law, even within one wide cultural sphere, such as continental European law. The terms, concepts and presuppositions on which systems are based vary from legal order to legal order. A comparativist is lost without knowledge of the cultural context.[48] When this cultural context is being established, the method of understanding is crucial.[49]

Comparativists would also benefit from viewing comparison as a process, during which they have to make several methodological choices and also justify them. On a general level, this can be illustrated by *Kennedy*'s rough model on the phases of legal comparison.

---

46 Husa, "Melodies on Comparative Law", p. 173. See also Husa, "Emancipation or Deprivation for the European Legal Mind? The Contribution of the Legal Traditions Approach", where the problem of an exclusive legal mind is addressed.

47 See also de Cruz, Comparative Law in a Changing World, p. 29.

48 Aarnio, "Oikeussäädöksiä tulkitsemassa – Interpreting Statutes. A Comparative Study", p. 253. See also *Legrand*'s view on interpretation as a cultural product in "The Impossibility of 'Legal Transplants'", p. 115.

49 An example of a field of law where contextual understanding is necessitated is labour law. Institutional arrangements on which this field of law rests depend much on the historical, political, cultural and economic context of countries and regions. See Weiss, "The Future of Workers' Participation in the EU", pp. 229–230. See also Liukkunen, Globalisaatio, EU ja henkilöstön osallistuminen. Tutkimus globalisaatiojuridiikasta ja eurooppaoikeudesta erityisesti rajat ylittävissä yritysjärjestelyissä, where a contextual understanding of national employee involvement models has been emphasised, and integrated into an analysis of the development of EC labour law.

First, a legal phenomenon is selected from one legal system, and might be compared with another legal phenomenon from another system. The phenomenon can be a rule, an institution, a practice, an approach, or some other item. All comparativists have their own preferences on how to choose phenomena and legal systems for comparison. Comparativists may choose to apply a limited, wide, formal or contextual definition. If in the course of the comparison a similarity between legal phenomena is identified, the comparativist determines whether it is a legal transplant or whether a system has otherwise affected the way a phenomenon is represented in another system.[50] Additionally, at this stage, the choice of the level of formality or contextuality affects the analysis. Generally speaking, similarities and differences can be understood by means of either technical or cultural factors. Legal phenomena that seem to be the same or similar may actually be fundamentally different when they are placed into appropriate context. The final phase that can be applied after description and analysis is evaluation.[51]

As *Legrand* stresses, in order for a legal phenomenon to be understood it must be placed in the context of the legal mentality and culture of each system. The evaluation phase as outlined by *Kennedy* is significant in the process of comparison because it enables a comprehensive analysis of the development of legal thinking in different systems and its effects on the differences in legal phenomena. Therefore, this present study aims at a comparison that pays particular attention to the differences in legal thinking of conflicts rules in the US and Europe.[52] In order to analyse legal culture, doctrinal history

---

50 See Kennedy, "The Method and Politics of Comparative Law", pp. 139–152. See also Legrand's critical view on legal transplants in "The Impossibility of 'Legal Transplants'".

51 See Kennedy, "The Method and Politics of Comparative Law", pp. 139–152.

52 As an example of comprehensive international study which analysed legal argumentation instead of rules and institutions, reference can be made to the 'Interpreting Statutes' study, which spanned continents. The main interest of the researchers was on how national higher courts interpret statutes. The courts in certain countries were asked a pattern of questions concerning interpreting statutes. From a comparative standpoint, the authors of the study were asked to consider, on the basis of the large comparative material,

also needs to be taken as an essential part of the development of legal thinking.[53] Legal development has necessitated a comparison that extends beyond the boundaries of Europe – and European legal thinking.

Lately, comparative law scholars have actually been discussing whether the legal systems of the world were approaching each other. Deepening European integration has maintained and accelerated this debate in Europe.[54] The harmonisation efforts of contract law have offered opportunities for comparative research seeking common approaches and similarities. One of the goals of legal comparison has been to promote integration in the field of contract law. However, comparativists have from time to time gone out of their way to emphasise the neutrality of their research and that no similarities are sought or assumed to exist. For example, the EU's eastern expansion has been said to have produced a clear division into two. In legal comparison, the old Member States are often paralleled by using the term 'cohesion', whereas when less developed countries are discussed, the verb 'to catch up' is easily used. This interpretative framework makes Denmark and Greece, for example, seem more similar than

---

whether there were striking or salient similarities and differences or variations between the interpretational approaches of legal systems. Moreover, in the light of salient similarities and differences, the authors were asked what explanatory, justificatory, or critical comment they would offer on the interpretational approach of their own legal system. It was emphasised that there must be certainty that genuine variations between systems had been found before turning to explanations for, or justifications for, or criticism of these variations. See in more detail MacCormick – Summers, Interpreting Statutes. A Comparative Study, p. 273.

53 *Zimmermann* has emphasised the necessity of combining a comparative law and legal history approach. He remarks that a combination of comparative and historical scholarship seems to be the most appropriate way of grasping the relationship between common law and civil law and also advancing mutual understanding and harmonisation. See Zimmermann, "Savigny's Legacy. Legal History, Comparative Law and the Emergence of a European Legal Science", p. 602.

54 See Legrand, "Uniformity, Legal Traditions and Law's Limits", pp. 318–322 and "European Legal Systems are not Converging".

they actually are, with Austria and Slovenia correspondingly more different.[55]

The progress of European integration has brought more of the brand of comparative research that aims at evaluating the legal systems of Member States in light of the harmonised set of EC norms. Generally speaking, there are two approaches to conducting this research: firstly, on the surface level, keeping to analysing the norms of different national legal systems, and secondly, by placing norm analysis in the context of legal culture. The latter approach is important in that it shows how far the harmonisation of the laws of EU Member States has in fact proceeded by means of EC directives. Such a comparison may, for example, address the transposition of directives in different Member States. It may show what kind of consequences might arise when EC legislation places itself in conflict with the legal culture and the basic structures of the legal systems of Member States. However, if comparison is conducted only on the surface level of national systems, by keeping to a set of statutory transposition norms, then possible conflicts and tensions will not emerge.

A search for similarities between legal orders has traditionally been emphasised in European comparative law. However, globalisation has lowered the boundaries between states and regions, uncovering the face of another kind of legal science. *Jayme* has stressed that an important point supporting pluralism in the method of legal comparison is that societies have become multicultural.[56] A multicultural society sees diversity – not similarity – of legal rules as the starting point. No one system is better than another, because all systems reflect their own cultural identity. *Legrand* has even set the prioritisation of diversity as the objective of comparative law. In this respect, the emphases of both *Jayme* and *Legrand* differ from those of *Örücü*, who believes that comparative law could lead the way for ideal systems, or at least reflect the 'better law' approach.[57] *Husa* has pointed out that

---

55 Kennedy, "The Method and Politics of Comparative Law", p. 201.

56 See, for example, Jayme, Multicultural Society and Private Law. German Experiences, pp. 1–6 and 9–11.

57 See Örücü, The Enigma of Comparative Law. Variations on a Theme for the Twenty-First Century, p. 56 and p. 213, where she concludes that the future

when diversity dominates, comparative research can only be authentically pluralistic if it abandons the one-dimensional division into good law and bad law. The European 'better law' rhetoric stems, according to both *Husa* and *Kennedy*, from political harmonisation, which comparativists should also recognize.[58]

However, some justification can be found for the 'better law' approach from recent developments in global governance. As *Raimo Väyrynen* notes, the international debate has been shifting from the omnipotence of the market to emphasising the role of politics and public authority. A balanced market economy is seen to require social values and political guidance. Global governance inevitably requires rules and institutions.[59] Moreover, the discourse on the method of legal comparison has received new tones beyond post-modernism. In essence, they reflect a move towards acknowledging the possibility of objectivity in comparative law, and synthesising the requirements "for interdisciplinarity and thoughtful hermeneutics".[60]

Thus, unavoidably, globalisation in some way involves a 'better law' approach which strives to promote global governance whilst respecting certain fundamental norms. Although diversity is recognized and one way to promote global governance is to ensure that it is

---

of comparative law will be tied in both theory and practice to appreciating diversity and whenever possible striving for commonality.

58 See Husa, "Melodies on Comparative Law", pp. 173–174.

59 See Väyrynen, "Globalisaation voimat ja vastavoimat". It should be noted that international development towards better rules and institutions sometimes occurs in a cyclic way. For example, *Weiss* has observed that national employee involvement rules have crucially contributed to the shaping of the fundamental right nature of involvement rights in the EU. In concrete terms, the 1989 Community Charter of the fundamental social rights of workers has already confirmed the fundamental right nature of rights on information and consultation. Gradually, Article 27 of the Charter has increased the coherence of employee involvement rights in Europe. And this bears even greater significance in the Union of 25 Member States. See Weiss, Recent Developments in German and European Labour Law, p. 171. See also Hepple, Labour Laws and Global Trade, p. 245, where the *soft law* approach of the EU as a part of an attempt to increase market integration is considered to make the fundamental social rights, which express common values, indispensable.

60 Peters – Schwenke, "Comparative Law beyond Post-Modernism", p. 829.

respected, additionally uniform regulation, binding and non-binding, is required, in order to secure operating models that are uniform enough in terms of certain fundamental questions. Thus, comparative law can be seen as a field that illustrates diversity and emphasises respect for differences, as well as identifying needs and opportunities for uniform regulation.

6 Private International Law, Legal Comparison, and the European Approach

Generally speaking, we can recognise the discussion within late modern private international law, advanced for example by *Jayme,* that seeks to emphasise the diversity of legal systems, because cross-border relations increasingly often need to be set in a truly global context. The call for open-mindedness and true internationalism in comparativists, often expressed by *Basil S. Markesinis*, is more topical than ever.[61]

In Europe, the debate has been focusing much on Europeanisation of the law. However, with regard to legal comparison, globalisation has increasingly often rendered the regional context insufficient and revealed regional differences more clearly. For various reasons, the ongoing debate in comparative law is of interest for the conflict of laws. Ultimately, it is the differences between legal systems that give private international law its fundamental justification. Against this background, one of the most important contributions of comparative law to choice of law is that it has drawn attention to the fact that a superficial comparison of two legal systems is rarely sufficient in order to gain true knowledge of a foreign law.

The significance of legal comparison for European private international law has increased as a result of legal, social and economic development. Above all, the materialisation of conflicts rules has in-

61 See, for example, Markesinis, "The Destructive and Constructive Role of the Comparative Lawyer".

creased the need for legal comparison.[62] Increasingly often, conflicts rules require a comparison of the favourability of different laws and thereby determination and application of the most favourable law. Since statutory law broadly forms the basis for conflicts rules in Europe, and efforts are being made to enact new common legal instruments, one should pay more attention to the way legal comparison is used when preparing new legislation.[63] The manner in which legal comparison has been carried out has been significantly varied in different EC legislative projects. For the final legislative outcome, how comparative information is gathered and eventually used by the legislator can be crucial. In Europe, the division between common law and civil law is only one of the reasons for the argumentation of fundamental differences that is used when states express their willingness to avoid unification of legal rules in certain fields.

During the process of unifying rules of the conflict of laws, legal comparison should not be limited to a mere rhetorical role. Comparison is necessary to enable a thorough consideration of the present legal status. Comprehensive comparison is especially significant when legislative measures are considered in order to unify a field where common conflicts rules do not yet exist. However, a need for comparison arises even when unified rules already exist, as in the conversion work of the Rome Convention. This, being in the form of an international convention, has not as such been capable of ensuring unified interpretation of the rules. In cases where such rules are being revised, the legislator should, *inter alia*, identify those existing rules whose interpretation has been especially variable or otherwise problematic.[64]

---

62 See also my forthcoming Article "The Method of Understanding and Internal Viewpoint – on the Interface between Comparative Law and Private International Law" (to be published in ZVglRW 2/2007).

63 Comparative research was a rich source of inspiration for the drafters of 19th and 20th century legislation in Europe. See Zimmermann, "Savigny's Legacy. Legal History, Comparative Law, and the Emergence of a European Legal Science", pp. 601–602.

64 The Commission has attempted this in the Green Paper on conversion of the Rome Convention, which points out certain problems of the existing rules with leaning on the case law of some Member States. See Green Paper on the

During the drafting of common conflicts rules for the EU Member States, legal comparison tends to limit itself to the legal systems of the Member States or Europe little largely.[65] From the standpoint of a global business environment, this is a limited framework. With the dynamics of globalisation, legislators need to be ever more aware of legal solutions adopted in legal systems outside their own country or even region. In the field of the conflict of laws, legislators should be aware of legal development in other countries and regions.

One example of interesting conflicts law development is the recent enactment of private international rules on contractual obligations in Russia. The Third part of the Civil Code of the Russian Federation, which contains Division VI 'Private International Law', came into force in March 2002. The new statutory conflicts rules of this Division are very similar to those of the Rome Convention, which illustrates the reflection of Europeanisation of the conflict of laws in Russian private international law.[66] It will be interesting to see whether Russia will follow the European conflicts law path that has taken a more dynamic direction with the Treaty of Amsterdam. Since the forthcoming Rome I Regulation will likely provide clear amendments to the Rome Convention, the Russian legislator has to decide whether to follow these amendments or to maintain the provisions modelled on the Rome Convention.

European private international law has recently entered a new phase, which has proved to be exceptionally dynamic from the EC legislator's viewpoint. Communitarisation of conflicts rules has come to mean that to a very large extent they become statutory, and part of EC law. At present, several ongoing legislative projects concern choice of law in the field of private law in the EU. The aim of these legislative projects arises politically from visions of a 'genuine area'

---

conversion of the Rome Convention of 1980 on the law applicable to contractual obligations into a Community instrument and its modernisation, COM(2002) 654 final.

65 However, as was said, for instance Switzerland with its advanced statutory conflict rules has sometimes been referred to by the Commission.

66 The author is grateful to Dr. *Anton Asokov* for providing detailed information of Russian conflicts rules.

based on freedom, safety and justice presented most recently in the Hague Programme.[67]

Under pressure to incorporate conflicts rules to a large extent as a part of EC law, the EC legislator might set aside some significant aspects of private international law. It is true that when compared with the effects of an international conflicts law convention, the effectiveness of EC law also clearly strengthens the status of unified conflicts rules from the viewpoint of contracting parties and national courts. In general terms, private interests are often emphasised in the need to develop more flexible conflicts rules to facilitate the internal market. At the same time, the public interest is underlined in order to provide sufficient protection in choice of law for contracts involving a weaker party, such as consumer and employment contracts. This means placing emphasis on the role of mandatory rules in choice of law.

Some questions regarding the current phase of development remain unresolved. One of these is that the EC legislator needs to seek an answer to the question how the relationship between conflicts rules of EC law and other international norm sources concerning choice of law should be resolved. The need to ensure coherence between the EU and the international legal order is also recognised in the Hague Programme, which sets the objectives to be implemented in the area of freedom, security and justice in the period 2005–2010.[68] Another vital question is to consider how far Article 65 EC Treaty can be used as a legal basis for conflicts law statutes since it explicitly refers to "proper functioning of the internal market". So far, the Commission has interpreted this reference broadly.[69]

---

67 See The Hague Programme: strengthening freedom, security and justice in the European Union.

68 See ibid.

69 For example, in the Rome II Proposal the Commission argues that "the Community legislature has the power to put flesh on the bones of this Article and the discretion to determine whether a measure is necessary for the proper functioning of the internal market". See Proposal for a Regulation of the European Parliament and the Council on the law applicable to non-contractual obligations (Rome II). COM(2003) 427 final, p. 6.

7 The Two Directions of European Conflicts Law

Unification of private international law has caused considerable changes in the basis of choice of law in Europe. Much of the debate has focused on unification work based on the Articles of Title IV EC Treaty that has proceeded quite rapidly. What is sometimes forgotten is that the conflict of laws has also been under unification within the sectoral policies of the EU. In several fields, conflicts rules have become a significant part of the EC legal order. What has changed alongside this unification work is the role of private international law in the EC legal order.

In essence, two distinct developments can be distinguished within the EU: on the one hand, coordinated unification efforts, which follow the ambitious objectives of the Hague Programme; and on the other hand, a mostly uncoordinated trend of specific choice of law rules that are scattered around sectoral instruments of secondary EC legislation. These rules are prepared separately for each legislative instrument and in a rather differentiated manner. For this reason, their application and interpretation can be highly problematic, not least because the rules do not always follow the basic systematics of private international law.

The Rome Convention has sometimes been used as an example of the materialisation of choice of law rules in Europe. Reference has then been made mainly to the regulatory approach to consumer and employment contracts or the status of internationally mandatory rules in the Convention. However, the materialisation of conflicts rules is particularly marked in the field of EU sector policies. Specific conflicts rules of internal market law serve a particular objective, such as improving consumer or employee protection or facilitating the activities of entrepreneurs. The trend is increasingly to include specific conflicts rules in instruments of EC secondary legislation that take the form of directives rather than regulations. This leaves the EU Member States room to decide how they transpose the choice of law rules into their national legislation.[70]

---

[70] See Liukkunen, "Kansainvälinen yksityisoikeus ja Euroopan integraatio", p. 351.

In the unification work that has been carried out on the basis of Title IV EC Treaty, the EC legislator has chosen to increase the efficiency and legal certainty of choice of law rules by using regulation as the only legislative instrument. The special conflicts rules of secondary law provide an exception, as they are scattered quite unsystematically around directives in various fields of private law.

In the field of private law, most EC legal instruments are directives. Only some instruments are regulations.[71] As *Basedow* points out, the legislative process in the case of directives is split into two separate phases, the first taking place at EC level and the second at the level of individual Member States, which transpose the directive into their own legal systems. Only the first phase produces a uniform legal text, whereas the second can lead to different national outcomes, or, in *Basedow*'s words, to "all kinds of national distortions". Although these distortions are diminished since the courts have a duty to interpret national law in conformity with the directive, differences of form and content in particular remain considerable after harmonisation. *Basedow* criticises piecemeal EC legislation, claiming that it cannot cope with national divergences and especially differences of structure, principles, and concepts.[72]

Along with all the general problems related to the use of directives as a means of harmonisation, in the field of the conflict of laws we face specific problems when conflicts rules, sometimes seemingly incidentally, are included in directives that mainly aim at harmonising substantive law. First of all, the 'second phase' of the legislative process causes particular uncertainties since for choice of law rules it is crucial that these be transposed in a similar way in each state. The nature of conflicts rules rarely allows national differences in interpretation. Secondly, even if the Member States wished to transpose the conflicts rules properly, they are sometimes faced with highly complex formulations that make this task difficult. For example, the EC legislator does not always point out clearly that a directive adopted in a sectoral policy area contains conflicts rules. This causes difficulties in transposition. It seems that transposition of a directive is typically

---

71 See Basedow, "The Gradual Emergence of European Private Law", p. 12.

72 See ibid., pp. 12–13.

carried out by the Member State authorities of the sectoral policy area in question, and that these authorities perhaps lack expertise in the conflict of laws. At worst, this can lead to a situation where Member States simply do not recognise the conflicts rules set out in the directive.

When adopting initiatives for EC regulations in the field of private international law, the EC legislator has emphasised that the proposed rules are detailed, precise, and unconditional, requiring no measures by Member States for their transposition into national law. If the Member States had room for *manoeuvre* in transposing conflicts rules, then uncertainty would be reintroduced into the law, which is precisely what unification is supposed to abolish. Therefore, regulation is the legal instrument chosen to guarantee uniform application in Member States.[73]

Against this, non-uniform transposition of conflicts rules contained in directives presents a serious problem for private international law. Another is that we will be soon in a situation where EC conflicts rules derive from directives in various fields of private law based on non-coordinated law-drafting and from regulations based on coordinated legislative work enabled by Title IV EC Treaty. These two types of rules seem to derive from entirely different views on conflicts law.

All this also has concrete consequences for individuals, or 'EU citizens' as well as companies. The tendency of scattered conflicts rules leads to greater difficulty in estimating the fairness of the rules from the standpoint of the contracting parties. From a systemic standpoint, the consequences are only beginning to appear; and they are causing serious problems of coherence for the developing EC legal order. One of the most serious of these is lack of coherency between the general conflicts rules and the specific conflicts rules of secondary legislation.

Traditional private international law theory tends to emphasise the role of this field of law as co-ordinator of the laws of different countries. In recent times, we have seen that the role of the conflict of

---

73 See Proposal for a Regulation of the European Parliament and the Council on the law applicable to contractual obligations (Rome I), COM(2005) 650 final, p. 7.

laws has experienced significant changes in Europe. On the basis of the Hague Programme, it might seem as if only one European direction existed in which private international law is being developed. However, as we have seen, in addition to unification work based on Title IV EC Treaty, another type of development can be distinguished. Side by side with legislative work based on Article 65 EC Treaty, there is a trend of bringing special choice of law rules to internal market law. This trend arises from the phenomenon known as the materialisation of private international law.

It should be emphasised that developments in secondary EC law that have led to enactment of specific conflicts rules have been fragmented. Conflicts rules have been included in directives on internal market law to a significant extent since the 1990s. One explanation for the growing use of conflicts rules is that they have been introduced to avoid over-intense harmonisation of the contents of Member State legislation, a direction in which Member States are increasingly being pushed by deepening integration. This has resulted in a 'non-neutral' choice of law legislation in the Community, which aims at a certain material result, such as maintaining or improving the protection of the weaker contracting party in cross-border legal relations or facilitating the business operations of business parties. At this point, suffice to say that the more EC conflicts rules scatter, the more difficult it is to maintain coherence between them.[74]

[74] The Commission has emphasised that the internal market can only work if the rules concerning it are correctly implemented by the Member States and effectively applied in practice. However, with few exceptions Member States are failing to transpose a large number of key internal market directives into national law by the deadline. See Communication from the Commission to the Council, the European Parliament, the European Economic and Social Committee and the Committee of the Regions: Report on the implementation of the Internal Market Strategy (2003–2006). COM(2004) 22 final, p. 14 and p. 16.

8 Outline of the Study

This study examines conflicts rules with regard to cross-border services within the EC legal framework. The main focus is on discussing core choice of law questions and recent developments in the conflict of laws from the European viewpoint. The two distinct developments of conflicts law pointed out in the previous section are of particular interest here. The purpose is not to limit discussion to problems of interpretation but to give a general view of conflicts rules that govern cross-border services, taking into account the multiplicity of conflicts questions involved. Moreover, this study seeks to pinpoint the specific features of European developments that cause fragmentation of conflicts rules.

In the study, the terms 'conflicts law', 'the conflict of laws', and 'private international law' are used interchangeably, as are the terms 'choice of law rules' and 'conflicts rules'. When discussing the European approach, the approach adopted by the European Community and its Member States is under scrutiny. Since the Community has legislative competence within the EU, the term 'EC law' is used to refer to legislative material of the Community. Particular attention is paid to the mutual relationship between conflicts rules that arise from different norm sources, and conflicts rules that amalgamate various fields of private law, such as company law and labour law. Important but sometimes hidden intersections of sets of rules that affect choice of law in cross-border services are explored. In this respect, attention is paid to the use of the country of origin principle in internal market law and the problems encountered, in particular as regards commercial law and consumer protection. Furthermore, fundamental labour rights and the tensions between fundamental rights and EU economic freedoms are examined.

Since the EC seeks to encourage service-providers to use either freedom of services or freedom of establishment for service provision, the impact of EC law on freedom of establishment also deserves attention. To explore this, developments in international company law have to be assessed. For a long time, incorporation theory and real seat theory co-existed in European international company law. However, ECJ case law has gradually diminished the role of real seat theory in company law. In addition, the impact of freedom of establishment on employee participation rights in company administration is addressed. Furthermore, the study discusses how real seat theory of international company law is reflected in international labour law. In this study, the term 'involvement' governs information and consultation as well as employee participation in company administration.[75]

With regard to international business contracts, a line is sometimes very difficult to draw between contracts of trade in services and other types of contracts. For example, a contract for sale of goods may involve service provision to the buyer. In order to grasp such 'mixed' contracts, and because the conflicts rules for international sale of goods are closely connected to the rules for sale of services, the most relevant norm sources of sale of goods are also briefly discussed. In this respect, the Hague Conventions on international sale are paid attention. Moreover, certain central issues concerning the choice of law for sale of services are brought up in the context of the discussion of the CISG provided by this study.

Specific rules exist for certain types of services in the EU, such as insurance law, social security law, consumer law, and labour law. For each specific type with its specific conflicts law problems, a separate study could be carried out. In order to delimit the scope of this study and to be able to explore the main issues deeply enough, I have chosen to look at only two specific types of contracts: consumer contracts, and employment contracts. When discussing these two types of weaker party contracts, particular attention is paid to recent development trends in internal market law in terms of choice of law.

An interesting question that arises when exploring European solutions on statutory conflicts rules is how far and in what sense the European conflicts approach should be regarded as European. This study sheds light on some aspects of this question, especially by the method of legal comparison. Firstly, a comparison is drawn between

---

75 Similar definition has been used in the Council Directive 2001/86/EC supplementing the Statute for a European company with regard to the involvement of employees (later: SE Directive). Under Article 2(h) of the Directive, 'involvement of employees' means any mechanism, including information, consultation and participation, through which employees' representatives may exercise an influence on decisions to be taken within the company.

the European and US conflicts approach. Secondly, aspects of changes and continuity that can be recognized in the approach of common law and civil law systems towards conflicts law are addressed. In several places, intra-European and Scandinavian[76] comparisons highlight relevant aspects of conflicts law development.

[76] In this study, the term 'Scandinavian' is used to refer to Denmark, Finland, Norway, and Sweden.

Chapter II Global vs. Regional

1 Introduction

It might well be useful to begin by considering the term 'private international law' as commonly used by Europeans. In this context, 'international' can be said to refer to disputes with connections to more than just one country. In contrast, 'private' reflects the division of civil law origin between private law and public law and means that only private law disputes are governed by this particular field of law. Likewise, public-law disputes with an international character belong to the sphere of public international law.

It is sometimes claimed that the term 'private international law' is not only more descriptive but also more idealistic than the term 'conflict of laws' which has prevailed in the US. By associating 'private international law' with idealism the implication is that a distinct body of law exists which is universally applied by most countries that would provide solutions to multi-state private-law disputes. Similarly, the term 'conflict of laws' can lay claim to a certain accuracy. It has been said that the term assumes, firstly, that in all cases involving more than one state every state involved would desire its law to be applied. Secondly, the term would indicate that these desires conflict; and thirdly, that a mechanism of superior authority exists to resolve such conflicts.[77]

In the US, conflicts law is divided into jurisdiction, choice of law, and also recognition and enforcement of judgments.[78] In Europe, private international law can be understood either in a narrow or in a broad sense. The former definition governs only choice of law. Increasingly often, the latter refers not only to jurisdiction, choice of law, and recognition and enforcement of judgments but also to inter-

77 See Scoles – Hay – Borchers – Symeonides, Conflict of Laws pp. 1–2.
78 See ibid., p. 3.

national legal co-operation in civil matters.[79] In the US, conflicts law is mostly state law rather than federal law. Thus, from the US standpoint, choice of law is a question of state law.[80] For European countries belonging to the EU, increasingly often private international law has come to mean regional law instead of pure national law. With ongoing developments in the EU, the core of conflicts law governing contractual obligations will most likely become part of EC law.

Alongside international efforts to unify the rules of private international law, common substantive rules have been created for international sale of goods because conflicts rules have not been able to guarantee enough uniformity. International harmonisation efforts go back a long time in commercial contract law. However, it was not until the conclusion of the international UN sales law, the CISG, in 1980 that international harmonisation made a breakthrough. On many occasions the CISG has been cited as the cornerstone of the harmonisation of international trade law.[81] It has also had a more general impact on the development of contract law in various countries.

The CISG brings a global approach to the harmonisation of international sales law. Although the Convention also affects choice of law, regional and national approaches still dominate in the field of conflicts law under scrutiny. One reason for this is that the work of the Hague Conference on Private International Law has not been successful. Since global markets mean global competition, it should be asked how far a regional approach in the conflict of laws can be successfully stretched. An example that illustrates some problems of the regionalisation of conflicts law in Europe is how consumer protection has been advanced by choice of law means in EC directives.

All told, the European approach to conflicts law is complicated. It should be emphasised again that in the EU it is no longer possible to consider the legal development of the conflict of laws without paying

---

79 See Jänterä-Jareborg, "Foreign Law in National Courts – A Comparative Perspective", p. 200 and fn. 16.

80 See Symeonides – Perdue – von Mehren, Conflict of Laws: American, Comparative, International. Cases and Materials, p. 6 and Scoles – Hay – Borchers – Symeonides, Conflict of Laws, p. 2.

81 Magnus, "Action Plan for a European Contract Law. European Contract Law and CISG", p. 1.

attention to two distinct developments: the co-ordinated unification under the Articles of Title IV EC Treaty, and the scattered unification provided by sectoral instruments of secondary EC legislation. For the first development, the Rome I Proposal is of utmost interest here. For the second, both consumer law and labour law can be used as examples of areas where fragmentary EC legislation on conflicts law exists.[82] This chapter considers certain conflicts law questions of consumer protection in the EU.[83] It also investigates the impact of the extension of party autonomy suggested in the Rome I Proposal on employment contracts.[84]

Legal comparison can offer much enlightenment when considering how far we can speak of a European conflicts approach and in what sense conflicts law has been Europeanised. This chapter contains a comparison between the US and European approaches, in particular from the standpoint of conflicts law methodology and objectives. The focus of the comparison is on contractual obligations.

2 CISG and Choice of Law for Trade in Services

Globally, the most important sale of goods convention is the CISG, adopted in Vienna in 1980 after profound preparation work that included comprehensive legal comparisons. The preparation process of the Convention is testimony to the significance of careful legal comparison when making an international convention with the aim of formulating widely acceptable rules. The CISG was adopted unanimously by a diplomatic conference of representatives from 62 states

---

82 Insurance law could be used as a third illustrative example of EC conflicts legislation that is fragmented by nature. See Second Council Directive 88/357/EEC on the coordination of laws, regulations and administrative provisions relating to direct insurance other than life assurance and laying down provisions to facilitate the effective exercise of freedom to provide services and amending Directive 73/239/EEC and Directive 2002/83/EC of the European Parliament and of the Council concerning life assurance.

83 The discussion on consumer protection continues in chapter III.

84 For the most part, labour law issues are handled in chapters IV and V.

and eight international organisations.[85] So far, the Convention has been ratified by 67 states. Together, the Contracting States to the CISG today control approximately three-fourths of global exports and imports. Eight of the world's ten leading exporting states are Contracting States of the Convention; the United Kingdom and Japan being the only two remaining outside.[86]

One demonstration of the success of the CISG is the fact that the UNIDROIT Principles and PECL were modelled on it.[87] In a sense, the UNIDROIT Principles seek to repeat something similar to the Restatements of Law used in the US: the objective of the principles is to 'restate' existing international contract law. The point of departure is that these principles are either literally or in substance taken from the CISG in so far as it addresses the same issues.[88] As to matters that the Convention is silent about, it is sometimes argued that the UNIDROIT Principles or PECL could provide interpretative assistance for application of the CISG. Although consensus on the issue is lacking, *Magnus* for example has thought this desirable.[89] By virtue of its Article 7, the Convention should be interpreted having regard to its international character and the need to promote uniformity in its application. In the absence of an international system for ensuring uniform application, the case law of the Contracting States plays a vital role in interpreting the Convention.

The EC legislator has been eager to use the CISG as a structural model in law-drafting.[90] In terms of its structure, the Directive on cer-

---

85 See Bonell, The UNIDROIT Principles of International Commercial Contracts and CISG – Alternatives or Complementary Instruments? For the preparation of the CISG, see United Nations Conference on Contracts for the International Sale of Goods, Vienna 10 March – 11 April 1980, Official Records UN Doc. A/Conf. 97/19.

86 The ten major exporting countries are the US, Germany, Japan, France, China, United Kingdom, Canada, Italy, the Netherlands and Belgium. See Magnus, "25 Jahre UN-Kaufrecht", p. 97 and fn. 10.

87 See further Magnus, "Action Plan for a European Contract Law. European Contract Law and CISG", p. 4.

88 See Bonell, "The UNIDROIT Principles of International Commercial Contracts and CISG – Alternatives or Complementary Instruments?"

89 See Magnus, Wiener UN-Kaufrecht (CISG), Einleitung zum CISG, para. 51.

90 See Magnus, "25 Jahre UN-Kaufrecht", pp 106–107.

tain aspects of the sale of consumer goods and associated guarantees is very similar to the CISG.[91] Likewise, the legislative reforms of certain Member States, such as Finland, Germany, the Netherlands and Sweden, have been strongly influenced by the Convention.[92] On these bases the Convention has been called the main source of European trade and contract law and it is often welcomed as such for the future as well. However, this does not exclude the possibility of developing particular sets of norms for the needs of European contract law.[93]

In general, the CISG has increasingly facilitated smooth cross-border transactions within the Union; thus, too, the smooth functioning of the internal market. Yet, not all EU Member States have been willing to ratify the Convention. The United Kingdom, Ireland, Portugal and Malta are those Member States that are not members of the Convention.[94] For the United Kingdom, the main reason for remaining outside the CISG is often claimed to be the great economic advantage the country enjoys as a centre of international arbitration. English law has traditionally borne a commercial emphasis, while the Commercial Court in London has long been the centre for the resolution of international commercial disputes.[95]

From the standpoint of the economic objectives of the EU, it has been claimed that the current 'imbalance' between Member States causes unnecessary transaction costs for professional cross-border sales. It has been suggested in several contexts that all EU Member

---

91 See Directive 1999/44/EC of the European Parliament and of the Council on certain aspects of the sale of consumer goods and associated guarantees.

92 In Germany, the CISG served as a model for the reform of the Bürgerliches Gesetzbuch (BGB). See also Magnus, "25 Jahre UN-Kaufrecht", pp 104–105 and "Action Plan for a European Contract Law. European Contract Law and CISG", p. 4.

93 See, for example, Magnus, "Action Plan for a European Contract Law. European Contract Law and CISG", p. 4.

94 For the reasons why the United Kingdom has not been induced to sign, see Forte, "The United Nations Convention on Contracts for the International Sale of Goods: Reason or Unreason in the United Kingdom".

95 See Fentiman, "English Private International Law at the End of the 20th Century: Progress or Regress?", p. 172.

States should join the CISG, which, if more countries ratified it, could become a real global regulatory instrument for international sales.[96]

Legal literature on the CISG is voluminous. Detailed analysis of the material contents of the Convention is needless here. Suffice to say that substantively the CISG comprises two entities: provisions on the formation of contracts, and provisions on the sale of goods. For the most part, the substantive provisions are based on common law but some elements of civil law are present.[97] Part I of the CISG determines the scope of application of the Convention, while Part II contains provisions on the formation of international sales contracts. The Convention is largely based on the traditional 'mirror image' rule, so that a contract is formed only when an offer and an acceptance match in every respect.[98] Part III of the Convention contains substantive rules that define parties' obligations, rights, remedies for breach, and risk of loss. In essence, the right goods have to be delivered at the right time and place under the obligations set out in the contract and the CISG. Passing of risk is connected in the CISG to the last significant act by which delivery is complemented by the seller.[99]

Although the material content of the CISG is extensive, not every aspect of the contractual relationship is governed by the Convention. For example, under Article 4 of the CISG the main rule is that the validity of the contract is not covered by the Convention. However, the non-mandatory rules in the Convention can turn out to be inconsistent with national mandatory rules.[100] From the standpoint of private international law, it is noteworthy that determining whether the contract to which the Convention applies violates the *ordre public* principle has to be settled under the applicable conflicts rules.[101]

---

96 See Magnus, "Action Plan for a European Contract Law. European Contract Law and CISG", pp. 1–3.

97 See Forte, The United Nations Convention on Contracts for the International Sale of Goods: Reason or Unreason in the United Kingdom. See also Magnus, "Action Plan for a European Contract Law. European Contract Law and CISG", p. 4.

98 See Bernstein – Lookofsky, Understanding the CISG in Europe, p. 5.

99 See in more detail ibid., pp. 4–5.

100 See further Lando, "The European Principles in an Integrated World", p. 15.

101 See also Bernstein – Lookofsky, Understanding the CISG in Europe, p. 5.

Article 1 of the CISG is noteworthy in terms of choice of law. It reads as follows:

> (1) This Convention applies to contracts of sale of goods between parties whose places of business are in different States:
> (a) when the States are Contracting States; or
> (b) when the rules of private international law lead to the application of the law of a Contracting State.
> (2) The fact that the parties have their places of business in different States is to be disregarded whenever this fact does not appear either from the contract or from any dealings between, or from information disclosed by, the parties at any time before or at the conclusion of the contract.
> (3) Neither the nationality of the parties nor the civil or commercial character of the parties of the contract is to be taken into consideration in determining the application of this Convention.

The CISG provides no definition of either 'sale' or 'goods'. When defining 'sale' and 'goods' within the meaning of the CISG, an autonomous interpretation has to be sought.[102] Yet, it should be noted that according to the national laws of most Contracting States, a sale of goods is a transaction, which involves transfer of a property right in a movable thing.[103] By virtue of Article 3(1) of the CISG, contracts for the supply of goods to be manufactured or produced are considered sales unless the party ordering the goods undertakes to supply a substantial part of the materials necessary for such manufacture or production. The term 'goods' should be interpreted broadly, to include all moveable things.[104]

A contract for the sale of goods may also involve services. Subject to certain conditions, the CISG also applies to mixed contracts. Under Article 3(2), the Convention does not apply to contracts when the preponderant part of the obligations of the party furnishing

---

102 See ibid., p. 18.

103 See ibid., p. 16 and Lookofsky, "In dubio pro conventione? Some thoughts about opt-outs, computer programs and preemption under the 1980 Vienna Sales Convention (CISG)".

104 See Lookofsky, The 1980 United Nations Convention on Contracts for the International Sale of Goods.

the goods consists of the supply of labour or other services. Hence, the decisive factor is whether services form a 'preponderant part' of the sale. If under the contract the 'preponderant part' of the obligations of the supplier consists of providing labour or services, then the CISG is not applied. It seems that in determining preponderance, the quantitative approach should be taken.[105] Accordingly, the Convention applies to the supply of goods even if the value of labour or services is the dominant element.[106] Nevertheless, if contracts of services and sale of goods are separate, choice of law is carried out separately for each contract.[107]

The CISG is not universal in character. By virtue of Article 1(1), it applies when the contracting parties have their places of business in different CISG States. However, application is based on the principle of party autonomy. Under Article 6, the parties may exclude application of the Convention or derogate from or vary the effect of any of its provisions. Thus, the CISG is fully optional, so that the contracting parties may choose to apply some other law instead, either entirely or partially. The choice can be implicit but it has to become evident with sufficient certainty.[108] The *materiellrechtliche Verweisung* of the CISG or any of its provisions is permitted. However, it is disputed whether the *kollisionsrechtliche Verweisung* of the CISG as such is permitted.[109] As *Magnus* emphasises, the Convention does not establish an international and independent legal order. Instead, it is part of the national law of each Contracting State, from which it cannot be detached.[110]

If a choice of another law has not been made, the Convention is applied automatically under the basic rule when the places of business

---

105 See Fawcett – Harris – Bridge, International Sale of Goods in the Conflict of Laws, pp. 958–959. See also Bernstein –Lookofsky, Understanding the CISG in Europe, p. 22.

106 See Bernstein – Lookofsky, Understanding the CISG in Europe, p. 18.

107 See Fawcett – Harris – Bridge, International Sale of Goods in the Conflict of Laws, p. 759.

108 See Magnus, Wiener UN-Kaufrecht (CISG), Art. 6, para. 9.

109 See Magnus, ibid., para. 64. Cf. Schlechtriem, Internationales UN-Kaufrecht, p. 17.

110 See Magnus, Wiener UN-Kaufrecht (CISG), Art. 6, para. 65.

of the parties are located in different states. If a party has more than one place of business, then the place that has the closest relationship to the contract and its performance is decisive. Moreover, when the parties have chosen the law of a Contracting State as applicable to their contract, the CISG applies automatically.[111]

The CISG does not define 'the place of business'. However, it is held that the term does not govern the mere place of contracting. Nor does it refer to the place where only preparations for concluding a single contract have been made. Instead, a permanent and stable business organisation can be regarded as a place of business. The criterion that states where places of business are located need to be Contracting States excludes contracts between parties from legal systems that exist in a single Contracting State.[112]

Article 1(1)(b), according to which the CISG applies when the rules of private international law lead to the application of the law of a Contracting State, is relevant only when the criteria provided by Article 1(1)(a) are not met. In other words, when the places of business of the parties are in different countries which are at the same time Contracting States, the CISG applies even if conflicts rules would point to the law of a non-Contracting State.[113]

The CISG does not dictate the applicable national law, so the choice of law is made on the basis of the conflicts rules of the forum. If the law applicable to the contract under the objective conflicts rules is the law of a Contracting State, then the Convention is applied as a part of the applicable law. And if the contracting parties have made a choice of the law of any Contracting State, then the CISG applies to the contract. *Jayme* has argued that the term 'private international law' used in Article 1(1)(b) should be understood broadly. According to him, such procedural rules of a legal system that call for application of uniform law in cases where the applicable foreign law is not ascer-

---

[111] See Jayme, Article 1, in Bianca-Bonell Commentary on International Sales Law.

[112] See ibid.

[113] See Honnold, "Article 6. The Contract and the Convention". See also Magnus, Wiener UN-Kaufrecht (CISG), Einleitung zum CISG, para. 42.

tainable, also fall within the scope of Article 1(1)(b).[114] However, it seems that the majority of opinions in the legal literature suggest that rules of private international law should be interpreted to mean conflicts rules which the forum applies to sales contracts with international connections.[115]

It should be noted that the Convention authorises declarations. During preparation of the CISG, the role of Article 1(1)(b) turned out to be somewhat controversial. This led to a possibility of declaration set forth in Article 95, according to which Contracting States may declare that they are not bound by Article 1(1)(b). This means that when Article 1(1)(a) does not apply and Article 1(1)(b) is not applicable because of a declaration, the CISG can be applied only if the parties have used party autonomy and chosen the Convention as applicable.

The US is among those states that have made a declaration concerning Article 1(1)(b). In Europe, declarations have been made by the Czech Republic and Slovakia. In addition, when Germany ratified the CISG it declared that it does not apply Article 1(1)(b) in respect of a country which has made an Article 95 declaration. However, this German declaration was not authorised by the CISG and has been criticised in the legal literature. Some have understood it as a national statement interpreting the term 'Contracting States' in Article 1(1)(b).[116]

The four Scandinavian countries have a made declaration which can be problematic in terms of application of Article 1(1)(b) in certain situations. The rules on the formation of contract in the CISG (Part II) are not applied in the Scandinavian countries.[117] According to *Lookofsky*, one of the reasons for this reservation was that the distinction made between formation and validity in the Convention appears to be troublesome: both formation and validity rules relate to the process by which a contract is born. However, *Lookofsky* remarks

---

114 See Jayme, Article 1, in Bianca-Bonell Commentary on the International Sales Law.

115 See Magnus, Wiener UN-Kaufrecht (CISG), Art. 1, para. 101 and the references there.

116 See Bernstein – Lookofsky, Understanding the CISG in Europe, p. 191.

117 Under Article 92 of the CISG, Contracting States may declare at the time of adherance that they will not be bound by Part II or Part III of the Convention.

that the Scandinavian states hardly achieve their aim since they have not made a declaration with respect to Article 1(1)(b). Application of this Article may lead to a situation where the rules on formation in Part II of the Convention have to be applied even in cases where only one contracting party is from a Scandinavian state.[118]

According to another declaration of the four Scandinavian countries, the Convention does not apply to an inter-Scandinavian sale where the places of business of the contracting parties are in the Scandinavian countries.[119] The reasons behind the declaration relate to the uniform regulatory approach adopted by the Scandinavian countries. They have enacted quite uniform statutes on sale of goods at the national level and they want to maintain the well-established intra-Scandinavian sales model.

3 Failure of the Hague Sales Conventions

The Hague Conference on Private International Law adopted the Convention on the Law Applicable to International Sale of Goods (later: the 1955 Convention) in 1955.[120] Only Denmark, Finland, France, Italy, Niger, Norway, Sweden and Switzerland have ratified the Convention, which entered into force in 1964. That the Convention has not gained much success is partly explained by the fact that only 17 of the Conference Member States participated in the session in which the Convention was accepted in 1951. At the time, those states – of which only one was a common law state and all the rest were civil law states

---

118 See Lookofsky, "Alive and Well in Scandinavia: CISG Part II" and Understanding the CISG in Scandinavia, pp. 181–183, where the author concludes that "the resulting complex state of affairs works to no one's advantage, and the Scandinavian States should all withdraw their ill-advised reservations to CISG Part II". See also Bernstein – Lookofsky, Understanding the CISG in Europe, pp. 189–190.

119 This declaration is based on Article 94 of the CISG.

120 Even in 1928, the need for a convention on the law applicable to international sale of goods was discussed at the Hague Conference. See Lando, "The 1955 and 1985 Hague Conventions on the Law Applicable to the International Sale of Goods", p. 156.

– represented the Western economic system quite homogeneously.[121] Accordingly, for the most part the outcome of the preparation reflects continental legal thinking. It has even been claimed by some that the unsuccessful story of the 1955 Convention can be explained by the 'insufficiently differentiated' legal thinking of the states.[122]

The 1955 Convention has been considered too rigid for the needs of international sales because in the absence of a choice of law clause, the applicable law is determined in accordance with fixed connection rules. The preparation for a new Hague Convention began after the CISG was finished in 1980. The purpose was to create a convention on international sale of goods that would complement the CISG in the field of goods trade and replace the 1955 Convention. This time, more widespread acceptance was sought for the planned Convention by inviting more than 60 delegates to the session.[123] However, the array of countries was too heterogeneous to be able to agree on simple and clear rules.

Coincident with preparations for the new Hague Convention, the conflicts rules for contractual obligations were becoming Europeanized. As a result, two significant international conventions emerged for signature in 1980: the Rome Convention between the EC Member States, and the CISG. An international sales contract is an archetypal contract of the law of obligations, and the conflicts rules of the Rome Convention were created with this very much in mind.[124]

A new Convention was concluded on the law applicable to international sale of goods at the Hague Conference on Private International Law of 1986 (later: the 1986 Convention). The 1986 Convention aims to govern choice of law particularly in cases where the CISG is not applicable or does not regulate on the issue to be resolved. Fur-

---

121 See ibid.

122 See ibid., p. 157. However, *Lando* himself does not agree with this kind of explanation.

123 All UNCITRAL Member States were invited to the preparation of the revision of the 1955 Convention regardless of their membership in the Hague Conference. See von Mehren, Explanatory Report on the 1986 Hague Sales Convention, p. 16.

124 Fawcett – Harris – Bridge, International Sale of Goods in the Conflict of Laws, p. 901.

thermore, the 1986 Convention seeks to eliminate possible conflicts with the CISG.[125] As in the 1955 Convention, the scope of application of the 1986 Convention has been made universal. Thus, its application is not territorially restricted and reciprocity is not required in applying its choice of law rules.

Nevertheless, clear and substantial differences exist between the 1955 and the 1986 Conventions. Both Conventions are based on party autonomy but the 1986 Convention also allows a choice of law clause that concerns only part of a contract. As a rule, in the absence of choice, the law of the state in which the seller's place of business was located at the time of conclusion of the contract is to be applied under the 1955 Convention. However, in three different situations the law of the place where the buyer has its place of business at the time of concluding the contract is to be applied. In contrast with the 1955 Convention, the 1986 Convention is not based on fixed connection factors. The presumption rules can be departed from if the contract is manifestly more closely connected with another law than that designated under the presumptions. The Hague Conference sought relatively simple and clear-cut conflicts rules with a more flexible 'proper law' approach.[126] The influence of newer European private international law is demonstrated by the fact that the 1986 Convention also allows application of internationally mandatory rules of the forum. The 1955 Convention does not provide that option; it only includes the classic *ordre public* principle. In addition, in contrast with the 1955 Convention, the 1986 Convention includes rules on the field of applicable law and form of contract.

The 1955 and 1986 Conventions apply to 'international sale contracts'. The closeness of the 1986 Convention to the CISG can be seen in the scope of its application. Provisions defining contracts for sale of goods are close to those of the CISG. Consumer sales have been excluded from the scope of the 1986 Convention, as they have been excluded from the scope of the CISG. Under the 1986 Conven-

---

125 See Bernstein – Lookofsky, Understanding the CISG in Europe, p.186.

126 See von Mehren, Explanatory Report on the 1986 Hague Sales Convention, p. 31.

tion, consumer sales are sales of goods bought for personal, family, or household use.[127]

While pursuing detailed choice of law rules and, thus, attempting better predictability, the 1986 Convention has led to a set of conflicts rules far too rigid for international sales. As a result, none of the Member States of the Hague Conference have ratified the Convention. Additionally, the status of the 1955 Convention has remained quite marginal in international exchange. It seems that the 1955 Convention will have a disharmonising, thus unwanted, effect on the rules of international exchange if it remains a special arrangement between only eight states.

Unsurprisingly, the 1986 Convention has not entered into force internationally. From a European perspective, the reasons for this are clear: although more extensive and detailed than the 1955 Convention, it hardly improves the choice of law rules set out by the Rome Convention for EU Member States. At present, the 1955 Convention causes evident problems for Europe, since only some EU Member States have ratified this Convention whose scope of application partly overlaps the Rome Convention. Difficulties may arise when both Conventions are applied simultaneously to one case: for example, when the law applicable to the form of a contract or the transfer of receivables is defined in accordance with the Rome Convention but the law applicable to the sale itself is determined by virtue of the 1955 Convention. It is therefore possible, and, to my mind, strongly advisable, that when the Rome Convention is converted into an EC regulation, the EU Member States that are parties to the Hague Convention will consider it necessary to withdraw from the Convention.

Several core conflicts rules in the 1986 Convention are similar to those of the Rome Convention. The most crucial difference between the two is perhaps expansion of the scope of freedom of contract in the 1986 Convention. However, as *Fawcett*, *Harris* and *Bridge* note, a simultaneous problem consists of the 1986 Convention being

---

127 See Lando, "The 1985 Hague Convention on the Law Applicable to Sales", p. 64.

highly detailed, which in choice of law easily leads to uncertainty.[128] In fact, it seems that the Convention will have very little, if any, future significance, despite its ambitious aspirations.[129]

4 Relationship between different Conventions

It is useful next to address the relationship between the CISG, the 1955 Hague Convention, and the Rome Convention. It is well known that the last two conflicts law Conventions are applied universally in the Contracting States bound to these Conventions. In addition, the CISG is an instrument of substantive harmonisation, with its application restricted to Contracting States.

As regards the CISG, Article 90 defines the relationship of the Convention to other international agreements. It provides that the Convention does not prevail over any international agreement which has already been or may be entered into and which contains provisions concerning matters governed by the CISG, if the contracting parties have their places of business in countries party to such an agreement. The 1955 Hague Convention takes precedence over the CISG when the contracting parties have their places of business in countries which have entered into the 1955 Convention. It should also be mentioned that by virtue of 1(1)(b) of the CISG, the rules deriving from the 1955 Convention determine the applicable law in countries that have ratified it.[130]

Article 21 of the Rome Convention solves the relationship between the Rome Convention and other international agreements by giving them precedence over the Convention. Thus, in EU Member States that are members of the 1955 Hague Convention, the latter takes precedence over the Rome Convention.

---

128 See Fawcett – Harris – Bridge, International Sale of Goods in the Conflict of Laws, pp. 901–902.

129 See also the criticism of the 1955 Convention presented by Magnus in Wiener UN-Kaufrecht (CISG), Einleitung zum CISG, para. 23.

130 See also ibid., Art. 1, para. 101.

The relationship between the CISG and the Rome Convention also deserves attention. As regards the CISG, it does not prevail over an international agreement containing provisions concerning matters governed by the CISG, if the contracting parties have their places of business in countries party to such an agreement. A corresponding approach has been adopted in Article 21 of the Rome Convention. Hence, both Conventions give precedence to other international agreements on the same matters. In the legal literature it has been suggested that due to its specific nature, the CISG should be given precedence over the Rome Convention.[131]

5 Regional Efforts with Global Reach: Rome I

By Article 2 of the Treaty on European Union, the EU Member States set the objective of "maintaining and developing the Union as an area of freedom, security and justice, in which the free movement of persons is assured and litigants can assert their rights in the courts and before the authorities of all the Member States, enjoying facilities equivalent to those they enjoy in their own country". Although, starting from Amsterdam, Member States have emphasised the need for an area of 'freedom, security and justice', doubts have been presented as to the contribution of this notion to the communitarisation of private international law.[132]

According to EU rhetoric, unification of conflicts law constitutes a part of establishing 'genuine' European law-enforcement area. The Community has taken several legislative initiatives under the Articles of Title IV EC Treaty, in order to adopt measures in the field of judicial co-operation in civil matters. The *Tampere* European Council in 1999 acknowledged the mutual recognition principle as the cornerstone of judicial co-operation in the EU.[133] This was followed in 2000 by the joint Commission and Council Programme of measures to

131 See ibid., Art. 90, para. 17.

132 See Meeusen, "Fifteen theses on Brussels I, Rome I and the European Union's Institutional Framework", p. 49.

133 European Council Tampere 15–16.10.1999: Conclusions of the Presidency.

implement the principle in civil and commercial matters. Measures relating to unification of conflicts rules relate to this implementation, since according to the Programme they help to facilitate the mutual recognition of judgments. It is argued further in the Programme that common conflicts rules reinforce mutual trust in judicial decisions given in other Member States and are a vital element in attaining the longer-term objective of the free movement of judgments.[134] In 2004, the Council endorsed the Hague Programme for strengthening the area of 'freedom, security and justice'.[135] The Programme translates this objective into concrete measures, which include the communitarisation of private international law.

The unification work under new Article 65 EC Treaty began in 2000 when the Brussels Convention was converted into the Brussels I Regulation, which the Rome II Proposal[136] followed in July 2003. In December 2005, the Commission presented a Proposal for the Rome I Regulation. Substantial differences exist in the scope of the Brussels I Regulation and the Rome Convention. The former covers both contractual and non-contractual obligations, whereas the latter covers only contractual obligations. Therefore, the proposed Rome II Regulation has been held as a natural extension of the unification of conflicts rules in the area of non-contractual obligations in civil and commercial matters. The aim of covering important lacunas of common conflicts rules has set the line of legislative work concerning conflicts rules.

In preparation of the Rome I and II Proposals, careful attention has been paid to the Brussels I Regulation, whose basic rule is that defendants have to be sued in the courts of the Member State where they are domiciled. The Rome I Proposal was preceded by consulta-

134 See Council Draft programme of measures for implementation of the principle of mutual recognition of decisions in civil and commercial matters, 2001.

135 See the Hague Programme: strengthening freedom, security and justice in the European Union.

136 Proposal for a Regulation of the European Parliament and the Council on the law applicable to non-contractual obligations (Rome II). COM(2003) 427 final.

tions on the basis of the Green Paper given by the European Commission in 2003.[137]

For the purposes of this study, the Rome I Proposal is interesting especially in three particular respects. First of all, attempts to broaden the party autonomy of the contracting parties deserve attention. Secondly, the attempt to boost legal certainty by introducing fixed connecting factor rules is a remarkable and controversial novelty in the Proposal. Thirdly, the definition given to internationally mandatory rules in the Proposal is noteworthy. Moreover, the universal scope of application of the Proposal should be kept in mind when assessing its content. Universal conflicts rules demonstrate a regulatory approach where regional unification efforts have global reach. In this respect, it can be claimed that the legal basis of the Rome I and Rome II Proposals, Article 65 EC Treaty, might cause problems when the objective is to enact conflicts rules with universal scope of application. In these Proposals, the reference to the internal market has been given a broad interpretation.[138]

5.1 Party Autonomy

Before exploring European developments as to party autonomy, it is appropriate to discuss the basic justifications for it from the standpoint of business parties. Firstly, use of the choice of law clause increases certainty in commercial transactions. Secondly, no less important is the need of the parties for freedom of the applicable law. The parties have credible motives for choice of law in international commercial contracts. In fact, the parties can be held to be in competition with one

---

137 Green Paper on the conversion of the Rome Convention of 1980 on the law applicable to contractual obligations into a Community instrument and its modernization. COM(2002) 654 final.

138 It is noteworthy that the draft Constitutional Treaty distinguishes the internal market and the area of freedom, security and justice. See in detail Meeusen, "Fifteen theses on Brussels I, Rome I and the European Union's Institutional Framework", p. 57.

another not only in the services or goods in question but also with regard to the laws of the legal systems they can offer as applicable.[139]

When discussing conflicts law questions concerning contractual obligations, one should not forget that in Europe private international law is being developed alongside work on harmonising European contract law. In recent years, the European Contract Law Project has been constantly in the spotlight. At present, the Common Frame of Reference is being drafted.[140] Harmonisation efforts concerning contract law have also affected the objectives set for the development of choice of law rules. The best-known proponent of European contract law, *Ole Lando*, has repeatedly pointed out problems in choice of law rules which in their most concrete form have to do with the application of a foreign law.[141]

General terms of contract are widely applied in trade. A large number of general terms of contract have been drawn up to facilitate the preparation of business contracts. Supranational sets of rules and principles have long played an important part in international trade. The UNIDROIT Principles and PECL have proved successful. When considering the need to modernise the existing conflicts rules on contractual obligations, wide discussion has taken place in Europe

---

139 See Hay – Lando – Rotunda, "Conflict of Laws as a Technique for Legal Integration", pp. 237–238. See also Hartley, "Pleading and Proof of Foreign Law: The Major European Systems Compared", p. 291.

140 After the Communication on European Contract Law of July 2001, the European Commission adopted another Communication in February 2003 entitled "A more coherent European contract caw. An action plan". The Action Plan introduces a common frame of reference which would provide common principles and terminology on European contract law. In 2004, the Commission issued a third communication which involves a revision of the acquis. See further Communication from the Commission to the Council and the European Parliament on European Contract Law. COM(2001) 398 final; Communication from the Commission to the European Parliament and the Council: A more coherent European contract law. An action plan. COM(2003) 68 final; and Communication from the Commission to the European Parliament and the Council: European Contract Law and the revision of the acquis: the way forward. COM(2004) 651 final.

141 See, for example, Lando, "Some Features of the Law of Contract in the Third Millenium".

over whether choice of law clauses should be allowed to refer to the sets of principles and rules of international trade.

National courts determine the applicable law according to the rules of the Rome Convention. Only the law of a state can be determined as the applicable law. However, arbitrators may be permitted by the arbitration clause to apply the *lex mercatoria*.[142] It has been argued that one of the most central benefits of allowing choice of law clauses referring to non-governmental rules in the forthcoming Rome I would be that they would allow the contracting parties to choose a neutral framework and so avoid the problems that could follow from applying a foreign law.[143]

The fact that a choice of law clause can only refer to a state law has long been seen by many as one of the major problems of the Rome Convention. This has been considered insufficient with regard to the needs of business life and, for example, prevailing *business to business* contractual usage, because in international transactions the usage has changed significantly since the Rome Convention was written. In this respect, the claim is that the rules on party autonomy in the Convention are outdated.[144]

One might argue that an international contract is more closely connected to an autonomous system of rules, such as the UNIDROIT Principles and PECL, than to any particular law of a state.[145] Thus, it has been considered only appropriate to allow choice of law clauses that refer to non-governmental rules and principles. This would further the use of the *restatement* type of principles and create the foundation for a unified contract law infrastructure for the internal market.[146] At the same time, the flexibility and predictability of cross-border trans-

---

142 Cf. Ramberg, International Commercial Transactions, p. 22.

143 See, for example, Berger, "The Principles of European Contract Law and the Concept of 'Creeping Codification' of Law", pp. 28–29.

144 See, for example, López Rodríguez, Lex Mercatoria and Harmonisation of Contract Law in the EU, pp. 332–333, where the author also refers to Article 10 of the Mexico Convention, which permits the reference to trade usages.

145 See Ramberg, International Commercial Transactions, p. 22.

146 See Wilhelmsson, "Sopimusoikeuden eurooppalaistuminen ja oikeudellisten toimijoiden roolit – useampi kokki keittää paremman sopan", p. 1116.

actions would improve. The impending increase in the use of choice of law clauses would also improve legal certainty.

In this respect, the Rome I Proposal contains an expected move. It suggests that the freedom to choose the law applicable to a contract would be expanded so that a choice of law clause could, in addition to the law of a state, refer to legal principles that have been accepted internationally or by the EC. Hence, for example, a choice could be made of either the UNIDROIT Principles or the PECL, or the CISG. However, a choice of law clause would not be permitted to refer to the *lex mercatoria,* because it is not considered precise enough.[147]

It has been argued that European mainstream conflicts law theory stresses the privacy of commercial transactions.[148] With this in mind, the extension of party autonomy suggested in the Rome I Proposal seems to be a natural development. To boost the impact of the parties' will, party autonomy being a key principle of the Rome Convention, Article 3(2) of the Rome I Proposal would authorise the parties to choose a non-State body of law as the applicable law for the entire contract or part of it.

Article 3(2) would read as follows:

> The parties may also choose as the applicable law the principles and rules of the substantive law of contract recognised internationally or in the Community.
>
> However, questions relating to matters governed by such principles or rules which are not expressly settled by them shall be governed by the general principles underlying them or, failing such principles, in accordance with the law applicable in the absence of a choice under this Regulation.

Under the proposed Article, in every type of contract, except consumer contracts, governed by the Rome I Proposal, the parties might also choose as the applicable law the principles and rules of the

147 See Proposal for a Regulation of the European Parliament and the Council on the law applicable to contractual obligations (Rome I), COM(2005) 650 final, Article 3(2) of the Proposal and its grounds on page 5.

148 See Kronke, "Capital Markets and Conflict of Laws", p. 303.

substantive law of contract recognised internationally or in the Community. As regards consumer contracts, party autonomy would be fully excluded.

A careful analysis of the proposed Article 3(2) reveals some uncertainties. First of all, the formulation of the Article is quite open. It allows a choice of any sets of principles or rules that are recognised internationally or in the Community. The problems of the Article do not lie in selection of the UNIRDOIT Principles or PECL as the applicable law. Rather, other sets of principles or rules might exist which the parties would like to use as the applicable law. Such sets of principles or rules might govern only a specific branch or sector. As to the content, these sets of principles or rules could be such that they favour one party of the contract in a way which is normally not allowed in the law of obligations of EU Member States. Hence, selection of such principles or rules as the applicable law would mean that the court could not apply the law of a state which at present can normally be applied under the Rome Convention in order to correct an imbalance between the parties. Additionally, the openness of the extension of party autonomy in the Proposal is criticised, for example, in the Comments of the Max Planck Institute for Foreign Private and International Private Law (later: the Max Planck Institute). According to the Comments, the sets of principles or rules should fulfil certain requirements which could be given in the recital of the future Rome I Regulation. They should have been established by an independent, impartial, and neutral body and their content should be balanced and protected against evasion and abuse of certain mandatory rules. Moreover, the rights and duties should be regulated by the sets of principles or rules in a fairly comprehensive way.[149]

Secondly, the sphere of application of the proposed Article raises another problem. Article 3(2) would permit a choice of internationally recognised sets of principles or rules even in the case of weak party contracts where choice of law would be allowed. This would also mean that parties to an individual employment contract and contract between principal and agent would be permitted to choose internationally recognised sets of principles or rules instead of the law of a

149 See Max Planck Institute's Comments 2006, p. 17.

state. However, the Rome I Proposal gives no reasons for extending the extension of party autonomy to these two types of weak party contracts.

From the standpoint of employee protection, serious difficulties might occur if a choice of sets of principles or rules were permitted. With its very long history, labour law is typically mandatory, with the protection of employees resting on the application of mandatory rules to the contract. Although several ongoing projects in Europe seek to 'restate' general principles of European contract law, consumer law included, labour law has not been a target of these projects. An explanation for this is the special nature of that field of law.

Article 6(1) of the Rome Convention contains a specific protection rule which has also been adopted in the Rome I Proposal. According to this rule, a choice of law clause in an employment contract cannot have the result of depriving employees of the protection afforded them by mandatory rules of the law applicable in the absence of choice. When determining the content of the mandatory employee-protective rules, the question whether the rules serve to protect the employee should be understood broadly.[150] In addition, the Giuliano – Lagarde Report supports the view that issues such as health and safety should also be understood as employee-protective rules referred to in Article 6(1). This means that the Article also governs mandatory rules of a public law nature.[151] All in all, it is essential for this protection rule to become materialized so that comparison is carried out between the laws of different countries.

The specific protection rule of Article 6(1) is vital, since in order to protect the weaker party it limits the effects of the use of party autonomy. Firstly, the rule does not override the law chosen by the parties. Secondly, it requires comparison between the chosen law and the law that would be applied if a choice had not been made. On the basis of this comparison, the rules most favourable to the employee are applied. The new Article 3(2) of the Rome I Proposal would mean

---

150 See Magnus in Staudingers Kommentar, EGBGB 30, para. 75.

151 Giuliano – Lagarde Report, p. 25 and Liukkunen, The Role of Mandatory Rules in International Labour Law – A Comparative Study in the Conflict of Laws, pp. 149–150.

that such comparison might need to be carried out between the set of principles or rules chosen by the parties as the *lex causae* and the law of the state which would be applied in the absence of choice. Hence, we could find a set of non-State rules or principles on one side of the scale, and the law of a state on the other. The uncertainties would not be removed by turning to the rule in Article 3(2), according to which the law applicable in the absence of choice would be applied to issues that are not expressly settled by the rules or principles chosen by the parties.

Since Article 3(2) of the Rome I Proposal would cause uncertainties and weaken the present employee protection, employment contracts should be excluded from its scope of application. Finally, extending party autonomy in employment contracts is not in line with moving in the opposite direction in consumer contracts, where party autonomy would be fully excluded. This would mean tipping the scales against employee protection without any justifiable reason.

5.2 Fixed Connecting Factors

In the Rome Convention, determination of the applicable law is based on the use of semi-open conflicts rules, which combine a number of connecting factors with an exception clause ensuring the application of the law closest to the contract.[152] The starting point of the Convention is application of the law of the country where the party whose performance is characteristic of the contract habitually resides. The presumption rules are supplemented by an exception clause under which the courts may apply any other law than that referred to in the presumptions, if this other law is closer to the contract. This formula with 'soft' presumption rules has left discretion to the courts and, thus, provided the flexibility necessary in international contracting and commercial practice. However, it is sometimes claimed that the disadvantage of such rules is the danger of *lex forism*.

---

152 See Jänterä-Jareborg, "Foreign Law in National Courts – A Comparative Perspective", p. 213.

The rule contained in Article 4 of the Rome I Proposal on determining the applicable law in the absence of choice differs significantly from the present rule in Article 4 of the Rome Convention. The Commission proposes replacing the presumptions in this Article with specified fixed rules. Altogether, the proposed Article 4 contains eight different fixed rules for different types of contracts, such as contracts of sale, contracts for provision of services, and contracts of carriage. As the Max Planck Institute's Comments (2006) argue, the general approach, which almost completely abandons the flexibility present in Article 4 of the Rome Convention, is not desirable.[153] With the technique of fixed connection rules, the Proposal resembles the 1955 Hague Convention whose failure has been claimed to be partly due to such rules.

For the purposes of this study, it is not necessary to go through Article 4 of the Rome I Proposal in detail. A look into how service contracts would be dealt with under the Proposal will suffice. Article 4(1)(b) of the Proposal contains rules on contracts for provision of services. The law applicable to service contracts in the absence of choice would be the law of the country where the service-provider habitually resides. Under proposed Article 4(2), "contracts not specified in paragraph 1 shall be governed by the law of the country in which the party who is required to perform the service characterising the contract has his habitual residence at the time of the conclusion of the contract. Where that service cannot be identified, the contract shall be governed by the law of the country with which it is most closely connected".

Various types of cross-border contracts exist for provision of services, while the notion of 'service' is a broad one. Services can relate to the sale of goods but they are also common, for example, in the construction, communication, tourism, and transport industries. To illustrate, complex chains of cross-border service-providers are typical in construction. It is clear that service contracts may well be more closely connected with another country than the country where the service-provider habitually resides.[154] The law of the service-pro-

153 See Max Planck Institute's Comments 2006, pp. 27–28.
154 See also ibid., pp. 32–33.

vider's habitual residence may have a distant connection to the contract compared, *inter alia*, to the law of the place where the service is provided. The possibility of applying the exception clause could ensure that the law closest to the contract would always be applied. Thus, the justifiable expectations of the parties could also be fulfilled. The fear of *lex forism* should not override necessary flexibility. The fact that the forthcoming Rome I Regulation is to form part of EC law should improve the possibility of uniform interpretation.

5.3 Internationally Mandatory Rules

It can be said that with the Rome Convention the principle of internationally mandatory rules has been established in European private international law.[155] Article 7(2) of the Convention concerns internationally mandatory rules of the forum.[156] It reads as follows:

> Nothing in this Convention shall restrict the application of the rules of the law of the forum in a situation where they are mandatory irrespective of the law otherwise applicable to the contract.

Internationally mandatory rules are referred to under different terms, such as *lois de police*, *lois d'application immédiate* or *Eingriffsnormen*.[157] Compared to 'nationally' mandatory rules, the internationally mandatory nature of provisions is 'strengthened'. The nature and purpose of the provisions indicate that they are so important that they must be applied to contracts irrespective of the otherwise applicable law. The exceptional importance of the provisions links

---

155 The Group which prepared the Rome Convention stated that Article 7 only embodied principles which already existed in the then Member States of the Community. See Giuliano-Lagarde Report, p. 26.

156 See Rinze, "The Scope of Party Autonomy under the 1980 Rome Convention on the Law Applicable to Contractual Obligations", p. 425.

157 My study, The Role of Mandatory Rules in International Labour Law – A Comparative Study in the Conflict of Laws (2004), analyses the use of mandatory rules in international labour law with a particular focus on internationally mandatory rules.

them mostly to the public interest.[158] In other words, these appear to amount to the kind of provisions of law that either protect or demonstrate the public interests of society. Accordingly, the function of protecting the interests of individuals or the aim of establishing a balance between contracting parties are by themselves not enough to make a provision internationally mandatory.[159] In general, this line of interpretation has been followed by German case law. The Federal Labour Court has stated that the nature of the provision is decisive; only provisions fulfilling the public interest can be regarded as internationally mandatory.[160]

Article 7(2) does not specify what internationally mandatory rules can be like. However, it is clear that these rules give effect to important state policies, which cannot be derogated from by a contract.[161] These rules are considered so important that the courts are entitled to apply them, regardless of the country whose law would otherwise, according to the conflicts rules of the forum, cover the legal relationship. Such rules protect interests that are regarded as integral to the country in question. Article 7(2) also governs internationally mandatory rules of EC law.[162]

Internationally mandatory rules are rules whose nature requires that they be applied, irrespective of choice of law clause, irrespective of what the law determined on an objective basis provides, and irrespective of how these rules are connected to the law in question. However, under the Rome Convention their application is always at the discretion of the court. When it comes to internationally mandatory rules of third countries, Article 7(1) of the Convention contains criteria about when such rules can be applied. Article 7(2) does not require a connection between internationally mandatory rules of the

158 See Rinze, "The Scope of Party Autonomy under the 1980 Rome Convention on the Law Applicable to Contractual Obligations", p. 427.

159 See Liukkunen, The Role of Mandatory Rules in International Labour Law – A Comparative Study in the Conflict of Laws.

160 See BAG 24.8.1989, BAGE 63, p. 17 ff.

161 See Plender – Wilderspin, The European Contracts Convention. The Rome Convention on the Choice of Law for Contracts, p. 154.

162 See Lando, "The EEC Convention on the Law Applicable to Contractual Obligations", p. 207.

forum law and the contract or case in question. Yet, application of internationally mandatory rules of the forum can depend on the connection of the case or the circumstances to the forum country.

The Rome Convention does not prevent the Contracting States from enacting some of their national provisions as internationally mandatory. However, the objective of uniform application restricts the latitude of the Contracting States in this respect. The question of internationally mandatory rules has not often been dealt with by national legislators in the Contracting Sates. For the most part, national legislations do not provide direction to the courts when they have to determine whether a rule is internationally mandatory.

By virtue of the Rome Convention, a distinction must be drawn between 'domestically' mandatory rules and internationally mandatory rules in choice of law. For example, consumer- and employee-protective domestically mandatory rules of the objectively applicable law have been given a special status in Articles 5 and 6 of the Convention. The objective of the specific protection rules contained in these Articles is to restrict the effects of a choice of law that might weaken the position of the consumer or the employee from what it would be in the absence of choice. Consumers and employees cannot by a choice of law clause be deprived of the protection provided by mandatory rules of objectively applicable law.

It has sometimes been claimed that the mandatory rules referred to in Articles 5(2) and 6(1) should be distinguished from internationally mandatory rules. Clearly, the rules referred to in these Articles need not be internationally mandatory. They should only be 'internally' mandatory protective provisions. However, some authors would give Articles 5(2) and 6(1) priority. From the standpoint of weaker party protection, another option is to apply those mandatory rules which give best protection to the consumer or employee.[163] I have written elsewhere that Articles 6(1) and 7 overlap so that it is not reasonably possible to divorce internationally mandatory rules from mandatory rules applied under Article 6(1). As I see it, if different

---

163 See, for example, Magnus, Staudingers Kommentar, EGBGB 34. See also Junker, "Empfiehlt es sich, Art. 7 EVÜ zu revidieren oder aufgrund der bisherigen Erfahrungen zu präzisieren?".

rules require application simultaneously under Articles 5 or 6 and 7, rules that are most favourable to the consumer or employee should generally be applied.[164]

The Green Paper of the Commission on the conversion of the Rome Convention prompted interesting debate on Article 7. One of the starting points of the discussion was that the Commission pointed out in the Green Paper that the ECJ had already adopted a definition of internationally mandatory rules in *Arblade*.[165] This definition followed German legal thinking in that it focused on the purpose of the rules in question. Accordingly, the question was about "national provisions compliance with which has been deemed to be so crucial for the protection of the political, social or economic order in the Member State concerned as to require compliance therewith by all persons present the on the national territory of that Member State and all legal relationships within that State".[166]

The Max Planck Institute and, as one might say, its Scandinavian counterpart, the Nordic Group for Private International Law, gave detailed commentaries on the conversion work concerning the Rome Convention.[167] There was a significant difference of opinion between the Max Planck Institute and the Nordic Group about the future definition of internationally mandatory rules. The Nordic Group would have rejected the approach based on looking at the interests served by the mandatory rule in question. It would have left internationally mandatory rules undefined, whereas the Max Planck Institute preferred a definition modelled on the basis of the particular statement of the ECJ in *Arblade*. Yet, some flexibility was noticeable even in the latter approach.

Article 8(1) of the Rome I Proposal is closer to the German view than the Scandinavian one. The Commission proposes a definition of internationally mandatory rules inspired by the ECJ judgment

---

164 See Liukkunen, The Role of Mandatory Rules in International Labour Law – A Comparative Study in the Conflict of Laws.

165 Joined Cases C-369/96 and C-376/96, Criminal proceedings against Jean-Claude Arblade and Arblade & Fils SARL and Bernard Leloup, Serge Leloup and Sofrage SARL, [1999] ECR I-8453.

166 See ibid., para. 30.

167 See Max Planck Institute's Comments 2003 and NGPIL Proposal 2003.

in *Arblade*. Under the Article, mandatory rules would be rules "the respect for which is regarded as crucial by a country for safeguarding its political, social or economic organisation to such an extent that they are applicable to any situation falling within their scope, irrespective of the law otherwise applicable to the contract under this Regulation". This definition is flexible and would probably remove at least some of the ambiguity attached to determining internationally mandatory rules. It is noteworthy that the proposed definition is quite close to the interpretation adopted by the German courts according to which internationally mandatory rules should always serve the public interest.

6 Consumers in Conflicts Law: Objectives and their Realisation

In European international consumer and labour law, the principle of protecting the weaker party that sets limits for freedom of contract is not solely based on substantive protective provisions. The means which choice of law rules provide for taking into account the protective provisions of a given national legal system play an important role in strengthening the legal position of the consumer and employee. As we have seen, this is illustrated by the specific rules contained in the Rome Convention.

Consumer protection has been held as the 'the pioneer and engine' of the Europeanisation of private law.[168] Harmonising consumer law has been based on the need to develop the internal market. However, harmonisation has not been well co-ordinated, while transposition of various consumer directives has caused problems because of the diversity of national laws in Member States.[169] Moreover, the levels of protection of the consumer legislation in the Member States differ since consumer directives are based on minimum harmonisation.

168 Joerges, On the Legitimacy of Europeanising Europe's Private Law: Considerations on a Law of Justi(ce)-fication (*justum facere*) for the EU-Multi-Level System.

169 See Lando, "Liberal, Social and 'Ethical' Justice in European Contract Law", p. 818. See also López Rodríguez, Lex Mercatoria and Harmonisation of Contract Law in the EU, p. 240.

Lack of common general contract rules in Europe also has consequences in terms of choice of law. The emergence of choice of law rules in directives on consumer protection is often used as an example of the fragmentation of European conflicts law. These directives have been used to mend the choice of law rules on consumer contracts in Article 5 of the Rome Convention that became insufficient because of increased e-commerce and consumer mobility.

In general, the consumer directives use a similar definition of consumer to that given in the Rome Convention. Article 5 of the Convention applies to a contract for the supply of goods or services to a person ('the consumer') for a purpose which can be regarded as being outside the consumer's trade or profession, or a contract for providing credit for that object. Contracts of carriage and contracts for the supply of services in a country other than that in which the consumer habitually resides have been excluded from the scope of Article 5.

The Rome Convention was prepared at a time when consumer protection in Europe was in its infancy. What has happened since then cannot be detached from the need to develop internal market law for the specific purposes of European integration. It is also well known that forms of consumer sale have undergone major changes after conclusion of the Convention. From the conflicts law standpoint, the main legislative approach of EC directives has been to cover legislative lacunas by complementing the Convention in areas that protection of the Convention rules does not reach, by enacting mandatory EC legislation on consumer protection. This means that core EC provisions on consumer protection cannot be derogated from by means of a choice of law clause referring to a law of a non-Member State. As the Rome I Proposal would no longer allow the use of choice of law clauses in consumer contracts, the relationship between the consumer protection directives and the Rome I Proposal has to be settled. However, the Proposal contains no suggestions as to how this relationship is to be arranged.[170]

---

170 See also Liukkunen, "Kansainvälinen yksityisoikeus ja Euroopan integraatio", p. 348.

The following table lists the key Articles of consumer directives which affect choice of law:

Directive 93/13/EEC	Article 6 2. Member States shall take the necessary measures to ensure that the consumer does not lose the protection granted by this Directive by virtue of the choice of the law of a non-Member country as the law applicable to the contract if the latter has a close connection with the territory of the Member States.
Directive 94/47/EC	Article 9 The Member States shall take the measures necessary to ensure that, whatever the law applicable may be, the purchaser is not deprived of the protection afforded by this Directive, if the immovable property concerned is situated within the territory of a Member State.
Directive 97/7/EC	Article 12 Binding nature 2. Member States shall take the measures needed to ensure that the consumer does not lose the protection granted by this Directive by virtue of the choice of the law of a non-member country as the law applicable to the contract if the latter has close connection with the territory of one or more Member States.
Directive 99/44/EC	Article 7 Binding nature 2. Member States shall take the necessary measures to ensure that consumers are not deprived of the protection afforded by this Directive as a result of opting for the law of a non-member State as the law applicable to the contract where the contract has a close connection with the territory of the Member States.

Directive 2002/65/EC	Article 12 Imperative nature of this Directive's provisions 2. Member States shall take the measures needed to ensure that the consumer does not lose the protection granted by this Directive by virtue of the choice of the law of a non-member country as the law applicable to the contract, if this contract has a close link with the territory of one or more Member States.

The table shows an approach which is noteworthy in terms of European conflicts law. The foreign *lex causae* may lack such mandatory regulation that in EC law has been laid down in order to protect the consumer. The consumer directives contain provisions with the effect that the minimum protection provided for by these provisions cannot be derogated from by choice of the law of a non-Member State if the contract has a close connection to a Member State.

One might argue that the consumer directives seem *de facto* to consider the EU as a kind of subject of choice of law in relation to non-Member States. The criterion for a close connection to the Member States established in all five directives is related to this. In essence, the directives set the minimum protection provided by EC law against regulation provided by third countries only one-dimensionally, in cases which have a close connection to the territory of Member States. The basic assumption behind this regional 'better law' approach, which exclusively focuses on the protection based on EC regulation, seems to be that EC law provides better protection than the law of non-Member States. As *Basedow* sharply observes, the consumer directives do not enact on the application of the mandatory rules in a non-Member State law which would grant better protection in analogous situations. The directives only provide for the application of mandatory EC legislation when a 'minimum' connection of the case with the Community is established. The directives defend the rights of consumers against third country suppliers and side against third country consumers opposed to suppliers from the Member States.[171]

The need to update Article 5 in the Rome Convention and improve consumer protection in choice of law has often been considered one of the key issues in converting the Convention into a Community instrument. Consumers should be protected irrespective of where or how they make a purchase. In this sense, the protection provided by the consumer directives is selective, with the requirement of a close connection with the territory of a Member State. An improvement suggested by the Rome I Proposal is that a choice of law clause would no longer be permitted in consumer contracts.[172] This would ensure that only the law of one state – the law where the consumer habitually resides – would be applied, so that comparison between two different laws would be avoided. Since even now the protection rule in Article 5(2) of the Rome Convention guarantees the consumer protection of the law of habitual residence, the proposed amendment would not significantly change the present situation. However, the amendment would remove uncertainty as to which rules should be regarded as the 'mandatory rules of law' referred to in Article 5(2) of the Convention.

Yet, some unresolved issues need to be dealt with in the near future. As mentioned above, the Rome I Proposal provides no answers about how the relationship between the future Regulation and the consumer directives concerning choice of law would be arranged. If a choice of law clause were no longer permitted, then equally the need would no longer exist for the above-listed provisions ensuring application of protective rules in the directives when choice of a non-

---

171 See Basedow, "Consumer Contracts and Insurance Contracts in a Future Rome I-Regulation", p. 279.

172 According to the European Commission, two options were available: either application of the law of the professional or the law of the consumer, and only the latter is truly compatible with the high level of consumer protection required by the EC Treaty. See Proposal for a Regulation of the European Parliament and the Council on the law applicable to contractual obligations (Rome I). COM(2005) 650 final, p. 6.

Member State law has been made.[173] Hence, the Rome I project offers an opportunity to cure existing problems of the one-dimensionality of conflicts rules in the consumer directives.

The definition of a consumer in the Rome Convention has often been criticised for being much too narrow. The consumer protection in the Convention has been seen as being based on the inadequate idea of 'passive' consumers who react to suppliers' activities in their own state.[174] According to Article 5 of the Convention, the rules providing consumer protection are applicable if conclusion of the contract was preceded by a specific invitation addressed to the consumer or by advertising; if the other party or its agent received the consumer's order in the consumer's country; and, thirdly, if the contract is for the sale of goods and the consumer travelled from her own country to another country and there placed the order, provided that the journey was arranged by the seller for the purpose of inducing the consumer to buy.

The Rome Convention and the consumer directives provide a regional definition of a consumer. For example, the definition used in EC law differs from the definition in the CISG. Under Article 2(a) of the Convention, it is not applicable to sales "of goods bought for personal, family, or household use, unless the seller, at any time before or at the conclusion of the contract, neither knew nor ought to have known that the goods were bought for any such use".

In the Rome I Proposal, the definition of a consumer contract is broader than in the Rome Convention. The proposed definition governs consumers habitually resident in a Member State. However, as the Max Planck Institute's Comments argue, there is no reason to limit the scope of application of Article 5 in the Rome I Proposal to consumers habitually resident in a Member State. This limitation would mean establishing two different groups of consumers in the EU. Instead, the consumer-protective rules of the Rome I Proposal should

173 See Liukkunen, "Kansainvälinen yksityisoikeus ja Euroopan integraatio", p. 352.

174 See Basedow, "Consumer Contracts and Insurance Contracts in a Future Rome I Regulation", p. 275. See also Straetmans, "The Consumer Concept in EC law".

apply to all consumers within the meaning of the proposed Regulation irrespective of their place of habitual residence.[175] We should not forget that the Rome I Regulation will have universal scope of application. The definition of a consumer has far-reaching consequences. Although the possibility of applying internationally mandatory rules is an important complement to the conflicts rules that apply to consumer contracts, it should not become the only expedient for protecting a large group of consumers who would not fit the criteria given in Article 5 of the future Rome I Regulation.

7 Tools of Unification and Harmonisation

It has sometimes been argued that the creation of large areas of uniform law is merely an illusion.[176] The unsuccessful efforts of the Hague Conference on adopting global conflicts rules on international sales, discussed above in this chapter, show how difficult it is to work out universal conflicts rules on international contracts.[177] Yet, in the field of international sales law we have been witnessing the global success story of the CISG. The CISG also offers a remarkable example of the interplay between substantive sales law and private international law. Although the CISG has diminished the role of conflicts rules it should be noted that conflicts rules have not lost their relevance in international sales law. For its part, the Convention enables discussion of tools for unification and harmonisation. The call for clarity and predictability of choice of law in international contracting has not lost its relevance. What has been said above about the inconsistencies between the Rome Convention and the Hague 1955 Convention is noteworthy in this respect for those EU Member States that have ratified the 1955 Convention.

The success of the CISG is demonstrated by the fact that in both the US and Europe recommendations are being made that when de-

175 See Max Planck Institute's Comments 2006, p. 41.

176 See Kronke, "Capital Markets and Conflict of Laws", p. 378.

177 See also Oliver, "Standarization of Choice-of Law Rules for International Contracts: Should there be a New Beginning?", pp. 385–386.

veloping regional rules further, the CISG should serve as a model. In the US, these recommendations also concern conflicts rules, whereas in Europe they often deal with the harmonisation of contract law. *Magnus* has emphasised the need to avoid Europeanisation of international contract law if this is at the expense of progress reached globally in the field of international sales law. He has proposed that when drafting European contract law, the CISG should serve as the basis. Furthermore, according to *Magnus* European sales law should correspond to the CISG as closely as possible.[178] This can be held desirable from the standpoint of business parties, since if the diversity of legal rules between Member States were reduced, then transaction costs would also be reduced. This would also mean that the four EU Member States that have remained outside the CISG should ratify it without reservations.

The model proposed by *Magnus* would also likely mean the desirability that Member States having declarations would give them up.[179] However, the Scandinavian countries are probably not willing to abandon their current intra-Scandinavian sales law model, which has functioned well. Similarly, the United Kingdom has its own reasons to maintain the *status quo* and not ratify the Convention. The Member States that are members of the Hague 1955 Convention and, thus, apply the 1955 Convention universally, would also need to consider withdrawing from the Convention. We have seen above that the coexistence of the Hague 1955 Convention with the CISG is problematic.

Since the CISG has already had a great impact on the European regulatory approach, it would also be natural to use it when drafting European contract law. This would also have relevance globally. If European contract law were modelled on the CISG, then the European model would better maintain its coherency with the global model set out by the CISG.

Yet, it should be noted that a certain reluctance of the contracting parties to use the CISG has been overshadowing the success story

---

178 See Magnus, Action Plan for a European Contract Law. European Contract Law and CISG, p. 8.

179 See, however, Lookofsky, "Alive and Well in Scandinavia: CISG Part II".

of the Convention. According to some surveys, the Convention has relatively often been excluded by contracting parties and even by general terms of contract.[180] It seems that use of the CISG could be increased by improving awareness of its content. When considering future challenges, the role of the rules on jurisdiction should not be forgotten. As to business parties, compared to arbitration, the enforcement of foreign judgments is not as readily available. At regional level, the EC has made the enforcement of foreign judgments more efficient with the Brussels I Regulation. However, at the global level the enforcement of judgments faces constant challenges. In arbitration, the situation is better since many states have ratified the 1958 New York Convention on the recognition and enforcement of foreign arbitral awards.[181]

Altogether, tools of unification and harmonisation are becoming more and more varied.[182] In Europe, unification of the conflict of laws is based on binding instruments, whereas harmonisation of contract law is based also on various non-binding instruments. It is likely that *soft law* will be used even more frequently in the future. In this light, it is appropriate that the current tendency in European choice of law favours acknowledging non-binding sets of rules and principles. However, future conflicts rules should also in this sense be clear enough.

As we have seen, careful consideration is required by the EC legislator in order to make the forthcoming rules of the Rome I Proposal efficient enough and to ensure that they fulfil the objectives of flexibility and legal certainty, weak party protection included. Fragmentation of conflicts rules has become a serious problem in European private international law. Therefore, the EC legislator needs to pay more attention not only to the basic systematics of conflicts law but also to the work carried out by other organisations in the field of private international law. An important step forward is that the EC has

180 See, for example, Smits, "Diversity of Contract Law and the European Internal Market", p. 161.

181 See Ramberg, International Commercial Transactions, p. 79. It should also be noted that a new Convention on Choice of Court Agreements was adopted by the Hague Conference of Private International Law in 2005.

182 See Kronke, "Capital markets and Conflict of Laws", p. 378.

sought membership in the Hague Conference on Private International Law.[183]

8 Common Law, Continental Law, and the European Conflicts Law Approach

This section discusses some basic observations concerning European conflicts approach from the standpoint of the division between common law and continental law. This division has traditionally resulted in significant differences in the normative systems of conflicts law in Europe. The purpose is not to offer a detailed analysis but to present some typical features of the issue. The following observations also serve the legal comparison between Europe and the US, which is carried out later in the chapter.

As is generally known, common law traditionally views judgments of the courts as the most important legal source. This is also true for private international law. Nevertheless, although the origins of English conflicts law are found in the common law as administered by courts in England, evidence is available at the national level, in the shape of statutory rules concerning torts, of successfully developing

183 According to the proposed Council Decision, the Community will accede to the Hague Conference on Private International Law by making a declaration that it accepts the Statute of the Hague Conference. According to the Memorandum of the European Commission, "From a political standpoint, membership would grant the Community a status consistent with its new role as a major international player in the field of civil judicial cooperation. From a legal standpoint, membership would enable the Community to fully participate in the negotiations of conventions in areas of its competence by expressing its views and positions and ensuring consistency and coherence between its own rules and envisaged international instruments. Moreover, the Community as such rather than its Member States would be the subject of the rights and obligations stemming from Hague Conventions in areas of its competence". See Proposal for a Council Decision on the accession of the European Community to the Hague Conference on Private International Law. COM(2005) 639 final. The Community applied for membership of the Conference in 2002 and the Conference adopted amendments to the Statute that allow the EC to become a member in 2005.

private international law by means of legislation.[184] In addition, implementation of the Rome Convention provides evidence of a regional development with statutory conflicts rules. These rules have now been in force in England for over a decade.

Broadly speaking, however, it should be emphasised that the common law understanding of the role of the law contained in codes has been fundamentally different from that of continental law. As *Trevor C. Hartley* puts it, in general terms in common law systems the purpose and function of codes of law have traditionally been only remedial. According to him, exploring attitudes to legislation reveals a difference in priorities between common law and civil law: civil law lawyers are more concerned with the structure of the law, and common law lawyers with its operation.[185]

The discourse of English conflicts law has been often characterised as pragmatic, and statutes have been seen as pragmatic attempts to solve pragmatic problems.[186] In English conflicts law, the general tendency has been to favour the principle of party autonomy, while the role of the *lex fori* in the conflicts process has been supposed neutral.[187] According to *Hartley*, English courts tend to give priority to doing justice to the parties, whereas continental courts give more weight to state interests.[188] *Hartley* has also argued that the ECJ often

---

184 Morse, "Making English Private International Law", p. 276 and pp. 293–302. See also Hay, "Flexibility versus Predictability and Uniformity in Choice of Law. Reflections on Current European and United States Conflicts Law", p. 393.

185 See Hartley, "The European Union and the Systematic Dismantling of the Common Law of Conflict of Laws", p. 814.

186 See Fentiman, "English Private International Law at the End of the 20th Century: Progress or Regress?", pp. 166–168. See also de Cruz, Comparative Law in a Changing World, p. 103.

187 See Fentiman, "English Private International Law at the End of the 20th Century: Progress or Regress?", pp. 179–183. See also Hepple, Labour Laws and Global Trade, p. 190.

188 See Hartley, "The European Union and the Systematic Dismantling of the Common Law of Conflict of Laws", pp. 813–815. Cf. O'Hara – Ribstein, "From Politics to Efficiency in Choice of Law", p. 1184.

gives more weight to state interests than party interests and generally follows a more civilian than common law approach.[189]

When it comes to contractual obligations, the conflicts rules in the Rome Convention seek to provide a 'statutory bridge' between common law and continental law in Europe. The basic principle of the Convention is party autonomy, so it seeks to do justice to the parties. At the same time, the Convention rules on the application of mandatory rules ensure consideration of state interests. Yet, one objective of the Convention is to enable the applicable law to be determined *a priori*. The communitarisation of conflicts rules in Europe can be said to be based on the idea of legislative intervention.

The question arises about the extent to which the common law and continental approach are losing their differences in European conflicts law. With the Rome Convention, it is clear that from the systemic standpoint we can recognize a marked dominance in the EU of the continental conflicts approach. This approach, based on the use of statutory rules, is also evident in specific EC legislation containing conflicts rules and supported by the role adopted by the ECJ. Many EC directives seek to ensure that important EC rules cannot be undermined by choice of the law of a non-Member State.

Although one would not fully share *Hartley*'s views on the state interest-oriented approach adopted by the ECJ, a critical overview from the perspective of choice of law reveals certain tensions. The judgment of the Court in *Ingmar* could be used as an example here.[190] In brief, the Court held certain provisions of the Directive on the coordination of the laws of the Member States relating to self-employed commercial agents[191] to be internationally mandatory. Hence, these provisions were to be applied regardless of the choice of law clause agreed by the contracting parties. The case was about a principal established in a non-Member State and an agent established in a Member State. Their contract contained a choice of law clause which

---

[189] See Hartley, "The European Union and the Systematic Dismantling of the Common Law of Conflict of Laws", pp. 814–815.

[190] See Case C-381/98, Ingmar GB Ltd v. Eaton Leonard Technologies Inc., [2000] ECR I-9305.

[191] Council Directive 86/653/EEC on the coordination of the laws of the Member States relating to self-employed commercial agents.

referred to the law of a non-Member State. The decision of the ECJ shows how the Court can use private international law to ensure policy interests in a way which clearly gives more weight to state than to party interests.[192]

The decision of the EC legislator to use a regulation as the only legislative instrument in conflicts law unification work based on the Articles of Title IV EC Treaty demonstrates great trust in the power of legislation in the EU. In essence, the use of regulations presupposes that all 25 (or in practice, with Denmark remaining outside, 24) jurisdictions of the EU understand and apply forthcoming conflicts rules in the same way.

The next question to be asked is whether underlying differences in national views on the role of state interests versus party interests are strong enough to maintain their relevance in the future. Enacting common statutory rules does not alone make fundamental differences in legal thinking disappear. *Peter North*, for example, has pointed out that when the Brussels Convention and the Rome Convention were adopted in England, many attempts were made to maintain much of the old and to limit the effects of the new. Although he sees pragmatic reasons behind this, rather than reasons stemming from the common law system as such, this exemplifies some of the difficulties in wholesale adoption of a new conflicts law approach.[193] This is, of course, not merely a problem of conflicts law, for we have already seen that the intensive debate about a European Civil Code, or a Common Frame of Reference, reflects different views on how and to what extent a common framework could be established for Europe.

At best, in a Community of 25 Member States, the emergence of statutory rules combining elements of common law and continental law might often turn out to be only a point of departure for the development desired by the legislator. Whether the degree of unification sought by the EC legislator in the field of private international law

---

192 See also, for example, Verhagen, "The Tension Between Party Autonomy and European Union Law: Some Observations on Ingmar GB Ltd v Eaton Leonard Technologies Inc.", pp. 135–154.

193 See North, "Is European Harmonisation of Private International Law a Myth or a Reality? A British Perspective", pp. 44–45.

will eventually be reached depends on various factors, not least how legal integration in general continues in a Union of 25 different jurisdictions. Although the Community is creating conflicts rules that will serve both intra-regional and international purposes, there is a danger that in law-making the former purpose will prevail. Regionality has its pros and cons. Mere regionality would be a sign of a blinkered attitude in issues where globalisation and the breakdown of borders are being confronted from every direction.

Some tend to emphasise that although the business environment has become global, the field of the law of obligations cannot be fully detached from its linkage to legal culture and tradition. If we assess the development of EC law concerning conflicts rules so far, it is easy to see that much use of legislation has not prevented different approaches to handling problems of interpretation. This is partly due to divergences in substantive law and legal cultures, which affect the practical result in conflicts cases. For example, the national culture of English conflicts law still has characteristics that differ from those of continental legal systems.[194]

Finally, we ought to remember that legislative and judicial development should go together.[195] This is how the different approaches of continental and common law in Europe could be interconnected. Law-drafting is only one stage of the development. How statutory rules work in practice is of decisive importance for the future of European conflicts law.

9 EU and US Comparison

Legal comparison of the approaches to conflicts law adopted by the two leading economic areas in the world may provide fresh insight into present challenges to the conflict of laws. This relates, on the one hand, to the current preparation of conflicts rules in the EU and the

---

[194] See Fentiman, "English Private International Law at the End of the 20th Century: Progress or Regress?", pp. 166–167 and Morse, "Making English Private International Law", p. 276.

[195] Morse, "Making English Private International Law", p. 302.

lively debate surrounding it and, on the other hand, to the current debate in the US as to whether a need exists for a third Conflicts Restatement. The Rome Convention has unified the conflicts rules on contractual obligations in the EU Member States at intergovernmental level, without forming part of EC law as such. The Second Restatement of Conflict of Laws (later: the Second Restatement) can be said to provide a framework for the federal states of the US in the same field.

Restatements of Law, which can be characterised as systematic collections of laws, provide non-binding common law rules with explanatory comments. Restatements are published by the American Law Institute established in the 1920s. They exist in several fields of law, such as conflicts law, contracts, and property. Although Restatements do not carry official authority and should be understood as guides to the law, they can have a unifying impact on US law.[196] Yet, it should be noted that it is hardly possible to speak about US conflicts law, given that each state has its own conflicts law.[197] Moreover, it should be noted that although US conflicts doctrine commonly refers to the 'rules and principles' in the Second Restatement, these rules and principles are not binding. Rather, they seek to guide the courts and, by so doing, contribute to the unification of US law on a fully voluntary basis. Although the Restatements can be said to resemble civil law codes, they do not enjoy the status of legislation.[198] This basic distinction should also be taken into account when assessing the US and European approach by comparing the Second Restatement and the Rome Convention.

The particular nature of the US legal system can only be understood by bearing in mind the common law model, which originates in English law. It is well known that the law of the US originally derived to a large extent from English law even though, in principle, the heavy influence of English law ended in the US when the country became independent. Although US law has many unique features, the basic

---

196 See de Cruz, Comparative Law in a Changing World, pp. 115–116.

197 See Symeonides, "The American Choice-of-Law Revolution in the Courts: Today and Tomorrow", p. 27.

198 See de Cruz, Comparative Law in a Changing World, p. 116.

approach to law is still similar to that of England.[199] However, concepts of law differ.[200] The fact that the law of the US consists of federal law, state laws, and constitutional law makes it necessarily different from the common law of England, and explains why the outcome of 'transplantation' of English law in the legal and constitutional setup of the US is profoundly 'American'.[201]

As regards US conflicts law, this is one of the few branches of American law that has its origins in civilian sources. *Joseph Story*, the intellectual father of US conflicts law, has been said to be mostly responsible for this development.[202] European doctrines started to spread in particular with *Story*'s book Commentaries on the Conflict of Laws, Foreign and Domestic (1834).[203] It is generally held that the doctrine has affected conflicts law more than any other branch of American law.[204]

It should be emphasised that in the common law system of the US, the conflict of laws addresses not only determination of the applicable law among the laws of different states, but also between individual federated states. Strictly speaking, a distinction can be made between three categories of conflicts: 1) vertical conflicts between federal law and state law, 2) horizontal conflicts between the states of the US and 3) 'international' conflicts between the laws of foreign countries, on the one hand, and the laws of the US or the laws of a state of the US, on the other.[205] The last group mentioned naturally governs conflicts between foreign countries handled by the US courts. In practice, only vertical conflicts are a matter of federal law.[206] Although US conflicts law does not differentiate between interstate

199 See for example ibid., p. 118 and Mattila, Vertaileva oikeuslingvistiikka, p. 436.

200 See de Cruz, Comparative Law in a Changing World, p. 118.

201 See ibid., p. 107.

202 See Symeonides – Perdue – Mehren, Conflict of Laws: American, Comparative, International. Cases and Materials, pp. 12–13.

203 See Scoles – Hay – Borchers – Symeonides, Conflict of Laws, p. 18.

204 See ibid., p. 68.

205 See Symeonides – Perdue – von Mehren, Conflict of Laws: American, Comparative, International. Cases and Materials, p. 4.

206 See ibid., p. 5.

and international conflicts cases in a doctrinal sense, the circumstance of foreign facts may affect the choice of law decision.[207]

In the US, the role of constitutional law in the field of conflicts law is not marginal although, for the most part, conflicts law issues are matters of private law. The US Supreme Court in the *Allstate Insurance Co. v. Hague* case provided a general test of constitutionality, applicable to both international and interstate conflicts. According to the Court, "for a State's substantive law to be selected in a constitutionally permissible manner, that State must have a significant contact or significant aggregation of contacts, creating state interests, such that choice of its law is neither arbitrary nor fundamentally unfair".[208] In Europe, the role of unified conflicts rules on contractual obligations has been a specific one. Because of the previously existing lack of competence of the EC to create conflicts rules that would form part of EC law, in 1991 unification began by an international convention between the Member States. This means that the fundamental principles of EC law have not been applicable to the Rome Convention. In addition, since it was only in 2004 that the ECJ received limited authority to interpret the Convention, the national courts have not been able to obtain any guidance on interpretation of the Convention for over a decade.

It could be argued that differences in choice of law thinking within the two regions under comparison would support mention of several European and US approaches. Yet, pan-European statutory rules and pan-American Restatement rules, although the latter are non-binding, enable comparison of the European and American ap-

---

207 Hay, "Flexibility versus Predictability and Uniformity in Choice of Law. Reflections on Current European and United States Conflicts Law", p. 302. See also pp. 292–293. *Fentiman* has argued that if the European integration developed further, the conflict of laws might be characterised as an internal rather than an external branch, which would enable use of US approaches. See Fentiman, "English Private International Law at the End of the 20th Century: Progress or Regress?", on p. 175.

208 Allstate Insurance Co. v. Hague, Supreme Court of the United States, 1981, 449 U.S. 302, 101 S.Ct. 633, 66 L.End2d 521. See also Peterson, "American Private International Law at the End of the 20th Century: Progress or Regress?", pp. 414–415.

proaches. However, along with a certain diversity within the regions, systemic differences should be emphasised before turning to conflicts law comparisons in detail. As has been underlined, the case law system of the US differs fundamentally from that established in the EU, which is largely based on a statutory approach.

9.1 Methodological Observations

When addressing US and European conflicts law approaches, it would be possible to begin by comparing Restatement rules as such to the common statutory rules of the EU Member States. However, a wider context is useful to enable a grasp of some of the differences in legal thinking that affect the outcome of the conflicts rules. Therefore, the aim in the following is to sketch a picture of the methodological aspects of choice of law in the US and Europe. This increases understanding of the main differences in conflicts law thinking between the two continents. The same comparison is also used later to assess the communitarisation of conflicts law currently occurring in Europe.

As *Basil Markensisis* has emphasised, history often provides the starting point if one wishes to explain methodological differences. In the history of US conflicts law, periods can be distinguished when interstate conflicts have received almost the entire attention of US conflicts scholars, at least within the mainstream of American conflicts law. In order to understand the relevance of the interstate context for US development, a brief look into some characteristics of the history of US conflicts law is in order.

In broad terms, three phases of private international law in the US have been distinguished by *Reimann*. He makes a rough division between the traditional first hundred years, the phase between the 1950s and 1970s, and the third development which has taken shape since then. Originally, when US conflicts discipline was founded, it was rich in international and comparative perspectives.[209] The first half of the 20th century was dominated by the vested rights theory ad-

[209] See Reimann, "A New Restatement – For the International Age", pp. 577–580.

vanced by *Joseph Beale*. Once a right was 'vested' in a particular person it was to be enforced by the courts.[210] The principal aim of the theory was to achieve predictability and uniformity by a jurisdiction-selective choice of law method. This idea was also behind the first Restatement of Conflict of Laws published in 1934.[211]

When the second period of the discipline began in the 1950s under the heavy influence of legal realism, the focus of US scholars turned from an international to an interstate perspective. *Cavers*, *Currie*, *Ehrenzweig*, *Leflar* and others emphasised that conflicts rules also serve public interests, or governmental interests. The emphasis on forum law became apparent in *Currie*'s 'interest analysis' and *Ehrenzweig*'s theory on the application of forum law and when it can be 'properly' applied. The most significant idea that came out of the conflicts revolution was interest analysis. During this period, the Second Restatement was adopted. This Restatement, whose drafting started in 1953 and was completed in 1969, can be considered an outcome of the US conflicts revolution.[212] Before the revolution, the conflicts rules had attempted to provide legal certainty and to achieve conflicts justice and interstate uniformity, regardless of the forum. With the conflicts revolution, a drastic change towards flexibility occurred.[213]

The Second Restatement was drafted from the perspective of a neutral forum.[214] One of the key characteristics of the Restatement is that its principles and rules are drawn from interstate cases; and they are made for the domestic context.[215] This can be explained at least

---

210 See Peterson, "American Private International Law at the End of the 20th Century: Progress or Regress?", pp. 416–417.

211 See Restatement of Law of the Conflict of Laws (1934).

212 See Reimann, "A New Restatement – For the International Age", pp. 577–578 and Symeonides, "The Need for a Third Conflicts Restatement (And a Proposal for Tort Conflicts)", p. 443.

213 See Symeonides, "The American Choice-of-Law Revolution in the Courts: Today and Tomorrow", pp. 413–414.

214 See Scoles – Hay – Borchers – Symeonides, Conflict of Laws, p. 60.

215 *Willis Reese*, who for the most part was responsible for drafting the Second Restatement, was a representative of a conflicts approach with a domestic focus. See Reimann, "A New Restatement – For the International Age", p. 578.

partly by the fact that international conflicts cases played a marginal role in American conflicts law when the Restatement was adopted.[216] Although the text of the Restatement bears interstate dominance, the conflicts rules can be applied in both interstate and international cases. Contrary to that in Europe, US conflicts law thinking is generally based on the view that statutory solutions do not fit in conflicts problems.[217] As has been said, in contrast with European statutory rules of mandatory nature, Restatements are non-binding by nature. It is up to the US courts whether they follow Restatement rules or not. The courts are free to modify or ignore them.

The original purpose was that the Second Restatement would have a transitional character.[218] The Restatement has been an important source of guidance for the courts, but in practice several conflicts approaches in the US are to be recognized.[219] As regards contract conflicts, *Symeon C. Symeonides* has distinguished different methodological camps: a majority of states follow the Second Restatement, but also many states follow the traditional approach or the combined modern approach.[220] In 2004, a total of 22 US jurisdictions followed the Second Restatement in tort conflicts and 24 in contract conflicts.[221] Hence, some states still tend to follow the traditional theory in contract conflicts, tort conflicts, or both of these.[222] However, it appears that some of these states have an incentive to follow the Second Restatement.[223]

---

216 See Reimann, "A New Restatement – For the International Age", p. 579.

217 See Scoles – Hay – Borchers – Symeonides, Conflict of Laws, p. 61.

218 See Symeonides, "The Need for a Third Conflicts Restatement (And a Proposal for Tort Conflicts)", pp. 443–444.

219 See Symeonides, "The American Choice-of-Law Revolution in the Courts: Today and Tomorrow", p. 89.

220 See ibid., especially the figure on p. 93.

221 See Scoles – Hay – Borchers – Symeonides, Conflict of Laws, p. 68.

222 See Symeonides, "The American Choice-of-Law Revolution in the Courts: Today and Tomorrow", pp. 70–77.

223 See ibid., pp. 83–88. See also e.g. American Motorists Insurance Co. v. ARTRA Group, Inc., Court of Appeals of Maryland, 1995, 338 Md. 560, 659 A.2d 1295.

From a quantitative standpoint, it is abundantly clear that the Second Restatement dominates US conflicts law. But from a qualitative standpoint, important caveats can be presented. The courts' real loyalty to the Second Restatement has been rather weak. This provides a reason for emphasising that basically no single choice of law methodology exists in the US. In fact, *Currie*'s interest analysis is heavily employed even in those federal states that generally follow the Second Restatement.[224]

Although US conflicts law is litigation-driven and we can recognise different methodological camps, some important characteristics of US choice of law methodology can be pinpointed by looking into the rules of the Second Restatement. From a methodological standpoint, Section 6 of the Second Restatement forms the core rule of the Restatement.[225] It provides the guiding principles of the choice of law process and, as *Scoles*, *Hay*, *Borchers* and *Symeonides* point out, in essence it establishes a test that guides the courts in applying all other Sections of the Restatement.[226] Section 6 provides that factors relevant to the choice of the applicable rule of law include (a) the needs of the interstate and international systems, (b) the relevant policies of the forum, (c) the relevant policies of other interested states, and the relative interests of those states in determining the particular issue, (d) the protection of justified expectations, (e) the basic policies underlying the particular field of law, (f) certainty, predictability and uniformity of result, and (g) ease in determining and applying the law to be applied. The list shows that courts are given a wide margin of discretion in what they emphasise in decision-making.[227] The factors listed in Section 6 are multiple and diverse, and have not been given in any order of priority. In addition, they often point in different directions in a

---

224 See also Symeonides – Perdue – von Mehren, Conflict of Laws: American, Comparative, International. Cases and Materials, pp. 299–303.

225 The origins of Section 6 are said to have been found in the article Choice of the Applicable Law (Colum. L. Rev.), written by *Elliot E. Cheatman* and *Willis L. M. Roose* in 1952. See Cheatman – Reese: "Choice of the Applicable Law".

226 Most of the other Sections in the Restatement incorporate § 6 by Reference. See Scoles – Hay – Borchers – Symeonides, Conflict of Laws, pp. 60–61.

227 See also Second Restatement § 6, Comment, pp. 11–17.

concrete case, which has also turned out to be one of their major problems. Yet, Section 6 shows that the Restatement has adopted an approach different from traditional US conflicts law practice and abandoned previous jurisdiction-selecting rules.[228] When considering relevant policies under Section 6, the courts should consider not only their own relevant policies but also those of all other interested states.[229] Among other things, the general principles enable the court to take into account, in determining the applicable law, who the contracting parties are.[230]

The guiding test of Section 6 reveals the ideology of the Second Restatement and the basic objectives of the choice of law process.[231] As *Symeonides* remarks, the better law criterion has been excluded from the list, which is broader and qualitatively different from the policies supported by *Currie*.[232] Yet the principles have incorporated at least part of *Currie*'s interest theory.[233] And the courts are able to add the better law criterion to the list since the Second Restatement is fully voluntary by nature. Section 6 has enabled the courts the use of wide discretion.[234]

It is noteworthy that in the US, the courts split a case into separate issues for determining the applicable laws.[235] In conflicts theory, this is called issue-orientation.[236] For US conflicts methodology, the

---

228 See Scoles – Hay – Borchers – Symeonides, Conflict of Laws, p. 60.

229 See Second Restatement § 188, Comment, para. f, pp. 14–15.

230 Moreover, specific Sections in the Restatement address specific types of contracts. See Hay, "Flexibility versus Predictability and Uniformity in Choice of Law. Reflections on Current European and United States Conflicts Law", p. 371, pp. 380–381 and fn. 436 on p. 381.

231 See Hill, "For a Third Conflicts Restatement – But Stop Trying to Reinvent the Wheel", p. 538.

232 See Symeonides, "The American Choice-of-Law Revolution in the Courts: Today and Tomorrow", p. 59.

233 See Peterson, "American Private International Law at the End of the 20th Century: Progress or Regress?", p. 422.

234 See also Duncan v. Cessna Aircraft Company, Supreme Court of Texas, 1984, 665 S.W.2d 414.

235 See Hay, "Flexibility versus Predictability and Uniformity in Choice of Law. Reflections on Current European and United States Conflicts Law", p. 377.

236 See ibid., p. 299.

issue-oriented approach is one of the starting points which also ensures that various policy concerns of interested states can be considered. Hence, when Section 6 is applied each particular issue receives its own consideration.

The issue-oriented approach shows that US conflicts law uses *dépeçage* in a different way from the European approach. In Europe, *dépeçage* means first and foremost that parties are permitted to select different laws for different parts of the contract. In general, in the absence of party choice involving splitting the applicable law, European courts seek a single law that applies to the contract in question. Although the Rome Convention allows the contracting parties, and even courts in certain situations, to use *dépeçage*, the European attitude to *dépeçage* has been repudiated.

As *Hay* points out, Section 6 of the Second Restatement enables consideration of social interests in certain contractual relationships, such as employment and consumer contracts.[237] In general, the way in which the Restatement pays heed to both forum policies and policies of other interested states is more broadminded than that of the Rome Convention rules. The case law of the US courts reveals that their conflicts law approaches also involve the use of public policy concerns in the initial choice of law process instead of ultimate means of preventing application of the *lex causae*.[238]

In Europe, the emergence of '*lois d'application immédiate*' has become a means of reconciling party autonomy with compelling forum policies and policies of other states related to the case.[239] In the Rome Convention, the possibility of taking into account policy considerations of the *lex fori* is ensured by Article 7(2) under which the courts can apply internationally mandatory rules of their own law. As has been emphasised, the wording of the Article is open. By virtue of Article 7(1), internationally mandatory rules of third countries can be applied only on certain conditions.

---

237 See ibid., pp. 373–374.

238 See ibid., p. 379 and Lilienthal v. Kaufman, Supreme Court of Oregon, 1964, 239 Or. 1, 395 P.2d 543.

239 See de Boer, "The EEC Contracts Convention and the Dutch Courts", p. 26.

Although Article 7(1) of the Rome Convention has its European model in the *Alnati* case[240], *Jayme* has noticed 'American ideas' deriving from the conflicts revolution behind it.[241] The role of Article 7(1) is limited because the Contracting States may make a reservation on the Article. This can be understood to mean that, in general, policy concerns of third countries can be ignored in countries with a reservation. However, it should be emphasised that Article 7 provides an exception to the main principle of the Convention, which is party autonomy.

As regards employment and consumer contracts, the protection of the weaker party is explicitly ensured by specific conflicts rules in the Rome Convention. These rules limit the effects of a choice of law clause. The policy of Articles 5 and 6 in the Convention differs from the US approach in that these Articles contain clear rules on determining the applicable law so that the court cannot choose any jurisdiction involved.[242] With Articles 5 and 6, the principle of the most favourable law has been used to ensure protection of the weaker contracting party.

Methodologically, the points of departure in the US and Europe also differ when it comes to the determining the applicable law in the absence of a choice of law clause. In Europe, the Rome Convention contains binding rules on determining the law most closely connected to the contract. The Second Restatement gives no such guidance on methodology. However, as mentioned, the Restatement guides courts in determining the applicable law separately concerning each component of a single case.[243] The next section looks into these differences in more detail.

---

240 Judgment of May 13, 1966 in Van Nievelt, Goudriaan and Co.'s Stoomvaartmij N.V. v. N.V. Hollandsche Assurantie Societeit and Others.

241 See Jayme, "The American Conflicts Revolution and its Impact on European Private International Law", p. 21.

242 See de Boer, "The EEC Contracts Convention and the Dutch Courts", p. 34.

243 See Hay, "Flexibility versus Predictability and Uniformity in Choice of Law. Reflections on Current European and United States Conflicts Law", p. 359 and 375.

9.2 Contractual Obligations

The Second Restatement governs conflicts rules on contracts and torts, whereas in Europe unified conflicts rules on torts between the EU Member States do not yet exist. So far, only a few federal states of the US have enacted conflicts legislation. As the first common law jurisdiction, Oregon followed Louisiana in 2002 by enacting a comprehensive statute for contract conflicts.[244]

In order to grasp the key contents of the Restatement rules with a focus on contractual obligations, it is useful to discuss two Sections especially noteworthy in international contracting. Section 187 of the Second Restatement (Law of the State Chosen by the Parties) reads as follows:

> (1) The law of the state chosen by the parties to govern their contractual rights and duties will be applied if the particular issue is one which the parties could have resolved by an explicit provision in their agreement directed to that issue.
> (2) The law of the state chosen by the parties to govern their contractual rights and duties will be applied, even if the particular issue is one which the parties could not have resolved by an explicit provision in their agreement directed to that issue, unless either
> (a) the chosen state has no substantial relationship to the parties or the transaction and there is no other reasonable basis for the parties' choice, or
> (b) application of the law of the chosen state would be contrary to a fundamental policy of a state which has a materially greater interest than the chosen state in the determination of the particular issue and which, under the rule of § 188, would be the state of the applicable law in the absence of an effective choice of law by the parties.
> (3) In the absence of a contrary indication of intention, the reference is to the local law of the state of the chosen law.

It has been said that Section 187 is followed by US courts more often than any other Section of the Restatement.[245] This Section ap-

244 See in detail Symeonides, "Codifying Choice of Law for Contracts: The Oregon Experience".

245 See Scoles – Hay – Borchers – Symeonides, Conflict of Laws, pp. 979–980.

plies when the parties have chosen the applicable law. Even if the contract does not explicitly refer to a state, the court may conclude that the parties have made a choice of law. In practice, the US courts have applied the Second Restatement so as to respect the parties' choice of law clauses. Some federal states have even promulgated statutes that clarify acceptance of choice of law clauses.[246] However, in US legal literature, more clarity has been demanded in order to ensure that party choice is respected. It has also been noted that case law favours the enforcement of choice of law clauses when the law chosen by the parties has a relationship of some significance to the transaction.[247]

Along with the guiding test established by Section 6, the cornerstone of the Second Restatement is 'the most significant relationship' formula. In the absence of a choice of law, the law of the state that has the most significant relationship with the parties and the dispute is to be applied to the particular issue in question.[248] Section 188 of the Restatement (Law Governing in Absence of Effective Choice by the Parties) contains conflicts rules that apply in the absence of party choice. According to the basic rule, the applicable law is determined by the local law of the state which, with respect to that issue, has the most significant relationship to the transaction and the parties under the principles stated in Section 6. Protection of the justified expectations of the parties is aimed at by listing the factors to be taken into account when determining the applicable law. By virtue of Section 188, these factors are (a) the place of contracting, (b) the place where the contract was negotiated, (c) the place of performance, (d) the location of the subject matter of the contract, and (e) the domicile, residence, nationality, place of incorporation, and place of business of the parties. The factors should be weighted according to their importance to the particular issue.

---

246 See O'Hara – Ribstein, "From Politics to Efficiency in Choice of Law", p. 1199.

247 See Scoles – Hay – Borchers – Symeonides, Conflict of Laws, p. 974.

248 See Symeonides, "The American Choice-of-Law Revolution in the Courts: Today and Tomorrow", p. 60.

Two things are noteworthy here. First of all, the list given in Section 188 is not exhaustive. Secondly, US courts have long recognized that they are not bound to decide all issues under the local law of a single state. Section 188 makes an explicitly selective approach to choice of applicable law governing particular issues. Each issue is to receive separate consideration if it is one which would be resolved differently under the law of two or more potentially interested states.[249]

In Europe, the conflicts rules of the Rome Convention are based on party autonomy, which is also the starting point in the US. But as has been said, in the European model the use of *dépeçage* is exceptional; a separable part of the contract that has a closer connection with another country may by way of exception be governed by the law of that other country. In the absence of choice, the applicable law is that most closely connected with the contract. Article 4 of the Convention contains presumptions for determining the most closely connected law. Under Article 4(2), the law most closely connected is the law of the country where the party who is responsible for characteristic performance habitually resides at the time of concluding the contract. Paragraph 2 does not apply if characteristic performance cannot be determined, and the presumptions provided by Article 4 on the issue are disregarded if it appears from the circumstances as a whole that the contract is more closely connected with another country. The exception clause not only complements the presumptions but also seeks to provide flexibility. Article 4 of the Rome Convention has been considered an innovation from the standpoint of continental lawyers. According to *Jayme*, it demonstrates the impact of the American conflicts revolution on European law-making.[250] However, the principle of the closest connection as such is not new in European private international law. For example, the Norwegian Supreme Court adopted the principle in 1923 in the famous *Irma v. Mignon* case.[251]

---

249 See Second Restatement § 188, Comment, pp. 576–586.

250 See Jayme, "The American Conflicts Revolution and its Impact on European Private International Law", pp. 18–21.

251 See Rt. 1923 II, p. 59. See also Thue, "Irma-Mignon-Formelen. En konfliktskapende regel".

As mentioned, in the absence of choice of law, the Second Restatement is based on the 'most significant relationship' test. This test has become the basis for choice of law in the US, both in contract and in tort. At first glance, this rule appears to parallel the principle of the closest connection found in the Rome Convention.[252] However, a significant difference of choice of law method exists between the US and Europe. The US approach is issue-oriented, whereas the Rome Convention rules seek to determine the law applicable to the entire contractual relationship, which is to be done *a priori*. In the US, the Second Restatement contains only a few cases where the state of most significant relationship is determined *a priori* through written rules.[253] While the Rome Convention contains presumptions on the closest connection, the Second Restatement does not give such methodological guidance. Nor does it provide specific presumptions for weaker party contracts.[254] Section 6 is meant to guide the courts in taking into account relevant policy concerns. However, the Second Restatement contains certain Sections based on specific connecting factor rules in the manner of Articles 4(3), 4(4), 5(3) and 6(2) of the Rome Convention.[255] As regards services, the Second Restatement contains Section 196, under which the law of the state "where the contract requires that the services, or a major portion of the services, be rendered" applies to contracts with servants, independent contractors, and agents as well as persons who exercise public profession, lawyers doctors, brokers, commission agents and factors.[256]

---

252 See also Kay, "A Defense of Currie's Governmental Interest Analysis", p. 194.

253 See Symeonides, "The American Choice-of-Law Revolution in the Courts: Today and Tomorrow", p. 61.

254 See Hay, "Flexibility versus Predictability and Uniformity in Choice of Law. Reflections on Current European and United States Conflicts Law", pp. 361–362.

255 In addition to Section 188(3), these are Sections 189–199 and 203 of the Second Restatement. See Hay – Weintraub – Borchers, Conflict of Laws. Cases and Materials, p. 531.

256 Second Restatement § 196, Comment, Para a, pp. 623–624. See also Scoles – Hay – Borchers – Symeonides, Conflict of Laws, pp. 1019–1023.

9.3 Divergence or Convergence

The question of divergence and convergence is next discussed, with consideration of the methodology and objectives of choice of law. In the light of what has been said above, in the current stage of development one might be tempted to somewhat modify *Hay*'s view, according to which the diversity in the US and European conflicts law approach is only marginally one of methodology. It is true that a common law system can deal with statutory choice of law rules, as we saw happening, for example, when the Rome Convention was implemented in England. Similar developments have occurred in the US, too. However, from the methodological standpoint, it is highly significant how various state and party interests can be dealt with. In particular, the European rule-based approach differs markedly from the US approach in this sense, taking into account how these two continents are divided on contractual orientation: relationship or issue orientation.

Hay has pointed out that the divergence between US and European approaches derives principally from different insights into the objectives of the conflict of laws.[257] Hence, we should consider whether any *rapprochement* in this area can be recognised. The present and future objectives of European private international law are often discussed in light of the Rome Convention as well as ongoing legislative work within the EU, i.e. the Rome I and Rome II Proposals. This means that an assessment is carried out partly on the basis of ongoing preparation of conflicts rules.

The US conflicts revolution was much criticised in continental Europe, where predictability and systemic integrity were emphasised. According to *Hay*, the criticism that American judges would be too active and too ready to exercise a law-making function has been seriously flawed, as has the criticism of interest analysis based on the doctrine of *Currie*. It is often emphasised by US scholars that American developments have affected the contents of European codifications, not least the Rome Convention, which have adopted a more

---

257 See Hay, "Flexibility versus Predictability and Uniformity in Choice of Law. Reflections on Current European and United States Conflicts Law", p. 394.

flexible approach to choice of law. *Hay* has noted a kind of *rapprochement* between the US and the European model, although the points of departure of the legal systems differ. In essence, he notes that while the US courts have pulled back, Europeans have attempted to go a step further towards the American interest or better-law analysis.[258] In general, the Rome Convention has demonstrated an important step towards more flexibility in European choice of law. The Rome I Proposal of the European Commission seeks to maintain the basic approach in the Convention, but as has been said, it also bears features that contradict the objective of flexibility.

Policies underlying conflicts rules are not always easily identified. But as *Hay* sharply points out, the difference between Europe and the US lies in the different concepts and goals of conflict of laws. American conflicts law appears to emphasise results in individual cases more than predictability. One can claim that this goes back to the fundamental difference between European and American conflicts law: the former is rule-based, whereas the latter is litigation-driven with legal solutions reached through casuistic evolution.[259] The rule-based approach has been strengthened in the EU with unification efforts based on new EC Treaty Articles introduced by the Amsterdam Treaty. In addition, this approach has been speeded up with the specific conflicts rules of EU sectoral policies. In the European model, much of the interaction between conflicts law and substantive law occurs when conflicts rules are being drafted by the EC legislator. The developments where the EC legislator seeks given substantive outcomes with the help of conflicts rules can be said to illustrate that Europe has more often begun to seek 'the materially best solution' and material justice instead of the 'spatially best solution' and conflicts justice. This trend cannot be fully explained by referring to needs based on important policy concerns or deepening integration. Some of the extreme examples of development in EU sectoral policies might indicate that this has also something to do with mixing up conflicts rules with substantive rules without sufficiently taking account the role and system of private international law.

---

[258] See ibid., pp. 302–304.

[259] See ibid., pp. 392–398.

9.4 Today and Tomorrow

According to *Reimann*, it appears that from the 1990s, a strong interest in comparative and international perspectives has again emerged in US conflicts law.[260] This interest relates to requirements of consolidation and standardisation.[261]At the moment, intense debate is going on as to whether the Second Restatement should be reformed or replaced by a third one.[262] This debate has its close counterpart in Europe, where preparation of the Rome I Regulation has prompted lively discussion among scholars, not least because this preparation has strong connections with the Rome II project concerning conflicts rules on tort. The entry into force of the Amsterdam Treaty in May 1999 marked a turning point in the development of European private international law. A true communitarisation of conflicts rules as part of the corpus of the *acquis communautaire* could begin. In the EC competence, 'judicial cooperation in civil matters' has during a relatively short period brought about a number of new statutes and legislative proposals.

When preparation of the Rome Convention began, the waves of the American conflicts revolution had reached Europe. Yet, the methodological framework remained relatively intact in Europe.[263] There is no reason to doubt the unifying role that the Rome Convention has played as the statutory basis for European choice of law. However, although the Convention explicitly emphasises the objective of uniform interpretation, which is also made clear in the Interpretation Protocols, problems of diversity have not been avoided. Some have argued that, in several respects, the Convention has failed to provide

---

260 See Reimann, "A New Restatement – For the International Age", p. 578 and 580.

261 See Scoles – Hay – Borchers – Symeonides, Conflict of Laws, pp. 105–118.

262 The Indiana Law Journal has devoted its Issue 2/2000 to the subject based on a Symposium where leading US conflicts scholars discussed whether or how a third restatement would improve the quality of conflicts law.

263 See, for example, de Boer, "Forty Years On: The Evolution of Postwar Private International Law in Europe", p. 5.

legal certainty.[264] This is demonstrated by the diversity in interpretations of the Convention rules found in national case law.

What we have not yet seen is how European courts will apply the unified conflicts rules that will replace the Rome Convention and become part of EC law. As stressed above, a fundamental difference exists between conflicts rules based on an international convention and conflicts rules based on an EC regulation. Despite its linkage to the EU, the Rome Convention has serious disadvantages. The efficiency of EC law is transcendent compared with an international convention. The objective of the EC legislator is to provide rules which European courts can apply uniformly. However, it is difficult to see how this expectation of uniform application could be linked to a decrease in the margin of discretion given to the courts in certain respects where flexibility would be needed by the Rome I Proposal.

As we have seen, the rules of the Second Restatement, which has received an essential role in US conflicts law, establish an approach that permits policy-oriented analysis of conflicts problems. The reasons why courts favour the non-binding rules of the Restatement are several. One of the most obvious is that it gives wide latitude in choosing the applicable law. It has been argued that in the sense that the Restatement combines flexibility with guidance, it constitutes a complete system. In addition, the Restatement carries the prestige of the American Law Institute, and has enough 'momentum'.[265]

On both continents, a homeward trend exists.[266] *O'Hara* and *Ribstein* criticise the US approach based on modern interest analysis for pro-plaintiff, pro-resident, and pro-forum biases. According to the authors, the US courts have developed open-ended approaches that facilitate more 'self-indulgent' judicial decision-making. The authors argue that this reflects a kind of 'race to the bottom' in choice of law. They emphasise that *ex post* determination of the applicable law has

---

264 See, for example, Lando, "Optional or Mandatory Europeanisation of Contract Law", p. 62.

265 See Symeonides, "The American Choice-of-Law Revolution in the Courts: Today and Tomorrow", pp. 120–126.

266 See Hay – Lando – Rotunda, "Conflict of Laws as a Technique for Legal Integration", p. 164.

prevailed over enforcing *ex ante* choice of law of the parties.[267] Altogether, the development towards '*impressionisme juridique*' is claimed to have gone too far.[268]

In Europe, pro-forum biases are claimed basically to relate to the unwillingness of the courts to apply foreign law.[269] Lack of common rules on applying foreign law and settling its content has been said to be partly responsible for *lex forism*. In this respect, the ongoing unification of conflicts rules has been considered to remain insufficient unless supplemented by common rules on applying foreign law. What is easily forgotten is that in practice European courts tend to shy away from conflicts issues.[270] It has been claimed that they will use any available reason to apply their own law by ignoring the conflicts law aspects of the case.

It has been argued in the legal literature that, in the US, the trend seems to be increasing towards turning 'interest analysis' into 'equity analysis' in issues such as products liability, personal injury, environmental law, and workers' compensation. The trend both reflects and reinforces American theories of 'better law' and 'multi-state justice', where equity is increasingly regarded as the pre-dominant, if not the only, criterion for private international law decision-making.[271] With the emphasis on equity and the *lex fori*, the US approach cannot be held similar to that of Europe. In Europe, materialisation of the conflict of laws has been based on emphasising the kind of better law approach which, at the policy level, is often directly linked to the specific needs of European integration. The emergence of internationally mandatory rules has opened for the courts a general possibility to consider the policies of the forum law. Internationally mandatory rules

---

267 See O'Hara – Ribstein, "From Politics to Efficiency in Choice of Law", pp. 1180–1182 and p. 1232.

268 See Scoles – Hay – Borchers – Symeonides, Conflict of Laws, p. 107.

269 See also de Boer: "Forum Preferences in Contemporary European Conflicts Law: The Myth of a 'Neutral Choice'", pp. 53–55.

270 See Lando, "The Principles of European Contract Law and the lex mercatoria", p. 393.

271 See Tetley, "A Canadian Looks at American Conflict of Law Theory and Practice, Especially in the Light of the American Legal and Social Systems. (Corrective vs Distributive Justice)".

have also been adopted by the EC legislator as a tool for safeguarding weaker party protection.

The elements mentioned appear to be at the heart of the EU–US comparison. Hence, it is not sufficient to say that the European 'better law' approach with its increasing materialisation reflects Americanisation of the conflict of laws. Also, more attention needs to be paid to the consequences of materialisation and the reasons behind it. But as *Hay* notes, a case law system is probably more open to interest analysis and 'better law' orientation than a code-oriented legal system.[272]

To a large extent, the federal states follow the guidance given by the Second Restatement. However, this does not tell how deep the real commitment to the Restatement is.[273] It should be emphasised that US courts have played a significant part in the process in which conflicts rules have taken shape.[274] In Europe, national courts have been significantly sidelined if one takes into account conflicts law development during recent years. The EC legislator has adopted the dominating role. History shows that the Dutch *Alnati* case[275] may be referred to when explaining the emergence of internationally mandatory rules of third countries in Article 7(1) of the Convention. And it is true that in some EU Member States, national courts have delivered decisions that have been important for the interpretation of the Rome Convention or, *inter alia*, the development of cross-border consumer protection in the EU. But decisions of interpretation of the Rome Convention have seldom extended their impact to other Member States.[276] As already emphasised, although the Convention itself explicitly emphasises the objective of uniform interpretation, this has

---

272 See Hay, "Flexibility versus Predictability and Uniformity in Choice of Law. Reflections on Current European and United States Conflicts Law", p. 392.

273 See Symeonides, "The American Choice-of-Law Revolution in the Courts: Today and Tomorrow", p. 120.

274 See also Hay, "Flexibility versus Predictability and Uniformity in Choice of Law. Reflections on Current European and United States Conflicts Law", p. 302.

275 Judgment of May 13, 1966 in Van Nievelt, Goudriaan and Co.'s Stoomvaartmij N.V. v. N.V. Hollandsche Assurantie Societeit and Others.

276 See, for example, Liukkunen, The Role of Mandatory Rules in International Labour Law – A Comparative Study in the Conflict of Laws.

not prevented diversity of interpretations. And even though the ECJ has played a crucial role in harmonising private law, the conflict of laws has not very often become an issue in the Court. One of the main reasons is that the Rome Convention establishes its own interpretation procedure, and the Court has received limited power to interpret the Convention only recently. However, in areas such as labour law ECJ case law has been vital when developing cross-border protection in a conflicts law sense.

Symeonides has considered what he calls 'the cyclical movement' between flexibility and certainty of conflicts systems in Europe and the US. He sees the European movement towards more flexibility as a result of small, controlled doses of flexibility.[277] It is clear that in Europe, integration has tipped the balance in favour of more flexibility in choice of law. And it would be a simplification to claim that flexibility has been sought at the expense of legal certainty. In this sense, it is easy to agree with *Symeonides*. The Rome Convention reflects the aim of achieving a balance between flexibility and legal certainty. As regards party autonomy, the Rome I Proposal takes flexibility a step further. When it comes to the fixed connecting factor rules that would be applied in the absence of choice, the Proposal takes flexibility a great step backwards. More predictability and legal certainty is attempted by rejecting the existing 'soft' presumptions provided by Article 4 of the Rome Convention.[278]

If the whole picture of conflicts law developments in Europe could be sketched with only the Rome Convention in mind, the development could be considered quite systematic and as such it would probably fit the expectations of many continental lawyers. However, in recent years it has become clear that in some respects the European move towards more flexibility has not occurred in small and controlled doses, as *Symeonides* suggests it has. Rather, when we take into account the entire development of European conflicts law concerning contractual obligations, some pieces of legislation turn out to be the result of less controlled and less systematic law-making efforts

277 See Symeonides, "The American Choice-of-Law Revolution in the Courts: Today and Tomorrow", p. 413.

278 See Juenger, "The Problem with Private International Law", p. 302.

within the EU. Specific conflicts rules serve the particular purposes of European integration. In various ways, these rules are based on interest analysis. Some rules reflect this heavily: methodologically, one interest analysis is carried out *a priori* during the law-drafting procedure, while another analysis is to be carried out each time the courts apply these conflicts rules. Numerous arguments could be presented against the existing approach towards increasingly specific conflicts rules. If any conflicts approach – be it regional or national – becomes heavily burdened by specific conflicts rules, then predictability suffers. This also causes a decrease in legal certainty.

Both European and US conflicts law are at the moment in a very interesting phase of development. In Europe, the experiences of the Rome Convention pave the way for the Rome I Regulation. In the US, recent scholarship has actively raised the issue of the need to reform the Second Restatement and the entire conflicts approach, which also has become fragmented, not least because the guiding principles in Section 6 often pull in conflicting directions.[279] With globalisation and internationalisation, it has been asked whether the Second Restatement fits today's needs. In addition, it has been asked whether the present conflicts approaches of the US courts fit the needs of the contracting parties.[280] According to *Symeonides*, the Second Restatement is out-of-date: it shies away from many conflicts and its few written rules are becoming more and more anachronistic.[281] Many US scholars favour a third restatement that would bring about more guidance and hence more predictability on conflicts law. Some case law developments have already been held as a positive sign of a new phase.[282] For example, the so-called *Neumeier* rules, developed by the New York

279 See Peterson, "American Private International Law at the End of the 20th Century: Progress or Regress?", pp. 442–443.

280 See, for example, Tetley, "A Canadian Looks at American Conflict of Law Theory and Practice, Especially in the Light of the American Legal and Social Systems (Corrective vs Distributive Justice)".

281 See, for example, Symeonides, "The Need for a Third Conflicts Restatement (And a Proposal for Tort Conflicts)", pp. 448–449.

282 See ibid., p. 448.

Court of Appeals in 1973 in *Neumeier v. Kuehner*[283], are often referred to as a set of rules for guest-statute conflicts, which has been successfully extended to torts beyond guest-statute conflicts. This has been seen as a successful use of the traditional conflicts approach.[284]

In the US debate about the need for reform, recommendations have been made that the drafters of a third restatement should carry out legal comparison that extends to foreign conflicts law.[285] Regrettably, the comparative work carried out by the EC law-drafters has so far been mainly within the borders of the EU. As has been said, Switzerland is almost the only non-Member State which has been referred to from time to time. In the US, it has also been argued that when drafting a new restatement, it will be necessary to determine whether future rules should be separated from other international conflicts law material or integrated with it.[286] It seems that an urgent need exists for a similar discussion of the 'international' role of regional conflicts rules both in Europe and the US. However, this question has so far been rather loosely debated in the EU institutions, although under the Hague Programme the Commission and the Council should ensure coherence between the EU and the international legal order and continue to engage in closer relations and co-operation with international organisations, such as the Hague Conference on Private International Law and the Council of Europe.[287]

In the American legal literature, the litigation-driven US approach has been called a tale-of-a-thousand-and-one-cases in which courts decide cases as if they were all unique and of first impres-

---

283 Neumeier v. Kuehner, Court of Appeals of New York, 1972, 31 N.Y.2d 121, 335 NY.S.2d 64, 286 N.E.2d 454. See Symeonides, "The American Choice-of-Law Revolution in the Courts: Today and Tomorrow", pp. 135–138 and Peterson, "American Private International Law at the End of the 20th Century: Progress or Regress?", pp. 442–443.

284 See also Schultz v. Boy Scouts of America, Inc., Court of Appeals of New York, 1985, 65 N.Y.2d 189, 491 N.Y.S.2d 90, 480 N.E.2d 679.

285 See Reimann, "A New Restatement – For the International Age", p. 585.

286 See ibid., p. 583.

287 See The Hague Programme: strengthening freedom, security and justice in the European Union, para. 3.4.5.

sion.[288] This tendency to treat each case as unique has led to fragmentation in conflicts law. Somewhat provocatively, European conflicts law might be claimed to appear to be a tale-of-a-thousand-and-one-statutes. Two elements support this. Firstly, an increasing number of various EC legal instruments contain conflicts rules. Secondly, the legal instruments that also contain rules on substantive harmonisation have regularly been EC directives of a complicated nature. As a consequence, each Member State may transpose them into its national legislation in its own particular way. Member States are obliged to transposition whatever content the specific directives take. So the contracting parties should be aware of the growing number of EC legal instruments and national statutes transposing them. The fact that the transposition legislation in each EU Member State may differ remarkably leads to fragmentation of the European conflicts law regime. Altogether, comparison of the US and European approach reveals that both face serious problems of fragmentation of normative systems.

10 How European is the European Conflicts Law Approach?

Within the limitations of a single study, one might ask if any possibility exists of providing a satisfactory answer to the question how far the European conflicts law approach has been Europeanised. However, global and regional developments of law and economics surely give rise to this question. Difficult though the question might be, the EU and US comparison has shown that regional conflicts approaches deserve consideration in a cross-continental framework. These are the real surroundings that parties to business transactions face in the global economy.

US conflicts law demonstrates expansion of the discretion of the courts in the choice of law process in a manner that has led to problems of fragmentation. Consideration of 'the relevant policies of the forum' is one of the most important factors listed in Section 6 of the

[288] See Kozyris, "Interest Analysis Facing its Critics – And, Incidentally, What Should be Done About Choice of Law for Products Liability", p. 578.

Second Restatement. Courts have often referred to this principle, which might also be seen as a demonstration of the influence of interest analysis.[289] At the same time, 'certainty, predictability and uniformity of result' are among objectives the courts should consider under Section 6.

European conflicts law demonstrates fragmentation due to the increase of statutes containing specific conflicts rules for specific issues. In the Rome I Proposal, the European Commission argues that the amendments contained in the Proposal would boost legal certainty.[290] Yet, the Proposal does not address the problem of fragmentation that endangers legal certainty. Similarly, the Hague Programme, which seeks to address the unification of conflicts law in a comprehensive way, does not take up this question up.

At present, the future is open since work on EC conflicts rules concerning contractual obligations is in progress. However, the Rome I Proposal and reactions to it can be seen as an indicator of present trends in European conflicts law thinking. Backed up by the objective of boosting the internal market, in this legislative project the European Commission has sought to take flexibility demands seriously, and at the same time to accept the basic limitations, already confirmed by the Rome Convention, to the extension of party autonomy. These limitations could also be seen as a manifestation of 'Social Europe' or 'Citizens' Europe', particularly in terms of weaker party contracts. Yet, from the standpoint of consumer and employee protection, the Rome I Proposal is problematic, albeit in different ways. From the standpoint of commercial transactions, the Rome I Proposal seems too rigid with its proposed list of fixed connecting factors.

The dynamics of regional unification of conflicts rules within the EU can be seen in the lively activity of the European Commission, with legislative initiatives in the area of 'freedom, security and justice'. Furthermore, the activities of the EC legislator in the field of in-

---

289 See Peterson, "American Private International Law at the End of the 20th Century: Progress or Regress?", pp. 429–431.

290 See Proposal for a Regulation of the European Parliament and the Council on the law applicable to contractual obligations (Rome I). COM(2005) 650 final, p. 3.

ternal market law have increasingly often reached conflicts issues. This raises questions as to how deeply and in what manner the conflicts law approach adopted has been communitarised.

First of all, the conflict of laws has become an instrument of regional and economic integration in Europe. Secondly, it has become a field of law which is used to maintain a certain legal diversity between EU Member States alongside substantive harmonisation. Yet, this does not mean that the conflict of laws would operate as a neutral coordinator. Rather, specific conflicts rules, which complement substantive harmonisation, are often enacted in order to ensure a given material outcome of choice of law. With European integration, materialisation of private international law has become one of the key characteristics of this field of law. Here, one might recognise the influence of the American conflicts revolution. However, the interaction between conflicts law and substantive law in Europe is based increasingly on the objective of ensuring *a priori* a given substantive outcome of choice of law, dictated by interests deriving from European integration. In this sense, the classical *Savignyan* search for the seat of an international legal relationship has been challenged in a particular way.

Given the objectives of the EU, the law-making manner adopted by the EC institutions affects the final outcome, be it an EC regulation or directive. On the surface, common statutory rules seek to be as comprehensive as possible. In the wider context, however, in the drafting of specific rules some fundamental questions of private international law, such as characterisation, have not been addressed.

It has often been emphasised that in Europe the continental approach to the conflict of laws in the field of contractual obligations prevails. This approach differs from the American, although we can claim to see various signs of *Leflar*'s better law approach or *Currie*'s interest analysis in Europe. The increasing materialisation of private international law has particular features deriving from the needs of deepening integration. As stated earlier, many specific sets of conflicts rules are found in EC directives which, for the most part, regulate substantive private law issues. When the Member States want to avoid extensive substantive harmonisation, conflicts rules are used to complement substantive harmonisation. As this study later shows, some pieces of EC legislation on the internal market are so complicated that the question whether they actually contain conflicts rules has proved very difficult to settle.

Chapter III New Developments in the Field of EU Economic Freedoms

1 Introduction

The European approach to the conflict of laws is necessarily affected by efforts to promote the four economic freedoms of the EU, the free movement of goods (Articles 28–30 EC Treaty), workers (Article 39 EC Treaty), services (Articles 49 and 55 EC Treaty), and capital (Articles 56 and 58 EC Treaty). EC law on the four freedoms has a broad scope of application. When defining the scope of the Treaty provisions on free movement, the economic nature of the activity is decisive.[291] However, it should be noted that Article 49 EC on services applies only to situations where no other Treaty freedom applies. Thus, it has a subordinate character.

A national measure restricting free movement can be justified either by an exception permitted by the EC Treaty or under criteria established in ECJ case law. The Court has held overriding reasons of public interest as justified grounds for restrictions. The case law of the Court shows that this is an open-ended class of justifications, so that the Court may add new justification grounds where necessary. The Treaty provisions themselves include an exhaustive list of justification grounds for exceptions.[292]

The relationship between EC law on the four economic freedoms and private international law is a complicated one. The current state of the law is reflected by tensions recognised, for example, in the fields of international company law, consumer law, and labour law. This chapter sheds light on some of the developments in EC law that reflect these tensions, in particular as to the rights of establishment and free movement of services. The developments under scrutiny can

---

291 See de Vries, Tensions within the Internal Market. The Functioning of the Internal Market and the Development of Horizontal and Flanking Policies, p. 37.

292 See ibid., pp. 49–50.

also be seen as efforts, direct or indirect, to redefine the role of the conflict of laws for the specific purposes of the internal market.

In general, services are much more prone to internal market barriers than goods, and service provision is often subject to much more complex rules than goods. Although some services can be provided at a distance, it is common that service provision requires the permanent or temporary presence of the service-provider in the Member State where the service is provided. In essence, some or all of the stages of the service provision process may occur in the Member State where the service is provided and be subject to requirements differing from those in the home state of the service-provider.[293]

The EU has set a general goal of allowing service-providers to practice cross-border service provision in the internal market either by establishing their operations in the Member State of their choice or by taking advantage of freedom of services. The aim is that service-providers should have a genuine opportunity to choose which of these two economic freedoms best suits their strategy. However, in regard to the definition of the internal market in the EC Treaty as 'an area without internal frontiers', and the objective, set out in the Internal Market Strategy for Services, of making the provision of services between Member States as easy as within a single Member State, it has been admitted that the internal market for services is still far from being a reality. The objective is hampered by many factors, one of these being the divergence of legislation between Member States.[294]

A cross-border service-provider seeking to enter the internal market, whether through establishment or cross-border service provision, may face complex questions of choice of law. Some of these questions concern the relationship between EC law on the four economic freedoms and conflicts law. This chapter discusses both free-

---

293 See Report from the Commission to the Council and the European Parliament on the State of Internal Market for Services presented under the first stage of the Internal Market Strategy for Services, COM(2002) 441 final, p. 6.

294 As the Commission puts it, two broad categories of problems can be singled out: those deriving directly or indirectly from legal constraints, and those deriving from non-legal factors. See ibid., p. 14.

dom of establishment and freedom to provide services from the standpoint of choice of law.

2 Freedom of Establishment and Conflicts Rules

In recent years, freedom of establishment has been significantly facilitated as a result of new legislative instruments of EC company law and case law of the ECJ, which have broadened the scope of this freedom. ECJ case law with regard to freedom of establishment has brought to light intersections of private international law and EC law which must be analysed by means of both the rules of freedom of establishment and the conflicts rules of international company law. The current legal state cannot be fully understood without such an analysis.

Discussion of the present challenges in international company law necessarily also involves the question of regulatory competition in company law. Assessment of the so-called *Delaware* phenomenon has often concentrated on disputing whether the related regulatory competition causes a 'race to the bottom' or a 'race to the top'. It has also been suggested that if the *Delaware* phenomenon took place in Europe, it would threaten broad expansion of the freedom of establishment. It seems the European discussion has sometimes suffered from a superficial understanding of the reasons behind the *Delaware* phenomenon in the US. In the following, the development of international company law in the EU is explored, with passing comparisons to the US approach.

2.1 New Phase of International Company Law

In Europe, conflicts rules of international company law have great relevance because substantive company law is still much in the hands of EU Member States. Cross-border transfers of company registered offices are not, at least not yet, allowed in the EU overall.[295] The European Company (*Societas Europaea*, later: SE) and European Cooperative Society (*Societas Cooperativa Europaea*, later: SCE) form an exception: their registered office can be transferred to another Member State.[296] However, that is subject to the condition that both the registered office and the headquarters of the SE and the SCE must be located in the same country.[297] The only option left for other forms of company is that they relocate their actual centre of administration under the secondary freedom of establishment.

From the viewpoint of private international law, the vital difference between Europe and the US is that in the US companies can reincorporate. The opportunity to transfer their registered offices provides significant competitive advantage for US companies. Moreover, it is the basis from which the *Delaware* phenomenon arises. Regulatory competition is also maintained in the US by what is known as the *franchise tax*, which is significant for the economies of small states.[298] The EU Member States do not have a similar tax and would be unable to introduce one.[299] The advantages of an efficient company law and judiciary are often referred to when explaining, in connection with the

[295] See, for example, Wymeersch, "Centros: A Landmark Decision in European Company Law", pp. 648–650.

[296] See Council Regulation (EC) No 2157/2001 on the Statute for a European company (SE) and Council Regulation (EC) No 1435/2003 on the Statute for a European Cooperative Society (SCE).

[297] See Article 7 of the SE Regulation N:o 2157/2001. See also Recital 27 of the Preamble, under which 'in view of the specific Community character of an SE, the "real seat" arrangement adopted by this Regulation in respect of SEs is without prejudice to Member States' laws and does not pre-empt any choices to be made for other Community texts on company law'. The requirement set out in Article 7 has been said to prevent a 'European Delaware effect'. See Werlauff, SE – the law of the European Company, p. 110.

[298] See Kieninger, "The Legal Framework of Regulatory Competition Based on Company Mobility: EU and US compared", p. 758 and pp. 764–765.

[299] See Schön, "Playing different games? Regulatory competition in tax law and company law compared", pp. 337–339.

Delaware phenomenon, the fact that most stock exchange listed companies have incorporated in the state of Delaware.[300]

The question whether regulatory competition in the area of company law could take place in the EU has prompted wide debate in Europe. EC law lays down an obligation to recognize a company that has been validly incorporated under the law of another Member State.[301] However, the difference between the US and European models lies in the question of reincorporation: in general, reincorporation is still not possible in Europe. If cross-border transfers of registered offices were allowed, then European companies would be able to move more freely, while their international competitiveness would improve. At the same time, Member States would probably enter into fierce regulatory competition for companies.

Indeed, regulatory competition in the field of company law has already been increasing within the EU. Reasons for this can be found in economic and regulatory development.[302] Both the legislative activity of the EC and ECJ case law have supported regulatory competition between the Member States. The Court has clarified the scope of freedom of establishment so as to boost regulatory competition for companies between Member States. The Court has ruled that it is against Articles 43 and 48 EC Treaty if a Member State refuses to register a branch of a company which has been established in accordance with the law of another Member State and has its registered office in that particular State but does not operate there.[303]

---

300 See, for example, Veasey, The Role of Judiciary in Corporate Law, Corporate Governance and Economic Goals, p. 3 and Wymeersch, "Centros: A Landmark Decision in European Company Law", p. 653.

301 See Micheler, "Current developments. Private international law", p. 526.

302 It should also be noted that company law is merely one element of the regulatory environment of undertakings. In Europe, the competition of corporate charters between the states is also based on taxation and other factors. See, for example, Van Hulle, "Introduction – European Corporate Law: United in Diversity", p. 2 and Wymeersch, "Centros: A Landmark Decision in European Company Law", p. 652.

303 See Case C-212/97, Centros Ltd v. Erhvervs- og Selskabsstyrelsen, [1999] ECR I-1459.

Thus, a company may be set up in a Member State merely because the country's legislation is more favourable, even if the company intends to operate solely or mainly in some other Member State. The Court has also affirmed that a difference exists between primary and secondary establishment. Under certain conditions, Member States are allowed to set limits for real seat transfers but not for establishment of branches and offices.[304] Nevertheless, the general grounds for limiting freedom of establishment in EC law remain relevant even then.

2.2 Incorporation Theory and Real Seat Theory

Because of the significant differences in the national company law regimes of Member States, the rules of international company law have maintained their essential role in Europe. European countries have long followed two leading theories on defining company statutes: incorporation theory (*Gründungstheorie*) and real seat theory (*Sitztheorie*). These theories have also influenced the text in Articles 43 and 48 EC Treaty.[305]

According to incorporation theory, the law applicable to a company is the law of the country of incorporation. Legal certainty, predictability, and easy determination of the applicable law have been considered benefits of incorporation theory, because the criterion applied, the establishment of a company, is clear and simple. Foreign companies are recognised without regard to their internal organisation or operations.[306]

Incorporation theory has been seen to reflect the principle of party autonomy of private international law. However, the same feature of incorporation theory which has been considered its greatest

---

304 See Case C-212/97, Centros Ltd v. Erhvervs- og Selskabsstyrelsen, [1999] ECR I-1459 and Case C-81/87, The Queen v. H. M. Treasury and Commissioners of Inland Revenue, ex parte Daily Mail and General Trust plc., [1988] ECR I-5483.

305 See Rammeloo, Corporations in Private International Law: A European Perspective, p. 9.

306 See ibid., pp. 16–17.

strength is, according to some, also its biggest weakness: international companies are tempted to choose the country of establishment whose law is the most favourable. Opponents of the theory argue that it urges countries to engage in endless competition over which country has the most favourable company law.[307] It has therefore been said that incorporation theory drives states into regulatory competition for companies. Incorporation theory or its modifications has been followed, for example, in the United Kingdom, the Netherlands, Denmark, Finland and Sweden.[308]

According to real seat theory, the applicable law is the law of the country in which the real seat of the company, the actual centre of administration, is located.[309] In terms of private international law, the starting point of the theory is opposite to that of incorporation theory: choice of law is based on the objectively applicable law. Thus, companies cannot freely select the applicable law; rather, the law most closely connected with the company must be applied. Real seat theory considers the location of the actual centre of administration as the closest connection.[310]

Some States have applied modifications of real seat theory in which a company's real seat can be transferred to another State without dissolving the company. Real seat theory is also known as 'protection theory', because the applicable law is determined with a view to the interests of the company's stakeholder groups, such as shareholders, employees, creditors, and customers, and of the public interest of the state in which the real seat of the company's administration is located.[311] This theory has been considered an efficient way of preventing evasion of national company law.[312] For example, real seat theory has gained a strong foothold in Germany, where it has been

307 See Rammeloo, Corporations in Private International Law: A European Perspective, pp. 16–17.

308 See Schall, "European Framework for the Mobility of Companies", p. 4.

309 See Werlauff, EU-Company Law. Common Business Law of 28 States, p. 5.

310 See Rammeloo, Corporations in Private International Law: A European Perspective, p. 11 and p. 14.

311 See Neville – Winther-Sorensen – Engsig Sorensen, Free Movement of Companies under Company Law, p. 190.

312 See Schall, "European Framework for the Mobility of Companies", p. 4.

closely connected with protecting the application of national legislation on employee participation in company administration.[313]

A crucial question for real seat theory is what follows if the formalities of company law in the country of the actual centre of administration are not observed. As a result, the company may no longer be considered a legal subject, or the company directors may lose their limited liability. Real seat theory's weakness is often considered to be its focus on supervision. In addition, it has been pointed out that, particularly in a global economy, it is increasingly difficult to determine the location of a company's actual centre of administration. Strengths of the theory are considered to include the fact that it prevents abuse of foreign law, provides equal treatment, and protects fair competition.[314]

For companies, incorporation theory is clearly more flexible than real seat theory. Incorporation theory can also boost the mobility of companies. It has, therefore, been regarded by many as the most suitable for the EU internal market.[315] Incorporation theory has its roots in Anglo-Saxon law. However, the choice made by each country to apply either incorporation theory or real seat theory has not always correlated with whether the country has an Anglo-Saxon or a continental legal system. It has also played no part whether the country stipulated on employee participation in company administration.

Legal doctrine involves some attempts to reconcile incorporation theory and real seat theory. For example, the German *Differenzierunglehre* is based on splitting the applicable law. According to this theory, the law applicable to the company and the law of the country on whose territory the company operates, as well as the law applicable to transactions between the company and third parties, constantly compete with each other. The applicable law is determined case by case, giving most weight either to the rules favouring business transaction or party protection.[316]

---

313 See Kieninger, "The Legal Framework of Regulatory Competition Based on Company Mobility: EU and US compared", p. 756.

314 See Rammeloo, Corporations in Private International Law: A European Perspective, pp. 11–14.

315 See ibid., p. 17.

316 See ibid., p. 21.

Until recent years, incorporation theory and real seat theory co-existed in the EU, while in practice conflicts rules remained untouched by EC law. The differences in conflicts law, together with the divergence in Member State company law, made the legal environment of companies highly complicated until the ECJ took a stand as to the relationship between freedom of establishment and conflicts rules on companies.

2.3 Progress of Incorporation Theory

The *Centros*[317] and *Inspire Art*[318] cases concerned incorporation decisions, not reincorporations, i.e. transfers of registered offices. In *Centros*, the Court made it clear that a company can, in the framework of freedom of establishment, set up a subsidiary or a branch in another Member State without carrying out economic activity in the Member State where it has been lawfully established. Hence, it is permitted to establish a company only nominally in one Member State and carry out economic activity in another. As the Advocate-General put it, a newly formed company may set up its principal and its secondary establishment anywhere within the Community.[319] It has been generally held that *Centros* was the engine for true regulatory competition between the Member States.[320] However, after *Centros*, some doubts

317 Case C-212/97, Centros Ltd v. Erhvervs- og Selskabsstyrelsen ECR [1999], I-1459.

318 Case C-167/01, Kamer van Koophandel en Fabrieken voor Amsterdam v. Inspire Art Ltd., ECR [2003], I-10155.

319 See also Opinion of Mr Advocate General La Pergola delivered on 16 July 1998, para. 20, where La Pergola also clarified that "in the absence of harmonisation, competition among rules must be allowed free play in corporate matters".

320 See, for example, Wymeersch, "Company Law in Europe and European Company Law", pp. 117–118.

still existed as to the non-applicability of real seat theory in view of EC law.[321]

Überseering[322] was a landmark case in that it made clear that real seat theory can no longer be applied by a Member State to companies that move to it. In *Überseering*, the ECJ ruled that companies should be accepted by the Member States as they are according to the law of their country of origin, irrespective of their real seat and irrespective of whether the real seat later changes.

Although the ECJ has not directly taken a position on how the conflicts rules for company law should be determined, decisions of the Court have *de facto* significantly strengthened the status of incorporation theory.[323] It has been suggested that this theory will gradually replace real seat theory in the Member States that have traditionally applied the latter. However, three remarks are in order here.

First of all, it is not completely clear as to how far a Member State, acting in the role of host state, can require a company established in another Member State to comply with its legislation. The point of departure, confirmed by *Inspire Art*, is that requirements based on the law of the host state are acceptable under the restriction grounds set out by EC law. In the legal literature, much discussion has taken place as to the extent to which the law of the real seat could be applied, for example, in the case of improper use of limited liability. This discussion has its roots in national divergence of traditions and of law and economics between the Member States. It is also a question of drawing a line, *inter alia*, between company law, insolvency law, and tort law when it comes to a company's director's duty to initiate insolvency proceedings. Some authors have found support for application of the law of the real seat from the Rome II Proposal and from the EC Regulation on insolvency.[324] In general, it has been considered self-

---

321 On German views concerning *Centros*, see Kieninger, "The Legal Framework of Regulatory Competition Based on Company Mobility: EU and US compared", pp. 745–746.

322 Case C-208/00, Überseering BV v. Nordic Construction Company Baumanagement GmbH (NCC) [2002] I-9919.

323 See also Schall, "European Framework for the Mobility of Companies", p. 7.

324 See Kindler, "'Inspire Art' – Aus Luxemburg nichts Neues zum internationalen Gesellschaftsrecht", p. 1086. See also Council Regulation (EC) No

evident that companies are bound by the general legal rules of the country where they engage in market activities. However, opinions differ on some issues, such as creditor protection. On the one hand, it has been suggested that duties concerning protection of the interests of members of a corporation or creditors should be governed by the law of the country of incorporation.[325] On the other hand, it has been suggested that liabilities deriving from the law of the host state may not be applied, but only so far as the law of the country of incorporation provides sufficient creditor protection.[326] The latter view seems to support comparison of favourability between the law of the country of incorporation and the law of the country of the real seat. However, no definite answers can be given, so it seems that this is an issue on which the ECJ could provide clarity.

Two other points show that real seat theory has not completely lost its relevance in Europe. Firstly, ECJ case law does not as a rule affect the application of national laws in cases involving companies from non-Member States unbound by freedom of establishment.[327] Secondly, the EC legislator has used real seat theory. In the field of company law, the EC Regulations on SE and SCE represent a compromise of sorts between incorporation theory and real seat theory.[328] Again, in the field of labour law the EC legislator has given real seat theory some relevance in rules on employee involvement.[329]

Eva-Maria Kieninger has pointed out that as long as the choice of the applicable law depends on the choice of the company's real seat, the freedom of companies to choose the applicable law remains only theoretical. The freedom to choose the *lex societatis* will become

---

1346/2000 on insolvency proceedings and Proposal for a Regulation of the European Parliament and the Council on the law applicable to non-contractual obligations (Rome II). COM(2003) 427 final.

325 See Kieninger, "The Legal Framework of Regulatory Competition Based on Company Mobility: EU and US compared."

326 See Schall, "European Framework for the Mobility of Companies", p. 9.

327 See also Wymeersch, "Centros: A Landmark Decision in European Company Law", p. 647.

328 See also Wymeersch, "Company Law in Europe and European Company Law", pp. 142–143.

329 See section 4 of chapter IV below.

real only if the company is given the opportunity to choose a corporate seat that is independent of the company's real seat.[330]

In the US, the principle of party autonomy is well-established in international company law. In the EU, the question of the role of party autonomy remained unanswered for a long time, and the freedom of companies to choose the applicable law materialized relatively late. The ECJ decision in *Centros* did not lead to all Member States applying the principle of party autonomy but *Überseering* finally clarified the situation. The decision has been interpreted to indicate that nowadays companies may choose the Member State of establishment.

2.4 Future Prospects

The influence of American and British company law has been increasing in Europe at both EU and national levels. It is widely thought that American and British concepts of company law offer a more modern, flexible, and liberal approach to issues such as corporate governance and creditor protection.[331] In international company law, attention has been increasingly paid to limitations hampering cross-border reincorporation within the Union. In this respect, the different competitive position between European and US companies has often been emphasised.

International company law is in an interesting phase of development in Europe. *Centros, Überseering,* and *Inspire Art* have provoked a new interest in conflicts law questions.[332] The effects of ECJ case law, discussed above, and the increased activity of the EC legislator give rise to the question of the future direction of international company law in Europe. Generally speaking, international company law could be developed on two bases.[333]

---

330 See Kieninger, "The Legal Framework of Regulatory Competition Based on Company Mobility: EU and US compared", p. 741.

331 See Schall, "European Framework for the Mobility of Companies", p. 12.

332 See also Van Hulle, "Introduction – European Company Law: United in Diversity", p. 1.

333 See Dammann, "Freedom of Choice in European Corporate Law", p. 480.

The first alternative would probably bring European international company law closer to its US counterpart, because the next step in strengthening party autonomy would be to allow cross-border transfers of registered offices. Nowadays, companies are able to choose the most favourable company statute mainly by using what is called the *pseudo foreign* arrangement. Among others, *Wymeersch* has emphasised the need for clear guidelines for cross-border transfers that would improve the possibility of companies to choose the optimal business form. Without a common legal framework, the internal market will remain fragmented.[334] The Commission is currently preparing a directive proposal on cross-border transfers of registered offices.[335] In addition, an important step towards allowing party autonomy was recently taken by the Directive on cross-border mergers of limited liability companies, which will enable cross-border restructuring within the internal market.[336] Another concrete step was taken in the *SEVIC* case, where it was held that lack of explicit statutory law on transformation of a company into a foreign entity does not justify denying companies from another Member State the right to merge with a German company.[337] These legislative projects and ECJ case law do not seem to give much support to another alternative, which would be the kind of extensive harmonisation of Member State company law that would render aims to strengthen party autonomy unnecessary.

Companies can currently be considered as being able to choose one of the 25 EU Member States as their country of establishment and

---

334 See Wymeersch, "Company Law in Europe and European Company Law", p. 121.

335 The ECJ has held that all the problems related to the manner of transferring the seat of a company incorporated under national law from one Member State to another have not been resolved by the rules on the right of establishment and such problems must, therefore, be dealt with by future legislation or conventions (Case C-81/87, The Queen v. H. M. Treasury and Commissioners of Inland Revenue, ex parte Daily Mail and General Trust plc., [1988] ECR I-5483, para. 23). The High-Level Group of Company Law Experts recommended that the Commission should urgently consider adopting a proposal for a Directive on transfer of registered office.

336 Directive 2005/56/EC of the European Parliament and of the Council on cross-border mergers of limited liability companies.

337 Case C-411/03, SEVIC Systems AG, [2005] ECR I-10805.

thus, too, the applicable law. In Germany, the *Bundesgerichtshof* has even held incorporation theory applicable to Lichtenstein, an EEA State which is not a member of the EU.[338] By analogy, this means that all 28 EEA States are governed by incorporation theory in Germany. In addition, this theory applies between Germany and the US on the basis of a bilateral agreement from 1954 between those countries.[339]

However, even though the decisions of the ECJ have paved the way for the freedom of companies to choose their country of establishment regardless of their real seat, it is nearly impossible within the EU to transfer registered offices across borders, something which can be considered central for creating a real 'company law market'.[340] Moreover, ECJ case law has distinguished between a company moving to a Member State and a company moving from another Member State. The *Überseering* case confirmed that real seat theory can no longer be applied to companies moving to a Member State by that State. This means, for example, that Member States must accept *pseudo foreign* companies that operate within their territory. A company can be set up in any Member State of the EU with its real seat and main activities placed in another. In principle, a company may also later transfer its real seat to another Member State. The receiving country is also then obligated to apply the law of the country of establishment. In cases of moving out, the legal framework is different. In the role of home states, Member States are able to set restrictions on moving out of companies established under their legislation.[341] This division between the moving in and moving out situations is not un-

338 BGH 19.9.2005, II ZR 372/03.

339 See in more detail Rehm, "Vom Außenseiter zum Liebling? Liechtensteinische Gesellschaften mit deutschem Verwaltungssitz als unternehmerische Gestaltungsoption. Zugleich eine Besprechung des BGH-Urteils vom 19.9.2005, II ZR 372/03".

340 See Kieninger, "The Legal Framework of Regulatory Competition Based on Company Mobility: EU and US compared", p. 742.

341 See Case C-81/87, The Queen v. H. M. Treasury and Commissioners of Inland Revenue, *ex parte* Daily Mail and General Trust plc., [1988] ECR I-5483.

problematic, because in practice it enables the home states of companies to prevent them from moving out.[342]

In private international law, one is faced with special conflicts questions when a company has been established in one Member State but its actual centre of administration is in another. In such cases the relationship between the law of the country of establishment and the law of the actual centre of administration must be determined. So far, the ECJ has not given its view on the extent to which the law of the host state can be applied. Member States are entitled to set restrictions on freedom of establishment, if the restrictions are acceptable in accordance with grounds for restricting freedom of establishment confirmed in EC law. In principle, this could be seen by Member States that previously followed real seat theory as a means to protect interests that real seat theory earlier safeguarded.

Generally, it is possible for courts of the country of the real seat of a company to prefer the *lex fori* instead of the *lex causae,* above all because the conflicts rules of international company law have remained mainly unwritten. A homeward trend is also apparent in international company law; courts tend to apply their own law to cases that have connections with more than one state. However, ECJ case law directs national courts in another direction. Although the decisions of the ECJ mainly concern the contents of freedom of establishment and do not explicitly aim to alter the conflicts rules of international company law, they have actually limited the freedom of choice of Member States as to making decisions on the contents of choice of law rules.

2.5 Excursion: Companies, Freedom of Establishment and Employee Participation

In the legal literature, it has been argued that the choice of the law applicable to a company, in other words the company statute, could in certain situations be used to avoid arranging employee participation in

342 See, for example, Ebke: "Überseering: 'Die wahre Liberalität ist Anerkennung'" and Kieninger, "The Legal Framework of Regulatory Competition Based on Company Mobility: EU and US compared".

company administration in those EU Member States that regard employee participation rules as a part of their company law.[343] This 'race to the bottom' could be enabled, for example, by the fact that the application of employee participation rules depends on the chosen company form. The debate arises from significant differences between employee participation rights in the Member States. The content of legislation on employee participation in company administration varies from one Member State to another, while some States have no such legislation at all.[344]

In some EU Member States, real seat theory traditionally ensured application of the employee participation regulation to foreign companies. Due to ECJ case law, the conditions for applying employee participation legislation must be re-evaluated, because real seat theory no longer guarantees that the legislation is applied to foreign companies. In the following, the matter is discussed from the viewpoint of German employee participation legislation. In Germany, wide debate has taken place over protecting employee participation in the new situation.[345] Germany can also be used as an example because the German employee participation model has influenced legislative solutions on employee participation in some of the new EU Member States.

Systematically, employee participation in company administration is considered in Germany to belong to the field of company law.[346] From the systematic division of the fields of law, it follows that

---

343 See Wymeersch, "Centros: A Landmark Decision in European Company Law", p. 643.

344 See also Weiss, "The Future of Workers' Participation in the EU", pp. 229–230. Incapability to resolve how to arrange employee participation has been one of the major issues that have slowed preparation of certain key company law directives. This was the main reason for the very slow progress of the preparation of EC rules on the SE.

345 Views on the German participation model are divided. Many company law scholars have criticized the model for severely hampering cross-border restructuring. See, for example, Hopt, European Company Law and Corporate Governance: Where does the Action Plan of the European Commission Lead?, p. 10.

346 See Junker, Grundkurs Arbeitsrecht, p. 441.

employee participation can be regarded as a part of the *lex societatis*. Thus, the application of employee participation rules to foreign companies is at stake, because real seat theory, used earlier in Germany to determine the company statute, can no longer be applied in order to determine the law applicable to a company that is established in another country but has its actual centre of administration in Germany.[347] Hence, Germany is unable to automatically require that companies established in another Member State should apply German employee participation legislation when their real seat is situated in the country.

Prior to the ECJ decision in *Überseering*, real seat theory guaranteed that German legislation on employee participation in company administration could be applied even to foreign companies. In other words, the theory required that companies established in another Member State but with their real seat in Germany should be dissolved and re-established in order to enjoy legal capacity under German law.

The status of employee participation in terms of the company statute and companies' freedom of establishment needs to be analysed from two viewpoints. When approaching the matter from the viewpoint of national legal system, the first question that needs to be resolved is whether employee participation in choice of law should be qualified as a matter of company law or a matter of labour law. When approaching the matter from the viewpoint of EC law, the status of national employee participation legislation should be considered in light of Articles 43 and 48 EC Treaty. The question that then needs to be answered is whether EC law enables countries to restrict companies' freedom of establishment in order to protect employee participation in company administration.[348]

From the viewpoint of national legal system, employee participation in company administration can, in principle, be qualified as either a company law or a labour law question. If it is qualified as a company law question, then applicability of employee participation rules is resolved on the basis of the company statute. If, on the other hand, employee participation is considered a labour law question, then

347 See, for example, Ebke, "Centros – Some Realities and some Mysteries", p. 1.

348 See Mitbestimmung modernisieren, p. 12.

applicability of employee participation rules is decided on the basis of the law of the country indicated by the conflicts rules of international labour law. Unification of the conflicts rules in international labour law in the EC does not, in principle, extend to employee participation rules. Thus, the applicable law is to be determined by virtue of the national conflicts rules of each Member State. The national rules may suggest application of employee participation rules in accordance with the principle of territoriality to all companies operating on a country's territory. However, certain countries have set restrictions on the application of their employee participation rules to foreign companies. Some countries apply their employee participation rules basically to domestic companies only.

The duty to arrange employee participation in company administration on the basis of the law of the country in which the company *de facto* operates by virtue of the freedom of establishment is next discussed from the standpoint of EC law. The question that arises is whether the application of national employee participation rules could be ensured by restricting freedom of establishment. In this context, attention needs to be paid to the grounds for restriction indicated by ECJ case law.[349]

According to ECJ case law, restrictions on freedom of establishment can be justified by overriding reasons of public interest and on grounds relating to the abuse of company law. The restrictions that Member States can set for freedom of establishment have to fulfil certain criteria confirmed by ECJ case law in order to be acceptable. Member State measures must be acceptable: they must be based on overriding reasons of public interest. They are allowed only if they do not violate the prohibition of discrimination, and if they accord to the principle of proportionality. Therefore, national measures must be suitable for guaranteeing the success of the desired outcome and cannot interfere with freedom of establishment more than is necessary in order to achieve that goal. Overriding reasons of public interest should

---

[349] See Liukkunen, Globalisaatio, EU ja henkilöstön osallistuminen. Tutkimus globalisaatiojuridiikasta ja eurooppaoikeudesta erityisesti rajat ylittävissä yritysjärjestelyissä, p. 205.

be interpreted in narrow terms because they provide an exception to freedom of establishment.

Protection of workers has been considered an overriding reason of public interest in ECJ case law.[350] Legal literature has suggested that German employee participation in company administration could also be defended by overriding reasons of public interest.[351] Thus, the protection of employees' right to be represented in company administration could be regarded as a reason for restricting freedom of establishment, provided that the other requirements are fulfilled.

However, this would require deciding how the employee participation legislation that governs only certain German company forms could be applied to foreign company forms. Here the matter becomes highly disputed. Some scholars in Germany have suggested that substitution could be used, as German legislation on employee participation only covers certain company forms referred to in German law. Foreign company forms corresponding to those regulated, for example, by the Co-determination Act (*Mitbestimmungsgesetz*) would be covered by this Act. This argumentation is based on the assumption that the comparability of different company forms would be relatively easily defined.[352] It is interesting to note that these efforts of German doctrine to extend employee participation legislation to foreign companies are not restricted by the fact that when the Co-determination Act came into force in 1976 the legislator intended to limit application of the Act to companies with their registered office in Germany. Since the Act is explicitly restricted to German company forms, it could be argued that

---

350 See Joined Cases C-369/96 and C-376/96, Criminal proceedings against Jean-Claude Arblade and Arblade & Fils SARL and Bernard Leloup, Serge Leloup and Sofrage SARL, [1999] ECR I-8453, para. 36.

351 See Roth, "Case law. Court of Justice, Case C-212/97, Centros Ltd v Erhvervs- og Selskabsstyrelsen, Judgment of 9 March 1999, Full Court", p. 155 and Dammann, "The Future of Codetermination after Centros: Will the German corporate law move closer to the U.S. model?".

352 See Franzen, "Niederlassungsfreiheit, internationales Gesellschaftsrecht und Unternehmensmitbestimmung", p. 260.

applying it to foreign companies would require an amendment to the legislation.[353]

It would be contrary to EC law to apply national employee participation rules so as to place foreign companies in an unfavourable position compared to domestic companies. It could be thought that foreign companies would not be placed in a less favourable position if the Co-determination Act was applicable without distinction to foreign and domestic companies with their real seat in Germany.[354] However, in that case it should be noted that the employee participation rules of the company's country of establishment might also apply.

In accordance with the principle of proportionality, the application of German employee participation legislation should be justified and proportional to the objectives set for such legislation. Thus, it would be contrary to this principle to apply the employee participation rules of the host country when the interests protected by the rules are already duly protected by the law of the home state. Therefore, it would have to be decided whether employees are sufficiently protected by employee participation arranged differently from the German system, for example, by using participation in the administrative board or management group, or by using a system where the number of employee representatives in company administration is smaller than in Germany.

Summing up, it might be said that keeping the above reservations in mind, the application of host state employee participation rules to foreign companies could, in principle, at least in certain cases be in accordance with EC law on freedom of establishment.[355] If this was not enabled, then the European legal framework set to increase the mobility of companies might diminish the social protection of employees. This is not just a theoretical question: since companies are able to operate as *pseudo foreign* companies, they can choose a country of establishment in which employee participation is not required

353 See also Dammann, "The Future of Codetermination after Centros: Will the German corporate law move closer to the U.S. model?", p. 200.

354 See Franzen, "Niederlassungsfreiheit, internationales Gesellschaftsrecht und Unternehmensmitbestimmung", p. 262.

355 See also ibid., p. 260. Cf. Kersting – Schindler, "The ECJ's Inspire Art Decision of 30 September and its Effects on Practice", pp. 1365–1366.

by law. In such cases, the extent of applicability of the employee participation rules of the country where the *pseudo foreign* companies actually operate needs to be determined. So far, ECJ case law has not clearly indicated the extent to which host state law could be applied to such companies irrespective of the company statute.[356]

It is interesting to note that the question of protecting employee participation rights was also brought up in the High-Level Group of Company Law Experts which the European Commission appointed in 2001 to suggest how to modernise company law. The Group discussed employee participation rights from the viewpoint of corporate restructuring and freedom of establishment. The Group made fairly general estimates: it can be required that employee participation be arranged in accordance with host state law if this fulfils the criteria accepted in EC law for restricting freedom of establishment. The Group considered that protection of employee participation is an objective that seems to justify measures of the host state. Moreover, the Group stated that the fact that participation rights are also protected in the EC legislation on SE supports the interpretation that these rights are legitimate.[357]

According to the Group, it would be a violation of the principle of proportionality for a host state to completely refuse to recognise a foreign company on the sole basis that the company does not apply the employee participation rules of the host state. Furthermore, it would be difficult to justify application of host state law when less than 50 percent of the company's employees work in the host state. Even when the connecting factor is sufficient, there would be a need for a provision which allows an agreed employee involvement system to be adopted.[358]

---

356 See, for example, Dammann, "Freedom of Choice in European Corporate Law", p. 486.

357 See Report of the High Level Group of Company Law Experts on a Modern Regulatory Framework for Company Law in Europe, pp. 103–105.

358 See ibid., p. 105. It should be noted that information and consultation as well as employee participation in company administration are covered by the concept of 'employee involvement' in the EC legislation on the SE. See Article 2(h) of the SE Directive.

A final point to mention relates to the private international law dimension on the grounds for restricting freedom of establishment. German doctrine involves suggestions that the employee participation rules in German legislation are internationally mandatory as referred to in Article 34 of the Introductory Code of the German Civil Code (*EGBGB*).[359] The Article is based on Article 7(2) of the Rome Convention.

It is possible to extend the application of the principle of internationally mandatory rules to international company law.[360] However, the question arises whether mandatory rules on employee participation in company administration can be considered internationally mandatory. Here, at least two aspects should be taken into consideration. Firstly, the rules in question should be mandatory by nature. Secondly, the nature and purpose of the rules should indicate that they are of such importance that they must be applied irrespective of the otherwise applicable law. If employee participation rules were considered internationally mandatory, then a court could apply them at its own discretion regardless of the *lex causae*. However, the court would also need to take into account EC law on justified grounds for restricting freedom of establishment.

It should be emphasised that reservations made by certain Contracting States to Article 7(1) of the Rome Convention have no relevance at this point. Therefore, although Germany, for instance, has made a reservation to Article 7(1), this does not rule out the possibility of applying internationally mandatory rules of third states. It seems unlikely, though, that a national court of any Member State would apply the employee participation legislation of a foreign country if such application meant departing from the company statute.[361]

---

359 See, for example, Franzen, "Niederlassungsfreiheit, internationales Gesellschaftsrecht und Unternehmensmitbestimmung", p. 263.

360 See Rinze, "The Scope of Party Autonomy under the 1980 Rome Convention on the Law Applicable to Contractual Obligations", p. 427.

361 See also Roth, "From Centros to Überseering: Free Movement of Companies, Private International Law, and Community Law", p. 200.

3 Freedom of Service Provision and Conflicts Rules

Along with the general conflicts rules on contractual obligations set out in the Rome Convention, internal market law has come to include several legislative instruments on services that affect choice of law in the Member States. Some of the conflicts rules are created to supplement the Convention, whereas some affect *de facto* choice of law even though the intention of the EC legislator would not have been to regulate on the issue. In the European choice of law discussion, certain developments of internal market law have received limited attention.

The most controversial internal market law initiative has turned out to be the Proposal for a Services Directive, introduced with great expectations in 2004. The aim of the proposed Directive is to remove the core legal impediments to the free movement of services between Member States. In addition, the aim is to simplify administrative procedures to promote opportunities to use freedom of establishment.[362]

The contents of the original Services Directive Proposal raised the question of the status of the country of origin principle in EC law and its relation to conflicts law. In recent years, this principle has turned out to be a source of serious conflicts law problems. Since it has been used in many legislative initiatives concerning cross-border services, the principle deserves attention here, starting with its origins in EC law.

3.1 *Raison d`être* of the Country of Origin Principle

In the *Cassis de Dijon* case, the ECJ gave a landmark decision, which introduced the principle of mutual recognition.[363] This was taken up by

---

[362] See Proposal for a Directive of the European Parliament and of the Council on services in the internal market. COM(2004) 2 final/3.

[363] See Case C-120/78, Rewe-Zentral AG v. Bundesmonopolverwaltung für Branntwein, [1979] ECR 649, para. 14: "There is therefore no valid reason why, provided that they have been lawfully produced and marketed in one of the Member States, alcoholic beverages should not be introduced in any other

the European Commission and used to develop a new approach to technical harmonisation.[364] From the principle of mutual recognition, the EC legislator deduced the country of origin principle, which takes the supervision exercised by the home state a step further. However, drawing a line between these principles has sometimes proven very difficult because of inconsistencies in the terminology used by the EC legislator.

Generally speaking, what is usually meant by the country of origin principle is that the activities of service-providers are also supervised by the home state when they operate in other Member States. But as will be shown later, the effects of the country of origin principle sometimes come very close to the principle of mutual recognition. The basic idea behind the country of origin principle is that service-providers are bound by the rules laid down for their operations in their home country and that they may operate in other Member States without having to observe any additional requirements of those States. Thus, the host country cannot require a service-provider operating temporarily on its territory to fulfil the requirements it has set for service-providers established on its territory.

Compared to the principle of mutual recognition, as defined by the ECJ, the country of origin principle, as applied in EC secondary legislation, is stricter. By virtue of it, the only additional conditions the host country can set for operations carried out on its territory are conditions specifically allowed in the EC legal instrument in question. If, for example, consumer or employee protection issues were not mentioned as supplementary conditions in an EC legal instrument, then a Member State could not require that a service-provider operating temporarily on its territory should observe rules that were stricter than those it observed in its home state. It is not clear whether a Member State could set requirements based on public interest when an EC legal instrument includes the country of origin principle and states

---

Member State". See also Graham, "Mutual Recognition and Country of Origin in the Case Law of the European Court of Justice", pp. 37–42.

364 Armstrong – Bulmer, The governance of the Single European Market, p. 149. See also de Vries, Tensions within the Internal Market. The Functioning of the Internal Market and the Development of Horizontal and Flanking Policies, p. 55.

that the only conditions Member States are allowed to set are those mentioned in the legal instrument. In EC law, harmonisation of a particular field has usually been considered to rule out the possibility of setting deviant national requirements.

So far, the country of origin principle has been used in internal market law by formulating the contents of the principle to suit the needs of the given legal instrument. In contrast, the principle of mutual recognition has well-established contents and has been applied in numerous legal instruments in several fields of EC law. The principle has usually been applied when the legislation of the Member States has been harmonised at Community level and, to complement the harmonisation, it has been considered necessary to mutually recognise the legislation and supervision implemented in other Member States. Usually, the EC legislator has aimed at creating adequately uniform legislation by harmonising when necessary and by widely following the principle of mutual recognition in the harmonised fields of law. The approach, based on the country of origin principle, is different: the Member States mutually recognise a field that is wider than the harmonised legislation. The term 'negative harmonisation' can be used to describe this approach: instead of harmonising legislation at Community level, the activities of the internal market are promoted by rendering national provisions unsuitable for a given purpose.[365]

From the viewpoint of promoting European integration, the country of origin principle aims at removing legal impediments, more specifically obstacles to trade posed by legislative differences between Member States. Criticism of the principle has been levelled in the legal literature for placing a one-sided emphasis on the interests of service-providers who should be able to operate on the basis of the law of their home countries. This means that, in a way, they should be able to take 'their own' law with them when they move within the Community. The question is also about the economic expense of the move, which can be avoided by using this principle. The interests of the demand side have been sidelined in favour of a 'supply-sided

365 See also Gekiere, "The Proposal of the European Commission for a Directive on Services in the Internal Market: An Overview of its Main Features and Critical Reflections", pp. 13–14.

economy' which, in the words of *Mankowski*, could move towards a 'lop-sided' economy.[366]

This brings us to one of the fundamental differences between the country of origin principle and conflicts law: whereas the country of origin principle can be one-sided, the basic rules of private international law take into account the interests of both the service-provider and receiver.[367]

To obtain a better grasp of the theme, the country of origin principle is next discussed starting from the E-Commerce Directive[368] and then in the context of the original Services Directive Proposal. It must be emphasised that the country of origin principle does not yet have an established content in EC law. It has been defined in EC legal instruments and initiatives in the manner most suitable for the given purpose. It should also be noted that in practice, the impact of existing EC law provisions on the country of origin principle is diminished by the limited scope of application of the principle and restrictions included in the legal instruments. However, in the following, two existing legislative initiatives are analysed in order to show that the Commission seems to have ambitions to extend application of the principle much further. Formally, this would occur in the name of the principle of mutual recognition, whose practical effects seem to make this principle almost interchangeable with the country of origin principle.

3.2 EC Legislation on Services

When considering the significance of the country of origin principle in the service sector, it should be remembered that the scope of application of free movement of services sets certain limitations to the application of the principle. The free movement of services refers to the

---

366 See Mankowski, "Wieder ein Herkunftslandprinzip für Dienstleistungen im Binnenmarkt", p. 386.

367 See also ibid., p. 390.

368 Directive 2000/31/EC of the European Parliament and of the Council on certain legal aspects of information society services, in particular electronic commerce, in the Internal Market (Directive on electronic commerce).

temporary provision of services in another Member State.[369] According to the ECJ, when deciding whether the question is about service provision or establishment, not only does the duration of the activity have to be taken into account, but also its 'regularity, periodicity or continuity'. Starting with *Schnitzer*[370], the ECJ has somewhat modified the concept of service provision and taken a step away from the starting point based on the time factor.

So far, the country of origin principle has only been applied in some EU service sectors. Initially, its scope of application was very limited. Also in the E-Commerce Directive, the principle has a limited scope of application. An e-commerce service offered in one country is easily received in another without the service-provider having to move or take other special measures. The E-Commerce Directive seeks to contribute to the proper functioning of the internal market by ensuring the free movement of information society services between Member States. Under Recital 59 of the Directive, co-ordination of national regulatory measures at EU level is necessary in order to avoid fragmentation of the internal market and to establish an appropriate European regulatory framework.

The E-Commerce Directive only applies to online operations, i.e. information society services, in which only the services, not the service-providers, move from country to country. Sometimes, though, online operations belong to a larger entity which may involve the movement of the service-provider. In the Directive, the country of origin principle guarantees above all that a Member State ensures that the services of service-providers located on its territory fulfil the requirements of its legal system. As a rule, the Member State is not allowed to restrict a service offering from another Member State on the basis of its own provisions. In general, the country of origin principle implies that as a rule, a service-provider that offers information society services in the Community cannot be expected to observe any other

369 See Case C-55/94, Reinhard Gebhard v. Consiglio dell'Ordine degli Avvocati e Procuratori di Milano, [1995] ECR I-4165, where the ECJ also stated that a service-provider can use some permanent infrastructure in the host state.

370 See Case C-215/01, Bruno Schnitzer, [2003] ECR I-14847.

provisions than those of its home country. In the Directive, this principle is taken relatively far in the supervision of the Member State.

One of the key elements in the European regulatory framework established by the Directive is the country of origin principle contained in Article 3(1). This reads as follows:

> 1. Each Member State shall ensure that the information society services provided by a service provider established on its territory comply with the national provisions applicable in the Member State in question which fall within the coordinated field.

The co-ordinated field is defined in the Directive.[371] By virtue of Article 3(1), a Member State has to ensure that the information society services provided by a service provider established on its territory comply with the national provisions applicable in the Member State in question which fall within the coordinated field. Under Article 3(2), Member States are not allowed, for reasons falling within the coordinated field, to restrict the freedom to provide information society services from another Member State.

However, these paragraphs do not apply to the field referred to in the Annex of the Directive. The list of excluded field includes the freedom of the parties to choose the law applicable to their contract; contractual obligations concerning consumer contacts; formal validity of contracts creating or transferring rights in real estate where such contracts are subject to mandatory formal requirements of the law of the Member State where the real estate is situated; and the permissibility of unsolicited commercial communications by electronic mail. Hence, the excluded field largely governs private relations, which means that the problems caused by the country of origin principle can be considered limited. Nonetheless, they remain noteworthy in terms of choice of law.

Article 3(4) sets out the conditions for deviation from the country of origin principle in the Member States. The starting point being

371 The co-ordinated field is defined in Article 2(h) of the Directive as "requirements laid down in Member States' legal systems applicable to information society service providers or information society services, regardless of whether they are of a general nature or specifically designed for them".

the country of origin principle, derogations can be used only narrowly. During negotiation of the Directive in the Council, it was noticed that introduction of the country of origin principle could affect choice of law. In order to avoid this, a separate provision was added to Article 1.[372] Article 1(4) reads as follows:

> 4. This Directive does not establish additional rules on private international law nor does it deal with the jurisdiction of Courts.

Despite this explicit rule, the Directive has caused confusion in the Member States as regards its impact on choice of law. For service-providers, the country of origin principle means that they cannot be required to follow any other provisions than those of their home country when they offer information society services in the Community. However, as has been said, the Directive contains certain exceptions to freedom of service provision and the country of origin principle, which should be taken into account when assessing the relevance of the principle.

It should also be noted that because of the nature of e-commerce the country of origin principle mainly concerns situations where only the service moves from one country to another, while the service-provider remains in the country of establishment. It is not clear whether the principle should be considered to be limited to the Member State's provisions on supervisory powers and not concern private relations. One cannot draw firm conclusions from the wording of Article 2, which contains a definition of the co-ordinated field of law.[373] However, it would be preferable to restrict application of the country of origin principle to public law issues.[374]

According to *Michael Hellner*, three alternative interpretations can be given to the country of origin principle contained in the E-Commerce Directive. First of all, the principle could be considered to establish a conflicts rule. Secondly, the principle could be considered to make the rules of the home country of the service-provider interna-

---

372 See Hellner, "The E-Commerce Directive and Private International Law", p. 108.

373 See ibid., pp. 110–111.

374 See ibid., p. 113.

tionally mandatory and, thirdly, it could be considered to set out certain limitations to the application of the designated law.

If the first alternative were accepted, then the content of Article 1(4) would be totally ignored. However, one of the arguments supporting this alternative is that when providing derogations from the country of origin principle, Article 3(4) takes as a starting point that the law of the country of origin is applicable.[375] In the legal literature, it has also been suggested that the Directive requires application of the conflict of laws of the state where the service-provider is established.[376]

If the second alternative sketched by *Hellner* were accepted and the country of origin principle were considered to make the rules of the country of origin internationally mandatory, then these rules would be applied to e-service-providers regardless of the otherwise applicable law. He argues that the advantage of this alternative would be that the interpretation would be more in line with Article 1(4) of the Directive. Secondly, some support for this interpretation could be found in ECJ case law, under which certain provisions in EC secondary legislation may have an internationally mandatory character. *Hellner* also refers to the fact that this has been confirmed by the Court in the *Ingmar* case.[377] It should also be noted that secondary legislation exists that is generally regarded as internationally mandatory without this being explicitly mentioned in the EC statute or confirmed by the ECJ. However, considering the country of origin principle as an expression of internationally mandatory rules would extend the sphere of such rules to a degree that would be contrary to the purpose of the principle of internationally mandatory rules.

---

375 See ibid., p. 114. *Hellner* also points out that both the European Commission and the European Parliament had intended to create a new conflict rule by Article 3(1). See also Mankowski, "Herkunftslandsprinzip und deutsches Umsetzungsgesetz zur e-commerce-Richtlinie", p. 138.

376 See for example Lurger – Vallant, "Grenzüberschreitender Wettbewerb im Internet – die Umsetzung des Herkunfts-landprinzips der E-Commerce-Richtlinie in Deutschland und Österreich", p. 196.

377 See Hellner, "The E-Commerce Directive and Private International Law", pp. 117–118.

According to *Hellner*, the third alternative would be to consider that the country of origin principle is simply a concretion of the country of origin principle in the EC Treaty. But, as the author admits, this solution would not take into account that the principle contained in Article 3(1) of the Directive is a novelty and clearly goes beyond the principle of mutual recognition. If mutual recognition had been the aim of the legislator, then a principle of the country of origin would not have been needed.[378]

Hellner is in favour of regarding the country of origin principle as an expression of the principle of internationally mandatory rules. Yet, he recognises problems even with this interpretation. He points out that the country of origin principle concerns only the law applicable to one of the parties, i.e. the e-service-provider. Secondly, problems arise because the country of origin principle only applies to the limited scope of the co-ordinated field. Hence, issues remaining outside will be dealt with under the conflicts rules in the Rome Convention. This results in *dépeçage*. Thirdly, the author points out that it is difficult to determine the issues which are subject to the law of the country of origin when it comes to contracts for the provision of both services and goods. Altogether, *Hellner* emphasises that the legal status is now much more complicated than it was before the Directive.[379]

The alternative interpretations of the country of origin principle discussed below clearly point out that there are different approaches with different implications available. Still another alternative would probably be that of regarding the country of origin principle simply as an expression of territoriality. Until the ECJ gets an opportunity to take a stand on the issue, the question of the nature of the country of origin principle remains unclear.

Further clarification would be needed in order to make the application of the E-Commerce Directive more coherent. When the Directive was being transposed, some Member States interpreted the country of origin principle to be a choice of law rule. Other countries considered that the principle did not change the way in which the law

---

378 See ibid., pp. 118–119.

379 See ibid., pp. 119–121.

applicable to contractual obligations is determined if the contracting parties have the right to choose the applicable law. The Directive seems to be too open to various interpretations, as it has been transposed so inconsistently.[380] This could have been avoided if enough attention had been paid to questions of private international law when the Directive was being prepared.[381]

3.3 The Proposed Services Directive and Conflicts Law

If the country of origin principle had been included in the forthcoming Services Directive, the prevailing legal status would have changed significantly since the contents of the principle suggested by the Commission were exceptionally far-reaching. According to the EC Treaty provisions on free movement of services, services may be offered in another Member State on the conditions the receiving State has set for the offering of such services. One of the problems was that the Directive would have limited the opportunities of a Member State to require that a service-provider coming from another Member State should fulfil the conditions it had set for service-providers located on its territory.

The original Proposal for a Services Directive concerned both service-providers' freedom of establishment and free movement of services. The country of origin principle, which was one of the key elements in the Proposal, would have been applied to service-providers offering services temporarily in another Member State.[382] The Pro-

---

[380] See Liukkunen, "Kansainvälinen yksityisoikeus ja Euroopan integraatio", p. 357.

[381] The Communication concerning transposition of the Directive does not pay attention to this problem. See Report from the Commission to the European Parliament, the Council and the European Economic and Social Committee – First Report on the application of Directive 2000/31/EC of the European Parliament and of the Council of 8 June 2000 on certain legal aspects of information society services, in particular electronic commerce, in the Internal Market (Directive on electronic commerce). COM(2003) 702 final.

[382] See Proposal for a Directive of the European Parliament and of the Council on services in the internal market. COM(2004) 2 final/3, see also

posal did not aim at extensive harmonisation of Member State rules on service operations; the basis of the Proposal was to introduce the country of origin principle. According to the principle, only the legislation of its home country was to be applied to a service-provider. Member States would only have been allowed to restrict the services delivered by a service-provider located in another Member State in special cases listed in the Directive.

For example, the Proposal excluded from the list of exceptions consumer protection provisions which would have enabled Member States to set additional requirements for companies temporarily offering services on their territory. According to the Commission, the most essential consumer protection requirements have already been harmonised in the Community, and therefore further requirements by the Member States could not have been allowed. In the Proposal, the Commission also suggested that the country of origin principle be extended to legislation on private relations.

Although the objective of the proposed Directive was to boost the internal services market, the original Proposal would likely have led to confusion over the law applicable to individual legal relationships. The scope of application of the proposed Directive was very wide. With a few rare exceptions, it covered the provision of all services. In practice, services requiring physical performance, such as health and beauty care services and building and repair services, would have undergone the greatest change.

The country of origin principle was set out in Article 16 of the Proposal. It reads as follows:

> (1) Member States shall ensure that providers are subject only to the national provisions of their Member State of origin which fall within the coordinated field.
> Paragraph 1 shall cover national provisions relating to access to and the exercise of a service activity, in particular those requirements governing the behaviour of the provider, the quality or content of the service, advertising, contracts and the provider's liability.

Mankowski, "Wider ein Herkunftslandprinzip für Dienstleistungen im Binnenmarkt", p. 386.

> (2) The Member State of origin shall be responsible for supervising the provider and the services provided by him, including services provided by him in another Member State.
> (3) Member States may not, for reasons falling within the coordinated field, restrict the freedom to provide services in the case of a provider established in another Member State, in particular, by imposing any of the following requirements:
> (a) an obligation on the provider to have an establishment in their territory;
> (b) an obligation on the provider to make a declaration or notification to, or to obtain an authorisation from, their competent authorities, including entry in a register or registration with a professional body or association in their territory;
> (c) an obligation on the provider to have an address or representative in their territory or to have an address for service at the address of a person authorised in that territory;
> (d) a ban on the provider setting up a certain infrastructure in their territory, including an office or chambers, which the provider needs to supply the services in question;
> (e) an obligation on the provider to comply with requirements, relating to the exercise of a service activity, applicable in their territory;
> (f) the application of specific contractual arrangements between the provider and the recipient which prevent or restrict service provision by the self-employed;
> (g) an obligation on the provider to possess an identity document issued by its competent authorities specific to the exercise of a service activity;
> (h) requirements which affect the use of equipment which is an integral part of the service provided;
> (i) restrictions on the freedom to provide the services referred to in Article 20, the first subparagraph of Article 23(1) or Article 25(1).

The scope of application of the country of origin principle was very unclear in the original Commission Proposal. According to the Proposal, the law of the service-provider's home country was to be applied to the entire service. In addition, the service-provider's liability for damages should, as a rule, have been determined on the basis of the home country.

The impact of the Proposal had not been properly considered, for example, from the standpoint of consumers. It is generally held that consumers can with good reason assume that the service-provider abides by the requirements of the consumers' home country, particularly when the services are performed in that country. This is also the case when the service-provider comes to the consumer's home country to perform a service. The choice between the law of the consumer's home country and the service-provider's home country can be highly significant in practice, because service legislation is little harmonised and national provisions often differ greatly. In certain situations, consumers would have been unprotected by the law of the state in which the service is offered, as the only law protecting them would have been the law of the service-provider's home country.[383]

Similarly, the Proposal seemed to suggest that the law of the service-provider's home country should be applied to employment contracts between service-provider and employees, unless the parties made a choice of law clause. Furthermore, the Proposal seemed to suggest that the law of the service-provider's home country should be applied to real estate deals made by the service-provider, unless otherwise agreed by the parties.

As to labour law, the original Directive Proposal regarded the Posted Workers Directive, based on the application of the host country regulation, merely as an exception to the country of origin principle. From the labour protection perspective, the well-established main principle was relegated to the role of an exception. The legal approach adopted in the Proposal was against the true spirit of the Posted Workers Directive and the related ECJ case law.[384]

---

383 See Position of the European Group for Private International Law on the draft directive of the European Parliament and the Council on services in the internal market, 23 November 2004.

384 From the perspective of the posting of workers, uncertainties also arose as to whether supervision of foreign service-providers could be safeguarded in the future. In particular, these uncertainties related to the fact that the Services Directive Proposal suggested a change to the present system of monitoring, giving more competence to the country of origin at the expense of the host state by eliminating some administrative requirements in the host state. See also Communication from the Commission: Guidance on the Posting of Workers in the Framework of the Provision of Services. COM(2006) 159 final.

As regards conflicts law, problems with legal certainty and coherency of EC law were obvious. When the original Services Directive Proposal was being prepared, the relationship between the country of origin principle and the existing conflicts rules was never appropriately examined. Nor was the relationship of the Directive Proposal and the Rome II Proposal, adopted in 2003 by the Commission, properly addressed.[385] Experts in private international law had to take up a critical position when evaluating the Directive Proposal. The worry was that the country of origin principle, in the form it took in the Commission's original Proposal, may affect choice of law unless conflicts questions are explicitly excluded from the scope of the Directive.

When the Directive Proposal was being discussed within the Council, it soon became clear that there is no general acceptance to extension of the principle's scope of application to conflicts rules concerning private relations. At its first reading, the European Parliament was clearly abandoning the proposed country of origin principle and replacing it with a provision on freedom to provide services. According to amended Article 16, Member States must respect the right of service-providers to provide services in another Member State than that in which they are established. The Member State where services are provided has to ensure free access to and free exercise of a service activity within its territory. Article 16 confirms that Member States can apply their own national requirements to service-providers established in another country only if they are non-discriminatory, necessary, and proportionate. In addition, the restrictions have to be justified on grounds of public policy, public security, public health, or protection of the environment. The Parliament also limited the scope of application of the Directive and introduced derogation for all provisions of private international law. In April 2006, the Commission issued an amended Proposal, accepting these amendments.[386] Political agreement of the Directive, seen by some as a 'watered-down' piece

---

385 See Proposal for a Directive of the European Parliament and of the Council on services in the internal market. COM(2004) 2 final/3, pp.16–17.

386 See Amended proposal for a Directive of the European Parliament and of the Council on services in the internal market. COM(2006) 160.

of EC legislation, was reached in the Council meeting of May 2006. A little later, in July 2006, the Council adopted a common position on the proposed Directive.[387]

In search for a model for how best to boost the internal services market, the Commission appears to have drifted onto a collision course with private international law. The adoption saga of the Services Directive shows a limited understanding of the vital role of conflicts rules in cross-border transactions. Private international law scholars tend to see the dilemma caused by the original Directive Proposal as a serious indication that the country of origin principle should not be used to interfere with the rules of private international law, be they on contractual or non-contractual obligations. This was also the specific approach taken when the E-Commerce Directive was being prepared, although the final outcome does not fully meet this aim.

3.4 On a Collision Course with Conflicts Law Again

From the standpoint of conflicts law, two other legislative initiatives of the European Commission give rise to more or less similar concerns as the original Proposal for a Services Directive. In these topical initiatives, the Commission has formally used the principle of mutual recognition. In practice, the principle is used in a way that comes very close to the legal effects of the country of origin principle. When looked at together, the initiatives seem to confirm that the use of the two principles is not consistent, and a clear distinction between the country of origin principle and the principle of mutual recognition, as defined by the Commission, is difficult to draw.

The amended Proposal for a Directive on consumer credit agreements is problematic from the standpoint of conflicts law.[388]

---

[387] See Common position adopted by the Council on 24 July 2006 with a view to the adoption of a Directive of the European Parliament and of the Council on services in the internal market. Brussels, 24 July 2006, 10003/4/06, REV 4.

[388] See Amended proposal for a Directive of the European Parliament and of the Council on credit agreements for consumers amending Council Directive 93/13/EC. COM(2005) 483 final/2. Cf. Proposal for a Directive of the Euro-

Opening of national markets to foreign creditors has been considered an important objective for establishing a genuine internal market. The proposed Directive would replace the existing Directive on consumer credit.[389] With the Proposal, the Commission seeks to ensure better consumer protection and improve the clarity of EC legislation. The original Proposal, adopted by the Commission in 2002, seeks to improve stability by provisions on responsible lending and on providing information and protection both when the credit agreement is concluded and during its performance.

In November 2005, the Commission adopted an amended Proposal following the opinion of the European Parliament. The Directive Proposal contains the principle of mutual recognition. By virtue of the principle, a creditor would have to comply with the legal requirements of its Member State of origin for an activity exercised in another Member State. In the Proposal, the Commission has explicitly remarked that the application of such a principle could lead to another result than the application of Article 5 of the Rome Convention on consumer contracts. However, it should be emphasised that the principle of mutual recognition would only have a limited scope of application in the proposed Directive.

Application of the principle of mutual recognition would mean that the contractual relationship between a consumer and a foreign creditor is not fully governed by the law of the habitual place of residence of the consumer. Instead, the law of the home country of the creditor would be partly applied. This would weaken the protection of consumers provided by the Rome Convention. Hence, the principle of mutual recognition would also contradict the conflicts rules of the Member States.

---

pean Parliament and of the Council on financial collateral arrangements. COM(2001) 168 final.

389 Council Directive 90/88/EEC amending Directive 87/102/EEC for the approximation of the laws, regulations and administrative provisions of the Member States concerning consumer credit, itself amended by Directive 98/7/EC of the European Parliament and of the Council amending Directive 87/102/EEC for the approximation of laws, regulations and administrative provisions of the Member States concerning consumer credit.

Under the Directive Proposal, in cases where the conflicts rules of the Rome Convention would lead to application of the law of the country of the consumer's habitual residence, that country should ensure that its rules would not be applied if they are different from or stricter than the provisions of the home country of the foreign creditor. Only certain exceptional situations would constitute an exception to this rule, which would lead to the splitting (*dépeçage*) of the law applicable to consumer contracts.

Since the Directive Proposal conflicts with Article 5 Rome Convention, it also fails to achieve the objective of 'improving clarity' of EC legislation. The effects of the principle of mutual recognition adopted in the Proposal come very close to those of the country of origin principle. Again, the Member States are confronted with an initiative that raises serious concerns about undermining the existing conflicts rules and weakening the weaker party protection provided by the Rome Convention.

The Commission Proposal for a Directive on payment services in the internal market raises similar concerns.[390] Again, the protection of consumers is at stake. The objective of the Proposal adopted in December 2005 is to establish a modern and harmonised legal framework for an integrated payments market in the EU. This is based on the fact that lack of harmonisation in the payment services market hinders the operation of the market.[391] According to the Commission, opening up national payment markets for foreign providers and ensuring a level playing field would increase competition and foster cross-border provision of services.[392] The proposed Directive has a wide scope of application and it would apply to both national and cross-border payment services.[393]

---

390 See Implementing the Community Lisbon programme: Proposal for a Directive of the European Parliament and of the Council on payment services in the internal market and amending Directives 97/7/EC, 2000/12/EC and 2002/65/EC. COM(2005) 603 final.

391 See ibid., p. 10.

392 See ibid., p. 1.

393 For example, public transport tickets bought by mobile phone would come within the scope of application of the Directive.

The Directive Proposal introduces an EU-wide licensing regime for payment institutions. Unification of national rules in the Member States would be based on the principle of supervision carried out by home states and on a single licence for payment allowing non-bank payment service-providers to offer their services within the Union. In general, the introduction of a common licence for payment institutions would mean that institutions with such a licence may freely offer their services in other Member States, while supervision of these institutions is carried out by the authorities of their home states.

Furthermore, the Proposal intends to leave maximum room for self-regulation, harmonising only what is necessary to overcome legal barriers to a single market. In certain issues, national exceptions would be possible; these would be subject to the principle of mutual recognition. This principle is provided in Article 78 of the proposed Directive. The principle would apply if a Member State has used the options given in Articles 50(1) and 64 of the Directive.[394]

Under the first subparagraph of Article 50(1) of the proposed Directive, the payment service user would bear the loss, up to a maximum of EUR 150, resulting from the use of a lost or stolen payment verification instrument (for example, credit card) and occurring before the user has fulfilled the obligation to notify the payment service-provider. According to Article 50(1), Member States might reduce the maximum amount of which the payment service user must bear the loss further, provided that such reduction does not apply to payment service-providers authorised in other Member States. Article 64 concerns national payment transactions. For purely national transactions, Member States might provide for shorter maximum execution times than those provided for in Section 2 of the Directive.

Application of a Member State's legislation based on use of the options given in Articles 50(1) and 64 of the proposed Directive

---

394 Article 78(2) of the Directive would read: "When exercising the options granted to them under the second subparagraph of Article 50(1) or Article 64 of this Directive, Member States may not restrict the activities of payment service providers authorised in another Member State and operating within their territory in accordance with the provisions of the present Directive either by way of freedom of establishment or by way of freedom to provide services."

would be restricted by virtue of Article 78 only to those institutions that have received their licence in that legislating state. Hence, the institutions that have received their licence in another Member State could not be required to follow such legislation in the state where they operate.

Two things are especially noteworthy here. Firstly, the rule contained in Article 78 would affect choice of law in contractual relationships. This would mean that the law of the home state of the institution would be applied to questions regulated by virtue of Articles 50(1) and 64 at national level. For the rest of the contractual relationship, the applicable law would be determined under the Rome Convention. Thus, *dépeçage* would occur. The same problem would occur with the Rome I Proposal, under which the law of the habitual place of residence should always be applied to customers.

Secondly, what makes Article 78 especially noteworthy is that it would be applied to institutions offering payment services in another country either by using freedom of service provision or by using freedom of establishment. This means that the Directive Proposal intends to extend the principle of mutual recognition to both service-providers that are only temporarily in another Member State and those institutions that move on the basis of freedom of establishment. So far, the EC rules on freedom of establishment have been based on application of the national rules of the country of establishment to undertakings that use freedom of establishment. The Proposal would seem to turn this principle upside down.

The concern that arises from the standpoint of private international law is that the Directive Proposal on payment services ignores the existing choice of law rules. It is in line neither with the Rome Convention nor with the Rome I Proposal adopted by the Commission in the same month, December 2005, as the Directive Proposal itself.

In contrast to the Directive Proposal on credit agreements for consumers, the Directive Proposal on payment services in the internal market shies away from the relationship between the proposed principle of mutual recognition and the existing conflicts rules. The effects of the principle of the mutual recognition have not been handled in the latter Proposal. Given the evidence the Services Directive project puts before us, reason exists to question why there is still an attempt to extend the use of the controversial principle of mutual recognition – with evident closeness to the country of origin principle – to contractual relationships.

3.5 Evaluation

As shown above, the country of origin principle used in EC directives has so far taken quite different forms in different contexts. The principle obligates a Member State, without harmonising national legislation in the Community, to accept operations on its territory which are supervised by another Member State, the country of origin, and to which operations the legislation of that foreign State is applied to the extent defined in each EC legal instrument. The host state is not permitted to set any other additional requirements than those allowed by the EC legal instrument in question.

The given and proposed EC legal instruments differ in the extent to which they rely on the country of origin principle. The significance of the principle depends on its defined scope of application, i.e. on what limitations or exceptions have been made to it. For example, the E-Commerce Directive contains detailed exceptions to the principle. However, this Directive is an example of a less successful piece of legislation whose impact on choice of law has remained unclear despite the EC legislator explicitly enacting on the issue.

The original Services Directive Proposal extended the country of origin principle to most services and to private relations. Application of the principle would no longer have concerned only a limited scope of application or cases in which a service is moved from one country to another. The principle would also have been applied generally to all services, except for a few special cases, and services which cannot be performed without people moving from one Member State to another.

The principle of mutual recognition concerns measures targeted by a Member State at private individuals and the related legislation. The ECJ has not considered the principle as being applicable to legislation on private relations. However, the two Directive Proposals discussed below suggest extending the principle of mutual recognition, which is very close to the principle of the country of origin, to contractual relationships between service-providers and consumers.

We have seen that, within the Community, legislative initiatives still exist on cross-border services which are highly controversial from the standpoint of private international law. The crucial point is that private international law is not a field of law to be glossed over without consequences. The discussion of recent legislative initiatives has also revealed a lack of co-ordination within the Commission. First of all, the Proposal for a Services Directive contradicted existing EC legislation and some other Proposals, such as Rome II, which had been given by the Commission in 2003. The same has occurred with the amended Proposal on credit agreements for consumers. The third example is the Proposal for a Directive on payment services in the internal market. These law-drafting projects, whose objectives have great relevance in terms of establishing a genuine internal market, have come to evince serious problems of legal certainty and coherency of EC law. Every justification exists to end by saying that the above analysis has highlighted urgent challenges for better regulation in the EU.[395]

395 See also European Parliament, Council, Commission: Interinstitutional agreement on better law-making (2003/C 321/01). According to the agreement, these three institutions agree to promote simplicity, clarity and consistency in the drafting of laws and the utmost transparency of the legislative process.

Chapter IV Hidden Conflicts Rules in EC Law

1 Introduction

This chapter seeks to shed light on 'hidden' conflicts rules in EC law. Two explanations can be offered for using the term hidden conflicts rules. On the one hand, the choice of law rules discussed below can be said to be hidden since they can be found in legislative instruments of EC law that mainly concern substantive harmonisation in the part of internal market law which is not mostly governed by the Rome Convention. These conflicts rules are often complicated by nature, which also makes their content sometimes very difficult to interpret. They have been typically initiated by those DGs in the Commission which are responsible for sectoral harmonisation measures. Hence, the broader view on conflicts issues has been often lacking in the preparation process. This is also a concrete explanation for the difficulties of setting these conflicts rules into the wider context of EC conflicts regulation. On the other hand, discussion of hidden conflicts rules seems justified with regard to such EC directives, which do not contain explicit conflicts rules but whose scope of application presupposes their existence when the directive is being applied in cross-border cases governed by it.

In the following, the latter type is examined first. Particular conflicts problems of the Directive on the Transfer of Undertakings[396] are discussed since these problems have become topical with the increase of cross-border restructuring. After that, light is shed on the first type of hidden conflicts rules. The aim is to highlight typical characteristics of conflicts rules increasingly often used in the field of EC company law and collective labour law. This also involves a specific conflicts law approach in Europe: in the EC legislation on employee involve-

[396] See Council Directive 2001/23/EC on the approximation of the laws of the Member States relating to the safeguarding of employees' rights in the event of transfers of undertakings, businesses or parts of undertakings or businesses.

ment, substantive company law rules and labour law rules are interconnected. Hence, specific conflicts rules contained in EC company law directives no longer concern merely company law issues. The newest directives also include conflicts rules that concern employee involvement rights, i.e. rules on information and consultation as well as participation in company administration.

2 Cross-border Transfers of Undertakings

In corporate restructuring, employees are protected by the Directive on the Transfer of Undertakings. This Directive contains a specific labour law definition of a transfer of undertaking. In transfers of undertakings as referred to in the Directive, employees have the right to retain the terms and conditions of their employment when they start working for the transferee. All rights and obligations deriving from employment contracts or relationships are transferred to the transferee.

Under Article 1(1), the Directive applies to any transfer of an undertaking, business, or part of an undertaking or business to another employer as a result of a legal transfer or merger. The manner in which the Directive's definition of the transfer of an undertaking is interpreted has been greatly influenced by the exceptionally extensive ECJ case law. In general, a transfer occurs when an economic entity has been transferred and the entity retains its identity. However, in each case, an overall assessment has to be made.

With globalisation and the development of the EU single market, cross-border restructuring that fulfils the definition of a transfer of an undertaking has become considerably more common. Without going into too much detail, it can be said that according to the Directive on the Transfer of Undertakings outsourcing can constitute a transfer of an undertaking. In certain cases a change of service-providers may also be considered a transfer. When the application of the Directive is being resolved, particular attention is paid to whether a significant amount of assets relating to the practice of the business has been transferred as well, and whether the new service-provider has employed the employees of the former service-provider in significant number and competence. Interpretation of these criteria issued by the

ECJ has proven difficult in certain transfers typical to the service sector. In offshore outsourcing the question is also about whether the undertaking retains its identity despite its relocation to another country.[397]

In addition to employment protection, the Directive contains provisions on information and consultation. In this respect, the Directive can be considered to belong to the group of EC information and consultation directives. According to Article 7(1) of the Directive, both transferor and transferee have to inform representatives of employees who will be transferred the date or proposed date of the transfer; the reasons for the transfer; the legal, economic and social implications of the transfer for the employees; and any measures envisaged in relation to the employees. Similarly to other information and consultation directives, the Directive leaves the definition of an 'employee representative' to national legislation or practice.

The provisions on the duty to inform and consult employees are applied according to Article 7(4) regardless of whether the decision to transfer an undertaking was made by the employer or an undertaking controlling the employer. In considering alleged breaches of neglect of the duty to inform and consult, the submission of insufficient information to the employer by the controlling undertaking is not an accepted excuse.[398] However, the Directive does not impose any obligations on the controlling undertaking.

Article 7(4) of the Directive also governs situations where the decision on transfer is made by a company located in another state that controls the transferor. Thus, the provisions of the Directive have cross-border scope. But it must also be asked whether the Directive should be applicable to cross-border transfers of undertakings. This question has increasing importance for employee protection in cross-border restructuring. It is also in the interest of undertakings to have certainty of the legal status.

---

397 See also Hepple, Labour Laws and Global Trade, pp. 172–173.

398 Similar provisions can be found in Article 2(4) of the Council Directive 98/59/EC on the approximation of the laws of the Member States relating to collective redundancies. See also Hepple, Labour Laws and Global Trade, pp. 182–183.

The cross-border application of the Directive may have to be considered in various cases of corporate restructuring. A typical case is that where the transferred undertaking or company is located within the EEA but the transferor and the transferee are both situated in different EEA Member States. Another example might be a transfer where either transferor or transferee is from a non-EEA State.

Determination of the cross-border scope of the Directive is problematic because the Directive does not provide rules on conflicts law. Although the ECJ has extensive jurisdiction on the Directive, the Court has not yet addressed the question of cross-border transfers. No guidance has been given by the recent Directive on cross-border mergers of limited liability companies either. This Directive does not govern labour law issues, except for arrangement of employee participation in company administration. Moreover, its scope of application differs from the Directive on the Transfer of Undertakings, which governs any transfer of an undertaking, business, or part of an undertaking or business to another employer as a result of a legal transfer or merger.[399]

The question of the cross-border application of the Directive on the Transfer of Undertakings was brought up for the first time when the Directive was being prepared. Originally, the European Commission intended to include rules on transfers in the territory of one or several Member States and on transfers where one of the parties to the transfer is an undertaking located in Member States territory.[400] According to the amended Commission Proposal, the Directive would also have been applied to cases where the transfer of an undertaking affects a company located in a Member State and involved in the transaction.[401] The proposed provision was not included in the

---

399 See Article 1(1) of the Directive on the Transfer of Undertakings.

400 See Proposal for a Directive of the Council on harmonisation of the legislation of Member States on the retention of the rights and advantages of employees in the case of mergers, takeovers and amalgamations. COM(74) 351 final/2, p. 5.

401 See Amended proposal for a Council Directive on harmonisation of the legislation of Member States on the safeguarding of employees' right and advantages in the case of mergers, takeovers and amalgamations. COM(75) 429, p. 6.

1977 Directive because an EC regulation on the choice of law rules for employment contracts was simultaneously being prepared and was thought to provide on these same issues.[402] However, the Proposal for the specific regulation did not proceed because of the Rome Convention, which was then currently being drawn up.

In the preparation for a directive amending the original Directive on the Transfer of Undertakings, the question of the cross-border application of the Directive was again raised. The Commission ordered an analysis of the cross-border application of the Directive from Professor *Bob Hepple*.[403] The purpose was to find out what kind of social and economic problems were involved with cross-border transfers of undertakings in the EU and how the Directive could be reformed in that respect. However, the Directive was not amended on the basis of the *Hepple*'s report of 1998.

2.1 Cross-border Application of the Transfers Directive

Article 1(2) of the Directive reads as follows:

> This Directive shall apply where and in so far as the undertaking, business or part of the undertaking or business to be transferred is situated within the territorial scope of the Treaty.

The Directive is to be applied to the extent that the undertaking or business is located in an area in which the EC Treaty is applied. Thus, according to its wording, the scope of the Directive is determined only on the basis of the geographical location of undertakings to be transferred. Article 1(2) does not pay attention to the destination of the transfer.

Hepple has pointed out that the Directive does not differentiate between cross-border transfers and transfers where the same law is

402 See Hepple, The Legal Consequences of Cross Border Transfers of Undertakings within the European Union, p. 7.

403 See Hepple, The Legal Consequences of Cross Border Transfers of Undertakings within the European Union.

applicable to both transferor and transferee.[404] Therefore, the Directive should be applied both to transfers within EEA States and transfers crossing EEA borders in the EEA area. According to Article 1(2), only the location of the undertaking matters, not the nationality of the transferor or the transferee. Thus, the Directive should be applied both to cases with connections with one state only and to cases in which one must first solve the law applicable to the transfer.[405]

It should be noted that application of the Rome Convention is limited by Article 20 of the Convention. By virtue of it conflicts rules of EC law as well as national transposition legislation concerning these rules take precedence over the Convention. The rules referred to in Article 20 can be specific choice of law rules included in EC law. Besides EC legislation, the Article refers to national rules issued to transpose them.[406] Because of the way it is written, Article 1(2) of the Directive on the Transfer of Undertakings is not a choice of law rule as referred to in the Rome Convention.[407]

2.2 Three Types of Conflicts Questions Involved

Legal questions involved with cross-border transfers of undertakings are highly complex from the standpoint of choice of law, and the prevailing legal situation cannot be considered clear.[408] To begin with, it

---

404 See ibid., p. 4.

405 According to *Jonas Malmberg*, it follows from Article 1(2) of the Directive that when the law of a certain Member State is applied on the basis of the choice of law rules, the national legislation implementing the Directive must then also be applied to transfers of undertakings, if the transferred business is or was practised on the territory of an EEA country. On this basis, *Malmberg* has discussed how the Brussels I Regulation determines the competent court, while the basic rules of the Rome Convention determine the law applicable to an employment contract. See Malmberg, "Arbetstagarens ställning vid gränsöverskridande företagsövergångar".

406 See also Giuliano – Lagarde Report, p. 39.

407 See also Hepple, Labour Laws and Global Trade, p. 176.

408 According to a working paper of the European Commission, the Commission aims to study the legal questions involved in cross border transfers of undertakings. See Commission Services Working Document, p. 11. This

is important to notice that the cross-border application of the Directive should not be considered solely from the viewpoint of the conflicts rules on employment contracts. Following *Hepple*'s division, one can speak about three types of conflicts questions being involved. Along with conflicts questions concerning individual employment contracts of employees affected by the transfer, consideration also needs to be given to questions relating to the application of collective agreements, and information and consultation rights of employees.[409]

In general, different conflicts rules apply to each of the three issue groups above. These are analysed in the following, particularly in two situations. On the one hand, attention is paid to cross-border transfers of undertakings where the undertaking's operations and employees remain in the original country after the transfer. On the other hand, another type of transfer is considered, namely where the undertaking's operations are transferred to another state and the employees continue to work for the transferee in the new state. The latter type of transfer is close to those where relocation of the undertaking to another country occurs in practice simultaneously with the transfer. Such relocation could occur, for example, when an undertaking is transferred between an Austrian transferor and a German transferee, with the undertaking being relocated to Poland.

Legal literature has rarely touched upon the subject of cross-border application of the Directive on the Transfer of Undertakings. When it has, most attention has been paid to the choice of law rules on employment contracts. The other two dimensions, conflicts questions on collective agreements and on information and consultation, have often received only marginal consideration. This is probably explained by the fact that determining the law applicable to employment contracts is significant, because that very law is also applied to

---

Commission staff working document contains guidelines on the application of the Directive based on ECJ case law.

409 See Hepple, The Legal Consequences of Cross Border Transfers of Undertakings within the European Union, p. 15. *Hepple* refers to 'exercising collective rights' but the context shows that by this he refers only to the application of collective agreements. Thus, it does not refer to the rights of information and consultation for which the Directive on the Transfer of Undertakings is also significant.

employee protection issues, such as grounds for dismissal, periods of notice, order of selection for redundancy and notice-period pay as well as possible severance pay. Determining the applicable law is crucial since the level of employee protection and the economic costs for companies based on it vary immensely between Member States. Now, as the Union has expanded to include 25 Member States, the differences between national legislations are more pronounced than ever.

In the absence of choice of law, the law applicable to an employment contract is determined in accordance with Article 6 of the Rome Convention. By virtue of that Article, the law of the habitual place of work is the one primarily applied. The protection clause in Article 6(1) limits the effects of the choice of law clause if such has been made.[410]

As a rule, when an employee continues working in the same country after the transfer of an undertaking, the law of that country is applied. If the country of employment changes because of the transfer, then the situation becomes more complicated. According to the first alternative interpretation, the law of the new country of employment could be applied on the basis that the habitual workplace has changed. Another alternative would be to continue applying the law that was applied at the moment of transfer. In that case it could be argued on the basis of Article 3(1) of the Directive that it aims at retaining the rights and obligations that derive from the employment relationship as they were at the time of the transfer. However, this could lead to a problematic result because of material differences between the legislations of the former and the new country of employment. Huge differences might exist, for example, in the level of regulation on pay and annual leave between the new and the former country of employment. It should also be noted that the Directive aims at only partial harmonisation and not at completely levelling the differences between the substantive rules of the Member States. Therefore, the most natural solution would be to determine the terms of employment on the basis of the habitual place of work. In this respect I do not fully follow the argumentation of *Hepple*, who says that the objectives of the Directive

410 See also section 4 of chapter V below.

cannot be achieved if the applicable law changes because of a cross-border transfer and, as a result, a less favourable law would be applied to an employee.[411] It appears, rather, that when the habitual country of employment changes, the law applied at the time of the transfer cannot be applied to the employment relationship on the basis of Article 3(1).

It could be argued that if the law of the present place of work provides lower minimum terms and conditions of employment, for example, on minimum wages or annual paid holidays, then the employee would be disadvantaged merely because of the transfer. However, applying the law of the previous workplace would be against the basic principles of Article 6(2) of the Rome Convention. Article 6(2) clearly states as a main rule the application of the habitual place of work when a choice of law clause has not been made by the parties. Thus, it appears that the only conclusion to be drawn is that when an undertaking moves to another country within the EEA because of a transfer, the transferee has an obligation to give the employees of the undertaking a chance to continue working for the undertaking in the new country under the terms and conditions of that country.

Hepple points out that the Posted Workers Directive also applies in certain situations where the transfer of an undertaking leads to the posting of an employee to another country.[412] The protection afforded by the Directive is based on application of the most favourable law. Article 3(10) of the Directive enables an extension of the list, set out in the Directive, of the host state rules on terms of employment that apply to a posted worker. Usually, however, this Directive does not play a part in transfers of undertakings because it is only applied to posting of workers to another state under the freedom to provide services.

In international labour law, mandatory rules of different degrees affect the choice of law for employment contracts. So far scholars addressing cross-border transfers have paid no attention to Article 7 of

---

411 Cf. Hepple, Labour Laws and Global Trade, p. 177.

412 See Hepple, The Legal Consequences of Cross Border Transfers of Undertakings within the European Union, pp. 23–24.

the Rome Convention.[413] Yet, on the basis of the Convention, the provisions on employment protection referred to in the Directive on the Transfer of Undertakings could be applicable, not only as part of the *lex causae* or by virtue of the protection rule of Article 6(1) of the Convention, but also as internationally mandatory on the basis of Article 7.

The protection rule in Article 6(1) means that when choice of law has been made, the mandatory rules on employee protection indicated by objective choice of law rules are applied if they are more favourable to the employee than the *lex causae*. If the provisions of the Directive were internationally mandatory, they could be applied regardless of the law applicable to an employment contract or to a contractual agreement on the transfer of the undertaking.

In general, at least the most central provisions on employee protection can be considered internationally mandatory on the basis of Article 7 of the Rome Convention.[414] It could be thought that the ECJ would interpret the core provisions on employee protection in the Directive on the Transfer of Undertakings as internationally mandatory. The Court could find support for such a line of interpretation particularly in the position it took in the *Daddy's Dance Hall* case.[415] According to that decision, protection of the rights provided by employment contracts as referred to in the Directive is of the public policy type in terms of its mandatory nature, and, thus, independent of the will of the parties to the employment relationship.[416] Although the definition of public policy in EC law differs for example from the definition of positive and negative *ordre public* in private international law, the

413 Although *Hepple* also mentions Article 7(2) when he describes the contents of the Rome Convention, he does not discuss its significance as to cross-border application of the Directive on Transfer of Undertakings. See Hepple, The Legal Consequences of Cross Border Transfers of Undertakings within the European Union, p. 9.

414 See in more detail Liukkunen, The Role of Mandatory Rules in International Labour Law – A Comparative Study in the Conflict of Laws, pp. 128–146.

415 Case C-324/86, Foreningen af Arbejdsledere i Danmark v. Daddy's Dance Hall, [1988] ECR 739.

416 See ibid., para. 14.

statements of the ECJ can be considered to show that the Directive provides fundamental protection legislation.

However, if certain provisions of the Directive were considered internationally mandatory, then the Rome Convention would enable application of the law most favourable to the employee. Thus, when the court has to choose between the *lex causae*, the provisions referred to in the protection rule in Article 6(1) of the Convention, and the internationally mandatory rules referred to in Article 7 of the Convention, it can choose to apply the law most favourable to the employee.

The question of the internationally mandatory nature of the provisions of the Directive on the Transfer of Undertakings in transfers crossing the EEA border is problematic because the wording of Article 1(2) limits the geographical scope specifically to the EEA. On this basis, the internationally mandatory nature of the provisions of the Directive would by virtue of Article 1(2) be restricted to transfers occurring only within the EEA area. However, it should be noted that the wording of this Article does not exclude cases in which the transferor and/or the transferee comes from outside the EEA. It should also be taken into account that the ECJ has already adopted quite a strong stand with regard to application of certain provisions of the Directive on Independent Commercial Agents on the protection of the weaker contracting party in cases of private international law.

The famous *Ingmar* case[417] concerned the Directive on self-employed commercial agents. The ECJ ruled that certain provisions of the Directive on Independent Commercial Agents had to be applied regardless of a choice of law clause. Hence, they were regarded as internationally mandatory. The Advocate General concluded that the Directive must be interpreted as meaning that it is, in principle, territorially applicable to a commercial agency contract if the commercial agent is based in a Member State and pursues activity in one or more Member States. He argued that the idea of the location of economic operators or of their conduct within the territory of the Community has, in several EC Treaty Articles, a place which cannot be overlooked in their interpretation and application. The reference to the ter-

---

417 Case C-381/98, Ingmar GB Ltd v. Eaton Leonard Technologies Inc., [2000] ECR I-9305.

ritory of a Member State of the Community legislator reflects the intention of the EC legislator to limit the benefit of the freedoms in question purely to economic operators already established on that territory, thereby promoting their mobility and the mobility of the services they provide throughout the common market. In this field, the territoriality of EC law constitutes an objective connecting method for individuals which entitles them to pursue their economic activity free from unjustified restrictions.[418]

In legal literature, the ECJ decision in *Ingmar* has been strongly criticised.[419] Authors have interpreted the decision as enabling the interpretation that single market legislation could similarly be applied to other cases in which the choice of law clause referring to a non-Member State has been made. This would remarkably narrow the scope of party autonomy in choice of law. However, the decision in *Ingmar* is noteworthy in terms of the discussion of hidden conflicts rules since it shows that EC secondary legislation can have an internationally mandatory nature without any explicit provision on the issue.

The Directive on the Transfer of Undertakings also includes provisions on the application of collective agreements. Under these provisions, the transferee is obligated to observe a collective agreement by which the transferor was bound at the time of the transfer. The question of whether certain collective agreement provisions should be applied as terms of employment is resolved on the basis of the choice of law rules on employment contracts in the Rome Convention. In their application, it has to be taken into account that the provisions of generally applicable collective agreements may also be internationally mandatory.

It is possible that when determining whether the Directive should be applied to cross-border transfers, the law applicable to a collective agreement also needs to be considered. The applicable law

---

418 See paras. 26, 36 and 55 of the Opinion of Mr Advocate General Léger delivered on 11 May 2000.

419 See, for example, Bogdan, "Ordre public, internationellt tvingande rättsregler och kringgåendeläran i EG-domstolens praxis rörande internationell privaträtt", pp. 341–342 and Jänterä-Jareborg, "När är harmoniserade gemenskapsregler internationellt tvingande?" pp. 411–412.

is determined on the basis of the conflicts rules of Articles 3 and 4 of the Rome Convention. Additionally, the internationally mandatory rules referred to in Article 7 may be applicable.

We have seen that the Rome Convention determines the applicable law for both individual employment contracts and collective agreements. However, employee involvement rights have a different status because conflicts rules on these rights have remained to a large extent unwritten in Europe. The Convention can be applied only to contractual obligations. Hence, the law which is to be applied to information and consultation obligations as provided in the Directive on the Transfer of Undertakings is determined on the basis of the Convention only if the question is about a contractual agreement on informing and consulting. This is done on the basis of Articles 3 and 4 of the Convention.[420]

The Directive imposes information and consultation obligations on both transferor and transferee. These obligations are implemented in each Member State in accordance with their national information and consultation systems. In other words, the Directive does not affect national structures of information and consultation. However, determination of the applicable law on the right to information and consultation as referred to in the Directive is significant because, for example, in certain cases the Directive allows some deviation from information and consultation obligations.

What is known as the *Flucht aus der Mitbestimmung* can take place when undertakings are transferred from countries whose legal systems guarantee strong employee involvement rights to states where these rights are weaker. To prevent this, *Hepple* suggested in 1998 that a special choice of law provision be included in the Directive. According to this suggestion, employee involvement rights would then have been determined on the basis of the law of the state in which the company is located at the time of transfer.[421] It is well known that no such provision was included in the Directive.

---

420 Naturally, Article 7 of the Rome Convention, for example, is also applicable.

421 See Hepple, The Legal Consequences of Cross Border Transfers of Undertakings within the European Union, p. 42.

With some exceptions, EC law contains no general conflicts rules on information and consultation of employees. In the current legal state, the question of the law applicable to information and consultation is to be resolved on the basis of the conflicts rules of each Member State. In some countries, the principle of territoriality and the radiation theory (*Ausstrahlungstheorie*) are observed when determining the law applicable to information and consultation.[422]

The correct interpretation of the traditional principle of territoriality is probably that the law applicable to information and consultation as referred to in the Directive is the law of the state in which the employees of the company habitually worked at the time of the transfer. In other respects, the law applicable to employee involvement is determined in accordance with the conflicts rules of the relevant Member State. In addition, attention should be paid to the special conflicts rules in the EC information and consultation directives. And if an agreement has been made about information and consultation, which is enabled, for example, in the European Works Council

422 For example, according to German legal practice, the scope of application of the Works Constitution Act (*Betriebsverfassungsgesetz*) is still determined in accordance with the traditional principle of territoriality. Thus, German law is applied to all places of business located in Germany, irrespective of the nationality of the employer or the employees or the terms of employment. The law is not applicable to places of business of German companies that are located outside Germany. However, the radiation theory, which states that public labour law 'radiates' on the kind of work abroad which is limited in its duration, complements the principle of territoriality in cases where Works Constitution Act is applied outside Germany. This can also concern places of work that are located in Germany but whose operations extend outside the German borders or the employees of a German-based place of business who are temporarily posted abroad. However, application of the radiation theory depends on the circumstances of each individual case and particularly on the duration of work done abroad. See, for example, Halbach – Paland – Schwedes – Wlotzke, Übersicht über das Arbeitsrecht, p. 360 and BAG 25.4.1978, BAGE 30, p. 266; BAG 27.5.1982, BAGE 39 and BAG 10.9.1985 – 1 ABR 28/83.

Directive (later: EWC Directive)[423], then the law applicable to that agreement is determined according to the Rome Convention.

3 Employee Involvement and Conflicts Rules in EC Law

Generally speaking, the facility to influence provided to employees by the rules on information and consultation should be matched with the influence that employees' representatives have in company administration on questions concerning business operations, economics, and the status of personnel. The Europeanisation of the rules on employee involvement rights is connected with an increased need to regulate companies' cross-border transactions at Community level. The need for cross-border regulation of these rights is also connected to the internationalisation of companies and to the increased mobility of employees within the provision of services.

Divergence of employee involvement rules in Europe underlines the relevance of the conflicts rules, taking into account that the EC does not aim at completely harmonising the legislation on employee involvement. The regulatory approach adopted in the EU derives from the need to respect the diversity found in the national traditions of the Member States.

Significant differences still exist between the employee involvement systems of the Member States.[424] There are differences between the continental and Anglo-Saxon labour law models. In practice, in the Anglo-Saxon countries statutory provisions on employee

---

423 See Council Directive 94/45/EC on the establishment of a European Works Council or a procedure in Community-scale undertakings and Community-scale groups undertakings for the purposes of informing and consulting employees and Council Directive 97/74/EC extending, to the United Kingdom of Great Britain and Northern Ireland, Directive 94/45/EC on the establishment of a European Works Council or a procedure in Community-scale undertakings and Community-scale groups of undertakings for the purposes of informing and consulting employees.

424 See also Weiss, "The Future of Workers' Participation in the EU", pp. 229–230 and Junker, "Betriebsverfassung im europäischen Vergleich", pp. 234–235.

involvement are mostly the result of the transposition of EC directives. Moreover, differences lie between the models as to whether they are based on the use of shop stewards or on work councils. The transposition of EC directives on information and consultation has provided a central foundation for employees' involvement rights in those Member States where employee involvement legislation has been almost nonexistent and collective agreement systems have not been developed.[425]

The developments deriving from EC labour law put in question whether we are witnessing a change in the collective labour law regimes where rules and institutions are traditionally seen so closely connected with the legal culture and structure of a particular national system that they are often deemed to be untransplantable. *Hepple* has argued that European developments suggest there may also be a borrowing of collective institutions. However, even then, transplants may serve as 'legal irritants'.[426]

From an EU perspective, an increasing need exists to ponder how national and regional regulation on transnational employee involvement rights should be developed from the standpoint of changes in business operations. However, the limits of EC legal regulation are met when the global protection of involvement rights is discussed, because the European model of protecting employee involvement rights does not extend beyond EU borders. So the obligations that EC legislation sets for informing employees and consulting them about business changes such as the transfer of production could not be efficiently imposed on a non-EU company, even if the company controls some EU companies. For example, in the US, rights of information and consultation do not form part of the statutory framework of em-

---

425 However, the use of employee participation in company administration, with the exception of SEs and SCEs, depends on national decisions in every Member State.

426 See Hepple, Labour Laws and Global Trade, pp. 270–271. Thus, the question is also what kind of transformations of meaning the new rule or institution will undergo once it is transplanted in another legal system. See Teubner, "Legal Irritants: Good Faith in British Law or How Unifying Law Ends Up In New Divergences", p. 12 and pp. 31–32.

ployee protection. If employees are given rights to information and consultation, this is done in the framework of collective bargaining.

For companies, globalisation of the economy is believed to have created a need for constant restructuring, or at least for being constantly prepared for it. For employees, globalisation means increasingly often greater pressure to adapt to changes and to be flexible. According to the policy adopted by the EU, if changes are anticipated, then certain restructuring-related social problems can be avoided. For their part, EC provisions on employee involvement aim to ensure this anticipation of changes.

From the standpoint of labour rights, one of the key factors for successful restructuring is to ensure that employee involvement rights are respected. In the EU, providing information and consulting employees at the right time has become an essential part of protecting employees at times when changes are made and employments terminated. EC law provisions are often procedural and concern not only the circumstances of regular information and consultation but also information and consultation during business changes. Development of the single market taken together with needs created by global competition have shifted the focus of EC legislation on employee involvement towards transnational cases. Nowadays, the view of the EC legislator on the role of the involvement rights in transnational restructuring can be said to be that employees' existing rights of information and consultation cannot be reduced as the result of transnational restructuring.

In recent years, the EC legislator has significantly improved involvement rights in cross-border restructuring. This has been carried out increasingly often by combining rules of company law with rules of collective labour law in EC legislation. What is interesting for this study is that putting together these two fields of law has been done by the EC legislator with the help of a third field of law, namely the conflict of laws. The special conflicts rules of EC collective labour law have gained less attention than, for example, posted worker or consumer legislation in the field of conflicts law.

The first directive illustrating the impact of company law on labour law through the means of private international law is the EWC Directive, adopted in 1994. It is usually emphasised that EC labour law is not inclusive enough in terms of its material field of application, that it only regulates certain issues. For decades the main focus was on the rules concerning equality and safety at work. Employee involvement came into focus as late as the 1990s, when EC legislation was extended to cover the institutional circumstances of employee information and consultation. This legislation has provided a basis for transnational involvement rights of employees in Member States.[427]

In recent years, the EC legislator's approach to strengthening employee involvement rights at transnational level has developed much further. The current approach is based on the view that information and consultation rights are fundamental social rights, which was already confirmed by the 1989 Community Charter of the fundamental social rights of workers.[428] Recently, this has been confirmed in the Charter of Fundamental Rights of the European Union. The title of Article 27 of the Charter is 'Workers' right to information and consultation within the undertaking'. According to this Article, "workers or their representatives must, at the appropriate levels, be guaranteed information and consultation in good time in the cases and under the conditions provided for by Community law and national laws and practices". 'Appropriate levels' can be considered as referring to those levels in the undertaking that have decision-making power concerning matters subject to information and consultation.[429]

However, it should be emphasised that the tensions of EU single market law become startlingly clear at the intersection of international company law and collective labour law on employee involvement rights. This is illustrated by the fact that preparation of company law directives has been very slow, mainly because the Member States have been unable to reach agreement on the role of employee involvement rights. Nevertheless, the EC legislation on involvement rights cannot be properly analyzed without the framework of company law. Altogether, in the systemisation of employee involvement

427 For example, Finland added provisions on transnational employee involvement to its legislation in the 1990s due to the impact of EC legislation.

428 See also Weiss, "The Future of Workers' Participation in the EU", p. 229.

429 See also Note from the Praesidium. Draft Charter of Fundamental Rights of the European Union, p. 27.

legislation, conflicts rules must also be observed. These rules are only partly included in EC law. However, European private international law has assumed the role of a 'mediator' between company law and collective labour law. This development is also partly the result of legal fragmentation and the aim to form an entity of 'the fragments of EC law' with the help of choice of law rules.

The role of private international law as the 'mediator' between two different fields of law can be linked to the materialisation of private international law. Special conflicts rules have been used in the EU to ensure that employee involvement rights are not reduced in transnational restructuring. These rules illustrate the problems involved with the fragmentation of the conflicts rules of secondary EC legislation from the standpoint of legal systematics. The mere fact that the conflicts rules are scattered throughout directives on labour law, and partly also contained in the company law statutes, makes them difficult to recognise and co-ordinate. Despite the emergence of different conflicts rules, EC legislation has not resolved some of the problems related to the conflicts questions of employee involvement. The unwritten conflicts rules of international company law may, in certain circumstances, affect the application of employee involvement rules in EC law, in particular employee participation in company administration.[430]

4 Real Seat Theory in Conflicts Rules on Employee Participation

It should be pointed out that although real seat theory has practically lost most of its relevance in European international company law, it still has a role in international collective labour law. The choice of law rules on employee information and consultation rights have been adopted in EC law in small steps and the beginning of the influence of company law in the field of EC labour law can be traced back to the first half of the 1990s.

430 This is based on an approach according to which employee participation in company administration can be qualified as a question of company law.

The EWC Directive, which was the first labour law directive on cross-border participation rights, can be considered to mark the beginning of the interaction between the norms of labour law and company law at the EU level. The Directive applies to both Community-scale undertakings and groups of undertakings that consist of a controlling undertaking and its controlled undertakings. The Directive contains conflicts rules based on international company law. In the arrangement of employee information and consultation, conflicts rules must be applied, for example, when the controlling company in a group is determined. Legal literature has widely ignored the conflicts rules on this matter contained in the Directive.[431] Their transposition has proven to be a difficult task for the Member States.

Article 3 of the EWC Directive provides a detailed set of conflicts rules that determine which law should be used to identify the controlling undertaking for the purposes of the Directive. The law applicable in order to determine whether an undertaking is a 'controlling undertaking' is the law of the Member State that governs that undertaking. Hence, the *lex societatis* is to be applied. However, if the applicable law would not be the law of any Member State, then another rule for determining the controlling undertaking applies. In this case, the law applicable is the law of the Member State within whose territory the representative of the undertaking is situated. In the absence of such a representative, the law applicable is the law of the Member State within whose territory the central management of the group undertaking that employs the greatest number of employees is situated. Hence, in this case, the real seat of the undertaking is given a decisive role.

5 Intertwining Company Law and Labour Law

With a view not only to the internal market but also global competition, EU legislation on SE and cross-border mergers of limited companies has been considered a significant step in improving the op-

431 See however Meeusen, "Directive 94/45 concernant les comités d'entreprise européens: aspects de droit international privé".

erating environment of European companies. The purpose is to promote the mobility of companies but at the same time the question is about furthering regulatory competition concerning companies' operating environments.

A question essentially related to the adoption of the new European company forms, the SE and the SCE, and to cross-border mergers is how the involvement rights of employees should be protected when changes take place in companies. Altogether, the legislation on employee involvement rights, which by nature extensively follows the principle of minimum harmonisation, has become one of the core issues of EC labour law. On the one hand, the cross-border dimensions of information and consultation rights are regulated particularly in the EWC Directive, which ensures that the personnel of large undertakings and groups simultaneously operating in more than one country are regularly informed and consulted. On the other hand, this core area of EC labour law includes provisions according to which involvement rights, employee participation in company administration included, should be arranged in cross-border restructuring.

In those EC statutes that have been issued in recent years, provisions on the right to participate in company administration are increasingly often connected to company law provisions.[432] This means that two different fields of law – company law and labour law – have been combined to fulfil the objectives of the internal market. As we have seen, the 'mediating' field of law between company and labour law is private international law. Conflicts rules have been drawn to serve the objectives set for both company and labour law. In other words, the rules of company law and labour law are combined using conflicts rules with the aim of taking into consideration the fundamental objectives of both fields of law. This has led to a significant strengthening of the status of international labour law and international company law.

Choice of law has gained in significance after introduction of EC legislation on SE and cross-border mergers of limited liability companies. A Regulation on the statute for an SE was issued in 2001,

[432] These EC statutes are the SE Regulation and the SCE Regulation and the related Directives as well as the Directive on cross-border mergers.

after more than 30 years of preparation. In an SE, employee participation must be arranged in stages, taking into consideration the employee participation models applied in companies participating in the establishment of an SE. Similar rules apply to arranging employee participation in an SCE. The most recent indication of the intertwining of labour and company law is the Directive on cross-border mergers of limited liability companies.

How should we understand the use of conflicts rules as a means of combining company law and labour law? This use arises above all from differing views among Member States on the status of participation rights in cross-border operations. As regards employee protection, the diversity of national rules is extensive, and the Member States have considered that comprehensive substantive harmonisation of the rules is not possible. Moreover, the purpose of the co-ordinating regulatory model is to limit harmonisation of substantive legislation on involvement systems. Special conflicts rules also serve the purpose of guaranteeing the continued application of national rules on involvement rights.

The efficiency of the EC regulatory approach based on the use of conflicts rules to be found in recent company law and labour law directives cannot yet be assessed. However, it can already be said that the fragmentary nature of the conflicts rules complicates their proper transposition. Moreover, not only in the field of EC labour law but also in the field of EC company law, evidence can be found of statutes that only partly grasp conflicts questions. For example, EC legislation on the SE has not made conflicts rules irrelevant. In a case where an SE is controlled by another undertaking, the applicable law is the law that applies to public limited liability companies in the country where the SE has its registered office.[433] Some issues, such as the question of an SE company's capital, maintenance of company capital, and changes to capital, are governed by the rules that apply to a limited liability company with a registered office in the Member State in which the SE is registered. A third point to mention here is that the

[433] See Recital 17 of the Regulation. See also Werlauff, SE – the law of the European company, p. 110.

Regulation on SE does not make it clear how the transfer of the seat of an SE affects the *lex societatis*.[434]

From the standpoint of employee protection, the use of conflicts rules in EC statutes on employee participation in company administration seems quite consistent. It is built on respect for the existing diversity among Member States. However, tension exists between the two objectives of recent company law statutes – to improve competitiveness and to protect continuation of employee rights to participate in company administration. In the case of an SE, this tension might materialise even when the SE is being established. In essence, on certain conditions, the SE cannot be registered before the question of the form of employee involvement has been settled. When the Member State in question has not transposed the subsidiary provisions on arranging employee participation provided by the SE Directive, an SE can be established by a merger and it can be registered only when an agreement is made on employee involvement in the SE.

The tensions between labour law and company law are particularly obvious in the global context of cross-border restructuring. Employee involvement rights are not nearly as well protected outside the EU as they are within, so a group of companies with operations that cross the EU border can have two different kinds of arrangements, depending on the location: within the EU area, arrangements providing employees with the minimum protection laid down in EC law must be made, while outside the Union, arrangements with less protection can be used. Hence, the specific conflicts rules relating to employee rights discussed in this section serve the arrangement of employee involvement only within the context of the internal market.

---

434 See Wymeersch, "The transfer of the company's seat in European company law", p. 692, fn. 122.

Chapter V Challenges for Service Provision and Labour Rights

1 Introduction

Labour law has a long tradition of protecting the weaker party to the contract and levelling down the unequal bargaining powers between employer and employee. Along with mandatory legislation, in many European countries collective agreements contribute to bringing a balance between the contracting parties to an employment contract.

In contemporary European private international law, the principle of protecting the weaker party, which imposes limits for freedom of contract, is not solely based on substantive protective provisions. The means that conflicts rules provide for taking into account the protective provisions of a given national legal system play an important role in strengthening the legal position of the employee in international contracting.

European conflicts rules enable adjustment of the outcome of choice of law by applying rules on mandatory provisions. In essence, the specific use of mandatory provisions, which limits the scope of party autonomy, reflects the effect of substantive labour law on choice of law. EC law ensures not only application of mandatory legislation but also of mandatory provisions of collective agreements of the country closest to the contract, in order to protect the employee in the framework of cross-border transactions. This legislative approach should also be seen as part of the materialisation of private international law in Europe.

In the EU Member States, the most important sources for conflicts rules on individual employment contracts consist of the Rome Convention and the Posted Workers Directive adopted in 1996, five years after the Rome Convention entered into force. As we have seen, the Convention sets out general conflicts rules on contractual obligations in the EU Member States, employment contracts included. The Directive applies to undertakings established in an EEA Member State that post workers to another Member State in the context of cross-border provision of services. Thus, the scope of application of the

Convention is considerably more extensive than that of the Directive. The latter applies merely to temporary postings in the framework of the provision of services and is based on Articles 47(2) and 55 EC Treaty.[435]

When determining the law applicable to an employment contract of a posted worker, the Convention and the Directive may both have to be considered. Since the Directive, along with providing a minimum standard, allows a variety of differences in transposition, it is especially relevant to be aware of Member State national rules concerning its transposition.

Recently, free service provision and labour rights have been put in the spotlight because of two cases referred to the ECJ: *Laval*[436] and *Rosella*.[437] The first is concerned with whether the Swedish model of applying collective agreements to posted workers is compatible with EC law. The second case is about plans to re-flag a ship and replace its personnel in this connection with a cheaper crew. In both cases, the fundamental question is whether industrial action is permitted for ensuring employee protection. Taking into account the fundamental nature of the right to industrial action, these cases concern in essence the question of how to find a balance between EU economic freedoms and protecting fundamental rights. From the perspective of private international law, the cases also relate to the question of the role of fundamental rights in choice of law.

These cases should also be seen in the wider framework of European integration. The EC was originally a project of economic integration, but gradually the integration has been taken on a course towards 'Social Europe'. The need to develop the social dimension of European integration lies at the heart of the development. According to Article 2 EC Treaty, "the Community shall have as its task, by es-

---

435 See also the judgment of the ECJ of 22 January 2002 in Case C-390/99 Canal Satélite Digital SL v Adminstración General del Estado, and Distribuidora de Televisión Digital SA (DTS), [2002] ECR I-607, paragraph 27 ff.

436 Case C-341/05, Laval un Partneri Ltd v. Svenska Byggnadsarbetareförbundet and Svenska Byggnadsarbetareförbundets avd. 1, Byggettan Svenska Elektrikerförbundet.

437 Case C-438/05, The International Transport Workers' Federation and The Finnish Seamen's Union v. Viking Line ABP and OU Viking Line Eesti.

tablishing a common market and an economic and monetary union and by implementing common policies or activities referred to in Articles 3 and 4, to promote throughout the Community a harmonious, balanced and sustainable development of economic activities, a high level of employment and of social protection, equality between men and women, sustainable and non-inflationary growth, a high degree of competitiveness and convergence of economic performance, a high level of protection and improvement of the quality of the environment, the raising of the standard of living and quality of life, and economic and social cohesion and solidarity among Member States". Also, Article 6(1) of the Treaty on European Union confirms that the Union is "founded on the principles of liberty, democracy, respect for human rights and fundamental freedoms, and the rule of law, principles which are common to the Member States".

2 Challenges for the Posted Workers' Regulation

To some extent, a tension can be noticed between EC law on the freedom to provide services and the principle of employee protection, especially when considering how far and in what manner Member States can apply their legislation and collective agreements to posted workers.[438] This tension was thought already to have been resolved in 1996, when the Posted Workers Directive was adopted. However, recent in-

---

[438] In the judgment in the *Wolff & Müller* case, the ECJ confirmed that "inasmuch as one of the objectives pursued by the national legislature is to prevent unfair competition on the part of undertakings paying their workers at a rate less than the minimum rate of pay, a matter which it is for the referring court to determine, such an objective may be taken into consideration as an overriding requirement capable of justifying a restriction on freedom to provide services provided that the conditions mentioned in paragraph 34 hereof are met. Moreover, as the Austrian Government has rightly pointed out in its observations, there is not necessarily any contradiction between the objective of upholding fair competition on the one hand and ensuring worker protection, on the other. The fifth recital in the preamble to Directive 96/71/EC demonstrates that those two objectives can be pursued concomitantly". See Case C-60/03, Wolff & Müller GmbH & Co. KG v. José Filipe Pereira Félix, [2004] ECR I-9553, para. 41 ff.

ternal market development has put pressure on the EC regulatory system of posted employees, the cornerstone of which is the above mentioned Directive. One example of this pressure is how the approach adopted in this Directive was recently abandoned by the European Commission in the original Proposal for the Services Directive.[439] Although this serious attempt to undermine the present protection of posted workers was turned down, it shows that within the EU, divergent views exist on how the social aspect of service provision should be dealt with.

In cross-border service provision, the status of posted workers has lately been put in the critical limelight mainly because of EU eastward expansion. The expanded internal market also amounts to an enlarged labour market with a new competitive situation, as many Eastern European countries with lower labour costs have entered the Union. The old and new Member States also differ in that the labour market systems and labour legislations of the new Members are often much less developed than those of the old.

As has already been emphasised, when cross-border services are provided, posted workers do not enter the labour market of the country where they temporarily perform work in the same way as employees who move to another country to work within the framework of EU free movement of workers. Typically, posted workers conclude their contracts in their home state and on the basis of these contracts carry out work for a limited period in the host state. And since they carry out their work only temporarily in another country than that where they habitually work, their employment contracts have connections with more than just one country.

To put the posted workers' issue fully into the perspective of this study, it has to be emphasised that the Posted Workers Directive is not a typical EC labour law directive, since it contains rules on choice of law. Unlike other labour law directives, the main legal effects of the Directive can be considered to belong to the sphere of international labour law that governs conflicts rules on individual employment contracts. The conflicts rules in the Directive also demonstrate that it combats social dumping and significantly carries a so-

---

[439] See also section 3.3 of chapter III above.

cially protective nature. In essence, the Directive lists the matters regarding terms and conditions of employment to which regulation of the host state must be applied. In addition to legislation, the Directive also provides rules on applying collective agreements to posted workers. However, the substantive content of regulation to be applied by the host state is not harmonised by the Directive.

The regulatory system of the Directive is in part very complex, mostly due to the fact that it is based on a political compromise, made quickly after a difficult preparation process.[440] So far in the discussion of posted workers' legal status, the legal literature has paid limited attention to the choice of law nature of the Directive and to its wider conflicts law framework provided by the Rome Convention.

The following explores European conflicts rules on posted workers, especially with regard to collective agreements. The perspective is delimited for the most part to collective agreements, since their role has proved to be especially problematic in cross-border service provision. The objective is also to highlight the framework in which the Posted Workers Directive should be seen in terms of the conflict of laws. The role of collective agreements in providing minimum terms of employment and the related right of industrial action have recently been discussed throughout Europe, mostly because of the questions posed by the *Laval* and *Rosella* cases. This chapter addresses both cases from the standpoint of fundamental labour rights and their relationship to EU economic freedoms. This chapter also sheds light on the Scandinavian labour law model and its compatibility with EC law, since *Laval* has prompted Europe-wide debate not only about the role of fundamental labour rights in a regional legislative context but also about the Scandinavian model itself.

440 On the preparation process in the Council see Biagi, "Guest Editorial. Fortune Smiles on the Italian EU Presidency: Talking Half-Seriously About the Posted Workers and Parental Leave Directives", p. 97 ff.

3 On the Role of Legal Comparison

As we have seen, materialisation of private international law has increased the need for legal comparison when determining the applicable law. Legal comparison is of great practical importance when applicable conflicts rules require a comparison between the norms of different legal systems in order to determine the rules most favourable for the employee. The principle of the most favourable law is followed both in Article 6(1) of the Rome Convention and in Article 3(7) of the Posted Workers Directive.

The fact that the Posted Workers Directive is a piece of legislation that increases the need for legal comparison when determining the applicable law is one of the reasons why transposition of the Directive is a useful target for comparative studies. When addressing the transposition of any EC directive, a variety of comparative methods are available.[441] In this chapter, comparison of the Scandinavian transpositions of the Directive's provisions on collective agreements is carried out from the viewpoint of conflicts law.

In comparative labour law studies, Scandinavian labour law is often considered a model of its own, distinguished by mandatory regulation which broadly stems from the activities of labour market organisations. Collective agreements are broadly used as a source of regulation, while a prerequisite for the proper functioning of the Scandinavian collective-bargaining system is that the labour market parties have far-reaching rights to take industrial action.[442] Although some modifications have occurred recently because of European integration, historical and societal reasons have enabled survival of this model.

Instead of looking so much at differences in substantive law, the idea in the following is, rather, to explore differences in national approaches towards the Posted Workers Directive – especially in the light of the options it offers for national transpositions on collective agreements. The characteristics of the Scandinavian labour law model are generally considered to explain the approaches adopted in Den-

---

441 See also section 5 of chapter I above.

442 Sigeman, "Nordic Labour Law. A Brief Presentation from a Comparative Perspective", p. 497 and 501.

mark, Finland, Norway, and Sweden. Yet, account should be taken that national transposition solutions also reflect certain differences of labour market systems in the countries under comparison.

4 The Posted Workers Directive and the Rome Convention

Basically, the Posted Workers Directive reflects the aim of establishing a balance between promotion of free movement of services in the EEA area and the need for minimum protection of posted workers.[443] The Directive is often considered as an implementation of principles established in ECJ case law.[444] The basic principle was adopted in the famous *Rush Portuguesa* case, where the Court held that "Community law does not preclude Member States from extending their legislation, or collective labour agreements entered into by both sides of the industry, to any person who is employed, even temporarily, within their territory".[445] The Directive clarifies the legal status of both posted workers and undertakings that post workers by determining the sphere of host state labour law regulation applicable to posted workers. However, under Article 3(7), the Directive follows the principle of the most favourable law and, hence, does not prevent application of more favourable provisions of the *lex causae*.

The Preamble to the Directive shows that it supplements the Rome Convention.[446] It can be argued that the host state rules on the matters listed in Article 3(1) of the Directive regarding terms and conditions of employment are to be considered internationally mandatory

---

443 See Proposal for a Council Directive concerning the posting of workers in the framework of the provision of services. COM(91) 230 final, pp. 2–4 and p. 13.

444 See Joined Cases C-62 and 63/81, Seco SA and Desquenne & Giral SA v. Établissement d'Assurances contre la Vieillesse et l'Invalidité, [1984] ECR 223; Case C-113/89, Rush Portuguesa Lda v. Office national d'immigration, [1990] ECR I-1417 and Case C-43/93, Raymond Vander Elst v. Office des Migrations Internationales, [1994] ECR I-3803.

445 Case C-113/89, Rush Portuguesa Lda v. Office national d'immigration, [1990] ECR I-1417, para. 18.

446 See Recitals 7–11 of the Directive.

in the sense of Article 7 of the Convention. In general, the Directive could be seen to complement either Article 7(1) on internationally mandatory rules of third countries or Article 7(2) on internationally mandatory rules of the forum. This question is later addressed separately in section 5.

In this connection, it is worth looking briefly at the specific conflicts rules for employment contracts included in the Rome Convention. As we have seen, the starting point is that the parties can freely select the law applicable to their contract. In the absence of choice, the applicable law is determined on the basis of Article 6(2) of the Convention. Firstly, the law of the country in which the employee habitually works, even if temporarily employed in another country, is applied. Secondly, if the employee does not habitually work in any one country, the law is applied of the country in which is situated the place of business through which the employee was engaged. However, if it appears from the circumstances as a whole that the employment contract is more closely connected with another country, then the employment contract is governed by the law of that country. These rules have been generally considered satisfactory, although problems might occur because the Convention does not provide guidance on the length of the work in another country that is considered temporary.[447]

Under the Rome Convention, the law of the habitual place of work (*lex loci laboris*) continues to be the applicable law, even when the employee is posted to another country for a limited period. The Convention contains no rules on the application of host country law, even if host country rules were more favourable than those of the

---

[447] In the Rome I Proposal, the Commission proposes that work would be regarded as temporary if the employee is expected to resume working in the country of origin after carrying out tasks abroad. Moreover, conclusion of a new employment contract with the original employer or an employer within the same group of companies would not preclude the employee for being regarded as temporarily carrying out work in another country. See Article 6(2)(a) of the Proposal for a Regulation of the European Parliament and the Council on the law applicable to contractual obligations (Rome I). COM(2005) 650 final. See also Liukkunen, The Role of Mandatory Rules in International Labour Law – A Comparative Study in the Conflict of Laws, p. 265.

normal place of work. In general, the only possibility of applying the rules of the host country is given in Article 7 of the Convention, provided that these rules can be considered internationally mandatory and that the conditions on applying such rules are met.

As we have seen, according to Article 6(1) of the Rome Convention, a choice of law clause in an employment contract cannot have the result of depriving the employee of the protection afforded by mandatory rules of the law that would be applied by virtue of Article 6(2) in the absence of choice. Article 6(1) does not repeal the law chosen by the parties. It only requires the primary application of mandatory employee protection rules of the law of the country in which the employee habitually works, or, secondarily, if no such country exists, the mandatory rules of the law of the country in which the business through which the engagement occurred is situated. The third alternative is to resort to the mandatory rules of the law indicated by the exception clause.[448]

As to posted workers, the Rome Convention thus ensures the protection afforded by the law of the habitual place of work, whereas the Posted Workers Directive safeguards application of the most significant host country rules. In this sense, the Convention and the Directive complement each other. Nevertheless, it should again be emphasised that the Convention sets out the frame of choice of law. Only in certain areas is the Convention supplemented by the Posted Workers Directive. The specific rules on employment contracts in the Convention are intended to protect the weaker party to the contract and this objective should affect their interpretation. Moreover, employee protection has a central role in the Directive, which also has another objective: facilitating cross-border provision of services within the EU. The latter objective demonstrates that the internal market also brings about economic objectives in the field of international labour law. Traditionally, ensuring sufficient employee protection has been typical of this field of law and it has preceded other kind of interests. A tension can be seen between the economic

448 See Rinze, "The Scope of Party Autonomy under the 1980 Rome Convention on the Law Applicable to Contractual Obligations", p. 424.

objectives of the Community and the social objective of employee protection.

4.1 Increasing Role of the Principle of the Most Favourable Law

In the field of substantive labour law, the favour principle, as I have called it, involves comparing rules within any given legal order.[449] Instead, in choice of law, the principle of the most favourable law leads to situations of application where the rules of different legal systems must be compared with each other. The protective idea of labour law can be seen in a tendency to create conflicts rules that lead to application of the law most favourable for the employee. Since in European labour law the central character of mandatory provisions is their minimum mandatory nature it has been considered only natural that this principle is reflected in conflicts law.

With the Rome Convention, the principle of the most favourable law was introduced in the field of European conflicts rules on employment contracts. As we have seen, the principle is included in the specific minimum protection rule of Article 6(1) of the Convention. By virtue of it, mandatory employee-protective provisions of the law referred to by objective connecting factor rules in the Convention are applied only if they are more favourable than the provisions of the *lex causae*.[450]

We have already seen that both the Posted Workers Directive and the Rome Convention are based on the principle of the most favourable law. I have examined elsewhere the applicability of the principle of the most favourable law in the case of internationally mandatory rules.[451] For example, an analysis of the Scandinavian countries and Germany shows that substantive labour law typically provides a minimum level of terms and conditions of employment.

---

449 See Liukkunen, The Role of Mandatory Rules in International Labour Law – A Comparative Study in the Conflict of Laws, p. 49.

450 See Junker, Internationales Arbeitsrecht im Konzern, p. 97.

451 See Liukkunen: The Role of Mandatory Rules in International Labour Law – A Comparative Study in the Conflict of Laws, pp. 135–138.

Whether found in legislation or collective agreements, labour law provisions can normally be deviated from to the benefit of the employee. As a consequence, their application should depend on their favourability to the employee even if they were regarded as internationally mandatory.

It should be noted that comparison of favourability has been attached to the application of every host state rule referred to in the Posted Workers Directive. Under Article 3(7) of the Directive, host state rules are to be applied only if they are more favourable to the employee than the otherwise applicable law. Since these host state rules should be regarded as internationally mandatory, it already follows from the provisions of this Directive that comparison of favourability has to be used in applying internationally mandatory rules. Thus, I have argued that justification exists for connecting the principle of the most favourable law to the application of internationally mandatory rules.

Regrettably, no concrete guidance on how to carry out comparison of favourability can be found in the Rome Convention or the Directive. Bearing in mind the diversity of substantive labour law in different countries, this comparison may, in practice, prove to be difficult for the courts to make. The nature of each labour law provision should be taken into account when deciding whether to apply the principle of the most favourable law. Some protective provisions in labour law allow no deviation.[452] Thus, they permit no comparison of favourability either.

It is also essential to note that, according to ECJ case law, the favourability comparison is one of the significant elements to be used in determining whether host state rules should be applied. The Court has emphasised that it has to be settled whether host country legislation brings the employee any genuine advantage.[453] Thus, a careful comparison between host and home country rules needs to be carried

452 Such provisions are typical in the regulation of health and safety at work.

453 See, for example, Joined Cases C-369/96 and C-376/96, Criminal proceedings against Jean-Claude Arblade and Arblade & Fils SARL and Bernard Leloup, Serge Leloup and Sofrage SARL, [1999] ECR I-8453.

out in order to determine whether host state rules should be applied under the Posted Workers Directive.[454]

Finally, it should be noted that the principle of the most favourable law also plays a role when determining the relationship between different conflicts rules on applying mandatory substantive rules in the Rome Convention. I have suggested that in situations involving a conflict between Articles 6(1) and 7(2) of the Convention, in each case the rule most favourable to the employee should be followed.[455]

4.2 Increasing Role of Internationally Mandatory Rules

The Rome Convention provided a breakthrough for the principle of the most favourable law in international labour law, and at the same time, the role of internationally mandatory rules became significant for ensuring employee protection. As stated, Article 7 of the Rome Convention enables the application of internationally mandatory rules of the law of the forum and also, on certain conditions, such rules of third countries. We have also seen that a definitional problem exists over how to define internationally mandatory rules. Only very rarely do labour law rules expressly include a statement concerning their being internationally mandatory. Rather, the internationally mandatory nature of each rule has to be determined separately.

In the absence of express legislation, identifying internationally mandatory labour law rules is left to the courts. To some extent, case law of the Contracting States provides guidance. In Germany, the Federal Labour Court has set a line of interpretation according to which, in deciding whether a labour law rule is internationally mandatory, one must consider whether the rule serves the public interest.[456] If it does, then it is to be considered internationally mandatory. However, it should be emphasised that since the ECJ has only recently received jurisdiction to interpret the Rome Convention and the Court

---

454 This is also the case with 'public policy provisions', which can be applied by virtue of Article 3(10) of the Directive.

455 See also section 5.3 of chapter II above.

456 See BAG 24.8.1989, BAGE 63, p. 17 ff.

has issued no decisions so far, differences between national interpretations cannot be avoided.

In the field of international labour law, there is not yet much experience of the application of internationally mandatory rules, although the Posted Workers Directive gives an open-ended list of such rules. By legislating on the issue, Contracting States may explicitly make certain mandatory provisions internationally mandatory. However, beyond the Directive, it remains quite an open question how far the national legislator could go in enacting on such rules. The Convention does not, for example, enable all domestically mandatory provisions on the terms of employment or collective agreements to be made internationally mandatory. Such an interpretation would go against the policy of the Convention, so that the conflicts rules of the Convention lose their relevance. It has to be taken into account that the central principle of the Convention is party autonomy, which the Contracting States are expected to respect, and Article 7 provides an exception rule to this principle.[457]

In many cases, it can be difficult to decide if a labour law rule is internationally mandatory, in particular when it comes to the rules of third countries. No common approach to this question is to be found in the EU Member States. However, the Posted Workers Directive can be considered to give some concrete guidance on the issue. The next section analyses how the Directive should be considered to complement the Rome Convention.

5 Posted Workers and Internationally Mandatory Rules

It has often been argued that the Posted Workers Directive specifies or tightens Article 7 of the Rome Convention; that the internationally mandatory provisions referred to in the Article would include the 'hard core' rules listed in Article 3(1) of the Directive.[458] For example,

---

457 See also Liukkunen, Lainvalinta kansainvälisissä työsopimuksissa – erityisesti lähetettyjen työntekijöiden kannalta, pp. 73–74.

458 See, for example, Davies, "Posted Workers: Single Market or Protection of National Labour Law System?", pp. 578–579 and the Report of the Working

according to the Green Paper on conversion of the Rome Convention, the Directive has to be seen as an implementation of Article 7.[459]

It has also been suggested that the Directive goes further than Article 7(1), so that it identifies the internationally mandatory rules of non-Member States, and it demands that they be applied by the home state. When the Contracting States ratified the Rome Convention, they were not obliged to give their courts the possibility of applying Article 7(1). But according to this suggestion, the Directive would have set aside reservations about the Article. For example, *Davies* has argued that the Directive identifies the applicable mandatory rules of the host state and requires the home state to apply them. According to him, when it comes to employment contracts the Directive simply overrides reservations that Contracting States may have made concerning application of Article 7(1) of the Convention.[460]

However, under the Directive the Member States, as host states, are obliged to apply those of their own mandatory provisions that are considered 'hard core' provisions on the basis of the rule of the most favourable law. Hence, the view according to which the Directive would demand that the home state ensures its courts apply the law of the host state where workers have been posted, finds no direct support in the Directive. Nevertheless, it might be thought that although the provisions of the Directive do not impose such an obligation, their effective application requires it in view of the objectives of the Directive.

In this light, the Directive complements Article 7(2) of the Convention, which concerns internationally mandatory rules of the forum, since the Directive requires application of the 'hard core' host country rules regardless of the otherwise applicable law. And as we have seen,

---

Party on the Transposal of the Directive concerning the Posting of Workers, p. 5, where it is stated that "in fact, the Posted Workers Directive gives expression to the principle laid down in Article 7 of the Rome Convention with regard to situations falling within the scope of the Directive".

459 See Green Paper on the conversion of the Rome Convention of 1980 on the law applicable to contractual obligations into a Community instrument and its modernization. COM(2002) 654 final, p. 36.

460 Davies, "Posted Workers: Single Market or Protection of National Labour Law System?", pp. 578–579.

the principle of the most favourable law contained in Article 3(7) of the Directive does not prevent host state regulation referred to in Article 3(1) of the Directive from being internationally mandatory. The minimum mandatory nature typical of labour law provisions makes it appropriate in certain cases to extend application of the principle of the most favourable law to internationally mandatory rules.

It is important to note that the Directive affects the way in which the content of internationally mandatory rules is construed in the field of labour law. The Directive supports the view according to which the line of thinking based on the idea of applying the most favourable law can play an important part in applying internationally mandatory rules. Additionally, ECJ case law in the field of free movement of services demonstrates the principle according to which host state legislation can be applied to posted workers if the law of their home state does not provide them with essentially similar protection.[461] This suggests the need for comparison of favourability between host state and home state regulation.

Nonetheless, regarding the list of applicable terms and conditions of employment contained in Article 3(1) of the Directive as an expression of internationally mandatory rules also means that the EC legislator has confirmed the internationally mandatory nature of essential collective agreement provisions. In fact, with the list of Article 3(1), the sphere of internationally mandatory collective agreement provisions becomes quite broad in substantive content.

Finally, it should be noted that EEA States that are not members of the EU, such as Norway, lack the framework provided by the Rome Convention to transpose the Posted Workers Directive. In cases that fall outside the scope of application of the Directive, the applicable law in EU Member States is determined in accordance with the rules of the Rome Convention. In other EEA States conflicts rules of domestic origin are to be applied instead. This can be seen as

---

461 See Case C-272/94, Criminal proceedings against Michel Guiot and Climatec SA, as employer liable at civil law, [1996] ECR I-1905.

problematic from the standpoint of coherency of choice of law in the EEA area.[462]

6 Scandinavian Countries – Comparative Observations

A brief introduction to the collective labour law models of the four Scandinavian countries helps to understand the particular framework of transposition of the Posted Workers Directive in these countries. No statutory minimum wage whatsoever exists in the Scandinavian countries. Instead, collective agreements are generally used to determine minimum wages. It can be said that the collective bargaining system of these countries fulfils the same function as the minimum wage system in some other countries.[463] Labour market policy and minimum wage policy emerge in cooperation between social partners, which also enjoy certain autonomy in providing terms of employment.

In general, the legal status and content of collective agreements vary between EU Member States. In the Scandinavian countries, the basic protection provided by labour law broadly stems from collective agreements. A characteristic feature of industrial relations is a very high rate of unionisation. The trade unions have been capable of upholding minimum terms throughout the labour market sector, including employers who are not members of an organisation concluding an industry-wide agreement. Although the *erga omnes* effect, by which the applicability of a collective agreement is extended to employers and employees who are not bound by the agreement, is

---

462 See Liukkunen, "Norwegian International Labour Law and the European Integration – Some Observations" p. 214.

463 Sigeman, "Nordic Labour Law. A Brief Presentation from a Comparative Perspective", p. 499. According to the Communication from the Commission, eight EU Member States (Germany, Austria, Cyprus, Denmark, Estonia, Finland, Italy, and Sweden) have no inter-sectoral national minimum wage, and collective agreements are the principal means by which wage rates are regulated. See Communication from the Commission: Guidance on the Posting of Workers in the Framework of the Provision of Services. COM(2006) 159 final, p. 16.

lacking in Denmark and Sweden, the Danish – Swedish model has an equivalent in its particularly efficient collective bargaining system.[464]

The statutory definitions of a collective agreement in Finland, Sweden, and Norway are nearly identical.[465] Under the Finnish Collective Agreements Act (*Työehtosopimuslaki*), a collective agreement is an agreement concluded by one or more employers or registered associations of employers and one or more registered employees' organisations. It concerns the conditions to be complied with in contracts of employment or in employment more generally. A collective agreement is binding upon the parties to the agreement themselves and those who have in writing joined the agreement. It also binds associations as well as individual employers and employees which are, directly or through intermediary associations, members of associations that are parties to the agreement.

By virtue of Section 23 of the Swedish Co-Determination Act (*Lagen om medbestämmande i arbetslivet*), a collective agreement is an agreement between an employees' organisation and employers' organisation or employer on terms and conditions of employment, or otherwise concerning the relationship between the employer and the employee. A collective agreement binds the signatory parties and also, within the area of employment it covers, those parties' members, including individual employers and employees. An employer bound by a collective agreement is normally obligated also to apply the agreement in relation to employees who are non-union members.[466]

In Norway, a collective agreement is defined in Section 1 of the Labour Disputes Act (*Arbeidstvistloven*). It is an agreement on terms and conditions of employment between the employer and the employee sides. 'Terms and conditions' are understood broadly.[467]

Only Denmark has no statutory definition of a collective agreement. According to the Danish legal literature, a collective agreement

---

464 Sigeman, "Nordic Labour Law. A Brief Presentation from a Comparative Perspective", p. 499.

465 See also Malmberg, "The Collective Agreement as an Instrument for Regulation of Wages and Employment Conditions", p. 197.

466 See Sigeman, Arbetsrätten. En översikt av svensk rätt med europarätt, pp. 59–61.

467 See Jakhelln, Oversikt over arbeidsretten, pp. 478–480.

is an agreement between an organisation of wage earners and an organisation of employers or an employer on wages and other terms of employment.[468]

In each of the four countries, the content of collective agreements is comprehensive and their coverage of employees is very high. General applicability of collective agreements, which extends their application beyond the normal personal scope, is used only in Finland and Norway. In Finland the general applicability of collective agreements has established itself as an essential element in protecting employees and determining minimum wages.[469] Minimum applicable terms of employment are largely determined by generally applicable collective agreements. General applicability is provided by the Employment Contracts Act (*Työsopimuslaki*). According to Section 7 of Chapter 2 of the Act, the employer must at least observe the provisions of a generally applicable collective agreement on the terms and conditions of the employment relationship that concern the work the employee performs or the nearest comparable work. The purpose of the system of general applicability is to provide minimum terms and conditions of employment for employees outside the sphere of normal applicability of collective agreements. Hence, general applicability of a collective agreement goes beyond its normal application set out in the Collective Agreements Act.[470]

No mechanism exists providing for general applicability of collective agreements in Denmark and Sweden.[471] Both countries have experienced quite strong resistance to the introduction of a system of general applicability. Danish labour law has been traditionally based on the idea of collective self-regulation, with social partners largely determining and administering the rules of the labour market. It has

---

468 See Kristiansen, Arbejdsretlig lærebog, pp. 46–48.

469 The most important function of the system of general applicability is to ensure that employees in non-organised companies get the same minimum level of wages and other terms of employment as other employees, i.e. employees within the sphere of normal applicability of collective agreements.

470 General applicability is confirmed by a special Commission appointed by the Government.

471 However, in Denmark the *erga omnes* effect has been used in the case of transposition of certain directives.

been argued that adoption of a system of collective agreements with an *erga omnes* effect would require serious reconsideration of some of the main principles of Danish collective labour law.[472] In Sweden, too, the autonomous collective labour law model has been strongly defended, with employers and trade unions firmly against the idea that the state would take responsibility for pay determination.[473] Both Danish and Swedish labour law models widely use the supplementary effect of a collective agreement. Usually, non-organised employers sign a so-called substitute agreement (*hängavtal*) with the trade union. Such an agreement, which is regarded as a collective agreement, provides that terms of employment of a national collective agreement of the industry in question are to be applied.[474] This practice is supported by the possibility of taking industrial action. If a non-organised employer refuses to sign a collective agreement, the normal trade union procedure is to declare a boycott against the employer. To make the action more effective, the primary boycott is supported by sympathy (secondary) action. This action is taken either by the trade union in question or by other trade unions. Usually, sympathy action aims at stopping deliveries to and from the employer and is highly effective.[475]

The situation in Norway differs from those mentioned above. Firstly, employers who are not organised in an employers' association are only governed by collective agreements if a substitute agreement has been concluded. Secondly, a system of general applicability of collective agreements was enacted when Norway joined the EEA Agreement in order to prevent social dumping of foreign employees. The purpose of the Act on the General Application of Collective Pay Agreements etc. (*Lov om allmenngjoring av tariffavtaler m.v.*) is to ensure that foreign employees enjoy terms of wages and other terms of employment

---

472 See Malmberg, "The Collective Agreement as an Instrument for Regulation of Wages and Employment Conditions", p. 209.

473 See Ahlberg – Bruun, "Sweden: Transition through collective bargaining", p. 1.

474 See Malmberg, "Collective Agreements and Competition Law in Sweden", p. 188 and Sigeman, Arbetsrätten. En översikt av svensk rätt med europarätt, p. 53 and p. 59. See also Kristiansen, Arbejdsretlig lærebog, pp. 148–149.

475 See Malmberg, "The Collective Agreement as an Instrument for Regulation of Wages and Employment Conditions", p. 208.

equal to Norwegian workers.[476] This Act seems to have been serving as an ultimate option, since it has been used very sparingly so far.

It has sometimes been claimed that the Posted Workers Directive has created unintended turbulence in the Scandinavian collective labour law tradition, although during preparation of the Directive guarantees were sought that the Scandinavian system could be maintained.[477] Before addressing the Directive's approach towards applying collective agreements from the Scandinavian standpoint, a brief look is in order into the role of collective agreements in the Rome Convention.

7 Collective Agreements and the Rome Convention

In many European states, collective agreements form an important source of the minimum terms of employment. Therefore, their role in choice of law is also of great interest in terms of posting of workers. As the specific conflicts rules in the Rome Convention determine the law applicable to employment contracts, these rules also govern collective agreement provisions that constitute a part of the law applicable to an employment contract. The conflicts rules on employment contracts were discussed in section 4. The Convention does not separately address generally applicable collective agreements. However, it is clear that these can form part of the law applicable to employment contracts. Altogether, collective agreements may form part of the applicable law or they can be applied under the protection rule set out in Article 6(1) of the Convention.

In European international labour law, a distinction needs to be made between the internationally mandatory nature of collective agreements and their internally mandatory nature. In principle, provisions of generally applicable collective agreements can be internationally mandatory by virtue of Article 7 of the Rome Convention. If collective agreement provisions in a given national legal system are internationally mandatory, this means that they can be applied regard-

476 See Evju – Holo, "Labour Law and the Labour Law Market in Norway", p. 138.

477 See Eklund, "Utstationering av arbetstagare", pp. 264–265.

less of the law applicable to the employment contract. In addition, collective agreement provisions can be applied as a part of the *lex causae* or by virtue of the protection rule in Article 6(1) of the Rome Convention.

8 Collective Agreements and the Posted Workers Directive

In general, the obligation of the Member States to apply collective agreements provided by the Posted Workers Directive is restricted and depends on the nature of the collective agreement system employed. However, the Directive demonstrates in two ways the significance of collective agreements as a source of minimum terms and conditions of employment. On the one hand, in the construction industry Member States have to apply collective agreement provisions on the terms and conditions of employment referred to in the 'hard core' list of Article 3(1), assuming the agreements have been declared generally applicable.[478] If the States so decide, such agreements may be applied on given conditions in other sectors as well. On the other hand, in the absence of a system for declaring collective agreements generally applicable, Article 3(8) enables the application of such collective agreements which are applied generally in the State.[479]

Article 3(8) of the Posted Workers Directive reads as follows:

> 'Collective agreements or arbitration awards which have been declared universally applicable' means collective agreements or arbitration awards which must be observed by all undertakings in the geographical area and in the profession or industry concerned.
>
> In the absence of a system for declaring collective agreements or arbitration awards to be of universal application within the meaning

[478] The Directive uses the expression "collective agreements or arbitration awards which have been declared universally applicable". However, this study uses the notion of 'generally applicable' collective agreements or arbitration awards.

[479] See Davies, "Posted Workers: Single Market or Protection of National Labour Law System?", pp. 580–581.

of the first subparagraph, Member States may, if they so decide, base themselves on:
- collective agreements or arbitration awards which are generally applicable to all similar undertakings in the geographical area and in the profession or industry concerned, and/or
- collective agreements which have been concluded by the most representative employers' and labour organizations at national level and which are applied throughout national territory,
provided that their application to the undertakings referred to in Article 1 (1) ensures equality of treatment on matters listed in the first subparagraph of paragraph 1 of this Article between those undertakings and the other undertakings referred to in this subparagraph which are in a similar position.

Equality of treatment, within the meaning of this Article, shall be deemed to exist where national undertakings in a similar position:
- are subject, in the place in question or in the sector concerned, to the same obligations as posting undertakings as regards the matters listed in the first subparagraph of paragraph 1, and
- are required to fulfil such obligations with the same effects.

In the absence of a system of *erga omnes* collective agreements, the Directive gives the option to use collective agreements that are otherwise applied widely enough. That possibility is given in Article 3(8) of the Directive. Member States can apply such collective agreements which affect all undertakings in the profession or industry with the same geographical sphere of application. This Article also permits application of collective agreements concluded by the most representative employer and labour organisations at national level and applied throughout the Member State. In addition, these collective agreements have to be applied equally to undertakings posting employees and to host state undertakings in a similar position.

To some extent, the Directive enables deviation from the 'hard core' list of host state rules in Article 3(1) with certain types of collective agreements. Member States may decide to make exemptions from minimum rates of pay by means of collective agreements within the meaning of Article 3(8). Such deviations may concern one or more sectors or activities, if the length of the posting does not exceed one month.[480]

Article 3(10) of the Directive allows extension of the 'hard core' list to provisions of a 'public policy' nature. Since collective agreements often broadly govern terms and conditions of employment, it is important to consider whether this possibility of extension can be used for collective agreements. According to Article 3(10), the extensions have to comply with the EC Treaty and undertakings have to be treated equally. Thirdly, the list may be extended only to provisions related to public policy (*ordre public*).[481]

Tore Sigeman has criticised use of the term '*ordre public*' in the Swedish version of this Article. He has argued that either the term 'fundamental principles' or the term 'internationally mandatory rules' should have been used instead.[482] However, in my view, the entire list of Article 3(1) is internationally mandatory by nature. This also means that extension of the list implies enacting certain rules as internationally mandatory. Therefore, use of this term in Article 3(10) would not have been suitable to specify the requirements set to the provisions that Member States can apply in addition to those explicitly listed in Article 3(1). Nevertheless, as *Sigeman* notes, the term '*ordre public*' can be considered ambiguous in this context. It is appropriate to approach the term of 'public policy' or '*ordre public*' used in Article 3(10) from the standpoint of EC law.[483] Hence, the concept should be given a narrow interpretation.[484]

The Directive explicitly allows application of collective agreements only to those matters mentioned in the 'hard core' list of Article 3(1). However, it should probably be considered that the intention of the EC legislator was to enable extension of the 'hard core' list simi-

---

480 See Article 3(4) of the Directive.

481 See in more detail Liukkunen, The Role of Mandatory Rules in International Labour Law – A Comparative Study in the Conflict of Laws, pp. 185–186.

482 See Sigeman, "Fri rörlighet för tjänster och nationell arbetsrätt", p. 473.

483 See Liukkunen, The Role of Mandatory Rules in International Labour Law – A Comparative Study in the Conflict of Laws, p. 186. See also Report on the Implementation of Directive 96/71/EC.

484 See ibid., p. 186.

larly with regard to collective agreements as to other sources of regulation.[485]

8.1 Scandinavian Approaches

The Posted Workers Directive aims to take into account the diversity of collective agreement systems in Europe. Yet, it gives more weight to the system of declaring collective agreements generally applicable, which is used in many Central and Southern European countries, than to the collective agreement model typical to most Scandinavian countries. This is not in line with the fact that collective agreements play a highly significant role in regulating the terms of employment in Denmark and Sweden without any statutory procedure on general applicability. Norway is the third Scandinavian country where substitute agreements play a significant role since the statutory system of general applicability has been used only a few times so far.[486] In sum, substitute agreements are used in all three countries and this method is not recognised in the Directive.[487]

A statutory system of general applicability of collective agreements was adopted in Finland in the 1970s and in Norway in the 1990s.[488] According to the legislation in both countries, a posted worker is entitled to minimum wages determined on the basis of a generally applicable collective agreement. However, Finland is alone among Scandinavian countries with an inclusive procedure for confirming general applicability.

---

485 See ibid., p. 188.

486 It was used for the first time in 2004.

487 See also Malmberg, "Collective Agreements and Competition Law in Sweden", p. 210 ff.

488 Since the 1970s Finnish legislation has contained provisions on generally applicable collective agreements, although a specific method of confirmation of general applicability was provided only in 2001. See also Liukkunen, "Yleissitovien työehtosopimusten soveltamisesta kansainvälisiin työsopimuksiin Suomessa".

8.2 Application of Collective Agreements through Substitute Agreements

In essence, the trade unions ensure the general level of wages and other terms of employment in Denmark and Sweden, and the cornerstone of the model is the possibility of industrial action. The practice in these countries analysed above has been characterised as an autonomous collective agreements model.[489]

It is noteworthy that in Sweden, determination of wage rates in the construction sector is carried out in a special procedure. This procedure also has to be followed by foreign service-providers. After conclusion of a substitute agreement, the applicable wage rates are decided in negotiations between the service-provider and the local trade union. Such negotiations are normally carried out separately for each construction site. In Sweden, this practice has been said to enable consideration of local characteristics.[490] However, it also means that foreign service-providers cannot beforehand receive information on the minimum wage rates they have to comply with when posting workers to Sweden. Yet, it should be noted that the pay scale in Sweden is small, which advances the efficiency of the system.

The Swedish implementation report, prepared by the Swedish authorities for the purposes of national decision-making concerning the Posted Workers Directive, argued that the transposition legislation should not affect arrangements for collective agreements in Sweden.[491] It was stated that the Swedish system of collective agreements is effective in preventing social dumping in the labour market. Moreover, it was argued that the social partners did not want to change the situation. According to them, it was appropriate that foreign employers comply with Swedish collective agreements when they carry out their activities in Sweden. The social partners also expressed their willing-

489 See also Bruun, Posting of workers: do the EU rules work? A Nordic Perspective, pp. 4–5.

490 See also ibid., p. 5, which states that a standard sectoral collective agreement sets out a framework for negotiations at local level, which makes the system flexible and enables taking account local peculiarities.

491 See SOU 1998:52, p. 90.

ness to contribute to delivering information on the collective agreement system and the content of the agreements.[492]

Although the role of collectively agreed rules was emphasised in the *travaux préparatoires*, it was decided not to include the application of collective agreements in the Swedish Posting of Workers Act *(Lagen om utstationerade arbetstagare)*.[493] The implementation report argued that Sweden will choose an 'indirect way' of transposition through rules of information and reference to the role of the social partners.[494]

The Swedish implementation report stated that the national solution of omitting collective agreements from the transposition legislation cannot be considered inconsistent with the objective of the Directive, since the system in Sweden will probably prevent social dumping. However, according to the *travaux préparatoires* room for doubt existed as to whether the objective of the Directive is met if collective agreed rules are excluded from the scope of the Posting of Workers Act. Preventing social dumping also means that foreign undertakings should not be able to benefit from differences in terms and conditions of employment to gain unfair competitive advantage. The *travaux préparatoires* stated that the question remains whether the mechanisms provided by the social partners in the Swedish labour market can be considered fulfilling the purpose of promoting free movement of services.[495]

The Swedish solution left it to the social partners to ensure the observance of collective agreements when workers are posted to Sweden. The national legislator underlined the well-established and efficient mechanisms of the Swedish collective agreement system. These features enabled it to be used in the case of posted workers. An essential element of the system is that foreign service-providers may face collective action taken by the trade unions when posting workers to Sweden in order to get them to follow the collective agreements.[496]

---

492 See ibid., pp. 87–89.

493 See Prop. 1998/99:90, p. 27.

494 See SOU 1998:52, p. 91.

495 See ibid., pp. 86–87 and pp. 89–91. See also Prop. 1998/99:90, p. 26.

496 See Eklund, "Utstationering av arbetstagare", p. 265 and Sigeman, Arbetsrätten. En översikt av svensk rätt med europarätt, pp. 69–70.

In practice, in the light of the Posted Workers Directive, Sweden decided on a transposition method involving 'indirect' application of collective agreements. It seems this solution was based on the traditional Swedish labour law approach. Moreover, the solution appears to be connected with respect for collective labour rights and their fundamental status. In the Swedish model, the application of collective agreements is connected to fundamental rights of employees. It seems that the Swedish legislator considered that the Directive does not intend to interfere with the mechanism of ensuring respect for collective rights, of which collective bargaining forms a fundamental part. It was thought that labour market mechanisms would ensure respect for the provisions of collective agreements with a minimum mandatory nature, as these mechanisms have done before. In this sense, the Swedish transposition solution could also be characterised as a 'collective rights model'.

Yet, the approach adopted in Sweden is somewhat problematic in respect of the policy of the Directive. The Directive lays down the system on how Member States are allowed or obliged to apply their regulation to posted workers. Thus, it is not possible to apply collectively agreed rules irrespective of the provisions of the Directive. If a Member State wants to apply collective agreements to posted workers, then these agreements and their application need to meet both the criteria and the conditions laid down in Article 3 of the Directive. Among other things, the rule of the most favourable law needs to be followed. However, it seems that the Swedish method of applying collective agreements has been operating from the beginning within the larger labour law framework.[497]

The Swedish solution and the grounds expressed by the legislator are close to the Danish decision to maintain the *status quo*, and thus entrust the entire manner of the application of collective agreements to the social partners. In Denmark, too, a tripartite discussion occurred between the authorities and the social partners on how to transpose the Directive in respect of collective agreements. The decision was not to enact on application of collective agreements in the

[497] See Liukkunen, The Role of Mandatory Rules in International Labour Law – A Comparative Study in the Conflict of Laws, p. 214.

transposition legislation. Thus, the option given in Article 3(8) was not explicitly used.

According to the Danish *travaux préparatoires*, the criteria set out in Article 3(8) would have been difficult to meet. One of the major problems would have been to create a system that guarantees equal treatment of domestic and foreign service-providers. The argument was that no large problems exist with social dumping that could not be tackled by the trade unions being able to attempt to reach an agreement with foreign service-providers. Behind this method lies the possibility of taking industrial action.[498]

In practice, in the light of Article 3(8) of the Posted Workers Directive, both Sweden and Denmark decided to use an indirect method of transposing the Directive.[499] It appears that also in Denmark this solution was based on a labour law approach and, in essence, it was connected with respect for collective labour rights.

With such transposition solutions, problems that might occur relate to EC law rules on the equal treatment of service-providers established in a Member State other than the host state. By virtue of EC law, foreign service-providers can be required to follow Swedish and Danish collective agreements only on condition that application of these agreements does not constitute unequal treatment of foreign service-providers compared with domestic ones in a similar position. If equal treatment between Swedish or Danish and foreign service-providers is not guaranteed, then this provides a competitive advantage for Swedish and Danish undertakings not bound by Danish and Swedish collective agreements when compared with foreign service-providers obliged to follow these agreements. Such unequal treatment would be against the EC Treaty and the Directive.

Similar problems might also arise in Norway, which is the third Scandinavian country that uses substitute agreements. When the Posted Workers Directive was transposed, Article 3(8) of the Directive was discussed in Norway. As in Denmark, doubts arose in Nor-

---

498 See Lovforslag nr. L 47, Folketinget 1999–2000, pp. 5–6. See also Notat om problemstillinger i forbindelse med gennemførelsen af udstationeringsdirektivet, pp. 60–61.

499 Cf. Report on the Implementation of Directive 96/71/EC, p. 7.

way as to whether the Norwegian collective agreements would meet the criteria laid down in the Article.

9 Evaluation of the Posted Workers Regulation

As we have seen, in order to fully understand the nature of the Posted Workers Directive, it is essential to take into account not only ECJ case law, but also the specific relationship between the Directive and the Rome Convention. One of the key elements in the Directive is that it places obligations on a Member State only when it occupies the role of a host state. As host states, Member States are obliged to apply those mandatory provisions that are considered 'hard core' provisions by virtue of the list given in Article 3(1) of the Directive.[500] These rules are applied regardless of the *lex causae* on the basis of the principle of the most favourable law. Hence, in this light, the Directive should be considered to complement Article 7(2) of the Rome Convention which concerns internationally mandatory provisions of the forum.

If the connection between the Directive and the Rome Convention is approached from the perspective of the Convention, the same conclusions can be drawn. When compared with the ideas underlying Articles 6(1), 7(1), and 7(2) of the Convention, it is justified to connect the Directive with Article 7(2) of the Convention. The Directive supplements the last mentioned Article by defining internationally mandatory rules of the host country in the case of posted workers within the framework of free service provision.[501]

As we have seen, some have argued that the Directive speaks for the conditions for the application of Article 7(1) of the Convention

---

500 This obligation has been based on the rule of the most favourable law in Article 3(7) of the Posted Workers Directive.

501 See Hoppe, Die Entsendung von Arbeitnehmern ins Ausland. Kollisionsrechtliche Probleme und internationale Zuständigkeit. Eine Untersuchung anhand praktischer Vertragsgestaltungen, p. 251.

being met when an employee is posted to another EEA State.[502] However, the Directive cannot be connected to Article 7(1) of the Convention; it does not require that a Member State, when acting in the role of home state, should guarantee that host state rules are applied. Yet, it could be argued that effective transposition of the Directive is better ensured if Member States explicitly regulate that, when occupying the role of home states, they apply the 'hard core' rules of another Member State in the case of a posting to that other country. This kind of legislation has been enacted in some EU Member States.[503]

In addition to employee protection, the emphasis of the objectives of the Posted Workers Directive is on promoting free movement of services. The Directive connects the application of host state rules on 'core' terms and conditions of employment to promoting freedom to provide services. Taking into account the nature of the provisions referred to in the 'hard core' list of the Directive, it is clear that the objective of the Directive is to make the most important rules of the host country explicitly applicable to posted workers. At the same time, the aim is not to govern all employee-protective rules of the host country.[504] It should be stressed again that, from the viewpoint of substantive law, the Directive only aims at partial harmonisation, i.e. to identify the applicable host state rules.

Although in EC labour law the role of collective agreements alongside legislation has strengthened in recent years, the regulatory approach of the Directive towards collective agreements can be criticised. From the standpoint of collective labour law, the Directive is clearly based on selective use of collective agreements for protection of posted workers. As to collective agreements with an *erga omnes*

---

502 The Directive does not require the Member States to ensure that – when in the position of a home state – they apply the host country provisions of another state referred to in the Directive.

503 Among Scandinavian countries, the legislation in Denmark, Norway, and Sweden provides for application of host country legislation to workers posted abroad. In this respect the legislation of these countries goes beyond the obligations set out in the Directive.

504 See Proposal for a Council Directive concerning the posting of workers in the framework of the provision of services. COM(91) 230 final, p. 15.

effect, maximum mandatory protection is afforded only in the construction industry. In other words, the obligation to apply collective agreement provisions in the construction sites concerns Member States with a system of collective agreements declared generally applicable. When an *erga omnes* system is lacking, the application of collective agreements is fully optional. In particular, from the viewpoint of the collective bargaining model of two Scandinavian countries, Denmark and Sweden, the protection provided in the Directive is selective: application of collective agreements is entirely at the discretion of the Member States.

The fact that in Denmark and Sweden collective agreement provisions are applied to posted workers through substitute agreements, might cause problems from the standpoint of coherency and transparency of choice of law. Although the desirable outcome in terms of employee protection is that minimum standards apply and are realised, it appears that the application of collective agreements should be carried out more openly. However, the Posted Workers Directive does not seem to have left these states any other option than to maintain their well-established labour market practices. In the absence of *erga omnes* collective agreements, Denmark and Sweden have not used the option given in Article 3(8) of the Directive, although their collective agreement systems would probably comply formally with the criteria of that Article.

In Norway, too, substitute agreements are still used in practice. Although Norway's transposition legislation includes the application of collective agreement provisions on minimum wages, the role assigned to collective agreements depends on the extent to which they are made generally applicable. The Act on the General Application of Collective Pay Agreements etc. has played a very limited role, since it has been used only few times so far. In Finland, the Employment Contracts Act provides a widely used system for confirming the general applicability of collective agreements.

Summing up, the comparison above has shown that the regulatory approach of the Posted Workers Directive causes obvious problems for some countries with regard to application of collective agreements. If Denmark and Sweden had used the option set out in Article 3(8) of the Directive and enacted on the application of collective agreements in the transposition legislation, then the nature of their collective agreement systems would have changed. In practice, this would have likely meant adopting an *erga omnes* system for countries that strongly defend their own tradition of collective labour law. In respect of applying collective agreements beyond their scope, this tradition rests on using substitute agreements to oblige non-organised employers to comply with the minimum terms and conditions of collective agreements.

In Denmark and Sweden the necessary prior information on applicable terms and conditions of employment is lacking. Foreign service-providers are not able to obtain advance information about applicable terms and conditions based on collective agreements. Recently, however, a collective agreement has been concluded between the central labour market organisations in Sweden to improve the position of foreign undertakings. Conclusion of this agreement could be seen as an attempt to clarify the present situation which the ECJ will consider in the *Laval* case. By virtue of the agreement, foreign undertakings may become temporary members of Swedish employer organisations and avoid the threat of industrial action. It has been argued that Swedish trade unions would also need to accept collective agreements with quite similar conditions with service-providers that do not join the employer organisations, since otherwise they endanger the principle of equality.[505]

It is important to note that the rules on applicable law in the EU remain a difficult jungle as long as posted workers and their employers cannot obtain advance information about which rules will be applied in the host country. The availability of such information beforehand was among the concrete aims of the Posted Workers Directive. Indeed, from the standpoint of foreign service-providers, the ambiguity of applicable rules in the host state can be claimed to impede free movement of services within the EU.

We have now seen that from the standpoint of the Scandinavian labour law model, the core feature of the Directive is that it provides conditions on how and when collective agreements can be applied to

---

505 See Bruun, "Posting of Workers: do the EU Rules work? A Nordic Perspective", p. 11.

posted workers. The problems with the Swedish and Danish transpositions were already taken up in my previous study.[506] Now the ECJ is confronted with these problems in the *Laval* case.

10 Challenges posed by the Laval Case

It has been emphasised that the Posted Workers Directive aims at levelling the imbalance between the parties to an employment contract by defining the extent to which mandatory labour legislation and collective agreements of the host state should be applied. As shown above, in terms of legislative approach the Directive can be considered a legal instrument of choice of law that should also be seen against the general set of conflicts rules that the Member States are bound by. Additionally, the Directive has to be seen in the particular framework set by ECJ case law.

In the *Mazzoleni* case[507], the ECJ held that national labour legislation on minimum pay may not necessarily be applicable to a foreign service-provider. The question was about whether host state rules should be applied to posted workers employed in frontier work. The Court referred to its well-established case law according to which service-providers should abide by the minimum remuneration requirements of the host State. But it also stated that "however, there may be circumstances in which the application of such rules would be neither necessary nor proportionate to the objective pursued".[508] In the *Portugaia Construções*[509] case, the Court confirmed that circumstances may exist in which application of host state legislation on minimum wages is not in conformity with Articles 59 and 60 (now 49 and 50) EC Treaty.

---

506 See Liukkunen, The Role of Mandatory Rules in International Labour Law – A Comparative Study in the Conflict of Laws.

507 Case C-165/98, Criminal proceedings against André Mazzoleni and Inter Surveillance Assistance SARL, as the party civilly liable, third parties: Eric Guillaume and Others, [2001] ECR I-2189.

508 See ibid., para. 30.

509 Case C-164/99, Portugaia Construções Ldª, [2002] ECR I-787.

Even while the Posted Workers Directive was being written, the question could be posed as to how it would be able to remove tensions between the principle of protecting employees and the aim of boosting service provision within the EU. The prevailing tensions have been highlighted by the *Laval* case, which is currently pending at the ECJ. The event behind the request for a preliminary ruling is a dispute between a Latvian construction company and the Swedish Building Workers' Union. Laval refused to sign a substitute agreement, which was required in accordance with the Swedish labour market practice. As a result, the Union boycotted the company. Laval demanded that the Swedish Labour Court should declare the industrial action unlawful.

The *Laval* case is about whether EC law restricts the possibility of engaging in industrial action to pressure a foreign service-provider to conclude a collective agreement. Additionally, the Swedish Labour Court seeks clarification as to whether the manner in which the Posted Workers Directive has been transposed in the host country has significance in the case. Moreover, clarification is sought as to how the assessment of the case should be affected by the fact that a different kind of industrial peace obligation is applied to a host state employer than to a foreign employer posting workers to Sweden.

The question of whether Sweden has properly transposed the Posted Workers Directive depends mainly on interpretation of Article 3(8) of the Directive. It has been said that this Article was included in the Directive specifically because of the special features of the Swedish and Danish collective agreement systems. The aim was that if they wanted to, these countries could by virtue of the Article apply their collective agreements to posted employees.[510] The purpose was not to make the countries amend their traditional collective agreement models. Rather, the idea was to take into account existing diversity.

The ECJ should now decide how the option given in Article 3(8) to apply collective agreements should be interpreted. Generally speaking, two different alternatives seem to be available. The Court could either accept the Swedish collective agreements practice, possi-

---

510 See, for example, Eklund, "Utstationering av arbetstagare", pp. 264–265.

bly with some minor modifications, or consider that it contradicts the Directive and freedom to provide services.

The first alternative would be to adopt a looser interpretation, according to which the Directive allows existing Swedish practice. As we have seen, this practice is based on involvement of the national social partners which ensure, without legislative support, that foreign service-providers abide by Swedish collective agreements. This alternative would guarantee the continuity of Sweden's current collective agreement model. It has been said that the model has functioned well in practice and it has been generally held efficient.[511] It may also be thought that the purpose of the Directive is not to turn collective agreement-based minimum terms of employment into statutory law 'by force', but only to ensure that they are properly observed. Among the arguments for this alternative is the view stemming indirectly from the Swedish *travaux préparatoires*, according to which the purpose of the Directive is not to transform the Swedish collective agreement system into an *erga omnes* system. However, even if this alternative were chosen, the manner of ensuring observance of the principle of the most favourable law, as explicitly referred to in Article 3(7) of the Directive, would have to be resolved. This would imply the need for some modifications to Swedish practice.

However, this alternative would, in general, result in a looser application of the Directive, which might be problematic. It could hamper freedom to provide services if foreign service-providers were unable to gain precise information beforehand on the obligations deriving from host state collective agreements. Determining the central terms of employment on the basis of collective agreement practices is a potential uncertainty factor for foreign undertakings.

According to the second alternative which the ECJ could follow, the option given in Article 3(8) of the Directive to apply other types of collective agreement in the absence of a system of general application means that Member States must separately stipulate on the matter. Hence, the national legislator should at least define when and

---

511 See also Malmberg, "Collective Agreements and Competition Law in Sweden", p. 210.

what kind of collective agreements fulfil the criteria referred to in Article 3(8).

In *Laval*, the question is also about the right to industrial action in order to make foreign service-providers sign substitute agreements. One of the central elements in the Swedish labour market system is that industrial action rights ensure the observance of collective agreements. According to Recital 22 of the Posted Workers Directive, the Directive is without prejudice to the law of Member States concerning collective action to defend the interests of trades and professions. The ECJ has to consider the relationship between the right to industrial action and freedom to provide services.

The Swedish Co-Determination Act (*Medbestämmandelagen*) prohibits industrial action that aims to circumvent a collective agreement concluded by other parties. However, due to specific provisions in this Act known as the *Lex Britannia*, this prohibition applies only when a trade union takes measures in respect of industrial relations to which the Act is directly applicable. The prohibition is not applicable to industrial action against a foreign employer temporarily carrying out its activities in Sweden with its own employees.

The objective of the *Lex Britannia* has been to enable trade unions to act to ensure that all employers comply with terms and conditions of employment normally used in the Swedish labour market. The legislator has argued that the legislation also creates favourable conditions for fair competition on equal terms between Swedish and foreign undertakings.[512]

The *Lex Britannia* was enacted to protect industrial action rights even when a foreign employer is bound by a collective agreement in its home country. However, in certain circumstances, the *Lex Britannia* may violate the EC law prohibition of nationality-based discrimination, as it places foreign undertakings bound by their own collective agreement in a different position to Swedish ones. It can be

---

[512] See Prop. 1990/91:162, pp. 5–6.

argued that the Act does not protect equality between service-providers in all circumstances.[513]

In its essentials, the *Laval* case relates to basic questions that arise as regards fundamental rights and EC law on economic freedoms. It concerns the relationship between the free movement provisions of the EC Treaty and industrial action rights. Also in the *Rosella* case, discussed later in detail, the legality of national industrial action has been contested by appealing to the EC law provisions on free movement.

These two cases concern the same fundamental issue: the clash of EU economic freedoms (freedom of service provision and establishment) with fundamental labour rights. They spotlight the fundamental rights versus economic rights discussion, which was also an issue in the *Schmidberger* case[514] and the *Omega* case[515]. In the former case, the Court explicitly considered that fundamental rights justified a restriction on the free movement of goods. National authorities were justified not to outlaw a demonstration that blocked free movement of goods, as it stood for the fundamental right of expression. In the latter case, the Court held that an obstacle to free movement of goods was justified because of the need to protect a fundamental right, which in this case was 'human dignity'. The ECJ explicitly stated that "since both the Community and its Member States are required to respect fundamental rights, the protection of those rights is a legitimate interest which, in principle, justifies a restriction of the obligations imposed by Community law, even under a fundamental freedom guaranteed by the Treaty such as the freedom to provide services".[516] The right to industrial action is protected in many international human rights documents. To consider the status of this right in international law, an excursion to ILO practice concerning it is next provided.

---

513 Cf. *Eklund*, who argues that the Lex Britannia is not very dissimilar to the extension of the use of collective agreements, which has been upheld by the ECJ. See Eklund, "The Laval Case", p. 208.

514 Case C-112/00 Eugen Schmidberger, Internationale Transporte und Planzüge v. Austria, [2003] ECR I-5659.

515 See Chu, "'Playing at Killing' Freedom of Movement", p. 85.

516 Case C-112/00 Eugen Schmidberger, Internationale Transporte und Planzüge v. Austria, [2003] ECR I-5659, para. 74.

11 Excursion: Right to Industrial Action and ILO Practice

Freedom of association is recognized as a human right in several international human rights documents, such as the International Covenant on Civil and Political Rights (Article 22). Article 8 of the International Covenant on Economic, Social and Cultural Rights expressly recognises the right to strike, provided that it is exercised in conformity with the laws of a particular state.

Article 6(4) of the European Social Charter recognizes the right to industrial action, including the right to strike. Article 11(1) of the ECHR reads as follows:

> Everyone has the right to freedom of peaceful assembly and to freedom of association with others, including the right to form and to join trade unions for the protection of his interests.

In the legal literature, it has been argued that the right to industrial action can be derived also from Article 11 of the ECHR.[517] The case law of the European Court of Human Rights confirms this view. In *Schmidt and Dahlström v. Sweden*, the Court argued in the following way: "Article 11 para. 1 (art. 11-1) nevertheless leaves each State a free choice of the means to be used towards this end. The grant of a right to strike represents without any doubt one of the most important of these means, but there are others. Such a right, which is not expressly enshrined in Article 11 (art. 11), may be subject under national law to regulation of a kind that limits its exercise in certain instances. The Social Charter of 18 October 1961 only guarantees the right to strike subject to such regulation, as well as to 'further restrictions' compatible with its Article 31, while at the same time recognising for employers too the right to resort to collective action (Article 6 para. 4 and Appendix). For its part, the 1950 Convention requires that under national law trade unionists should be enabled, in conditions not at variance with Article 11 (art. 11), to strive through the medium of their organisations for the protection of their occupational interests".[518]

---

517 See Jakhelln, "The Rights of Seafarers", p. 12.

518 Case Schmidt and Dahlström v. Sweden, 5589/72, [1976] ECHR 1 (6 February 1976), para. 36.

In *Gustafsson v. Sweden*, the Court clarified that the words "for the protection of [their] interests" in Article 11(1) show that the Convention safeguards freedom to protect the occupational interests of members of trade union by trade-union action.[519] In *National Union of Belgian Police v. Belgium* the Court found that the Convention "safeguards freedom to protect the occupational interests of trade union members by trade union action, the conduct and development of which the Contracting States must both permit and make possible".[520] *Henning Jakhelln* has emphasised that the ILO Conventions and other comparable international conventions should be paid attention to in interpreting Article 11 ECHR.[521] This has been confirmed by the Court.[522]

Since the ILO Conventions seek to provide a global framework for fundamental labour rights, as most recently confirmed by the ILO Declaration on Fundamental Principles and Rights at Work, the case law of the ILO deserves attention here. It is interesting to note that despite its nature as a fundamental labour right, the right to strike is not explicitly provided for in the ILO Constitution or in the Declaration of Philadelphia, nor specifically recognized in ILO Conventions Nos. 87 and 98, which are often referred to as the basis of the right to collective action.

However, it was already taken for granted in the first report prepared for discussion of Convention No. 87 at the 1947 International Labour Conference that these ILO instruments establish this fundamental right as their corollary. In the conclusions to the report, this was stated in connection with the special case of public servants and voluntary conciliation.[523]

---

519 See Case Gustafsson v. Sweden, 15573/89, [1996] ECHR 20 (25 April 1996), para. 45.

520 Case National Union of Belgian Police v. Belgium, 4464/70 [1975] ECHR 2 (27 October 1975).

521 See Jakhelln, "The Rights of Seafarers", p. 12.

522 See also Case Gustafsson v. Sweden, 15573/89, [1996] ECHR 20 (25 April 1996), para. 53.

523 See ILC, 30th Session, 1947, Report VII, Freedom of Association and Industrial Relations.

At present, among the ILO normative instruments only Article 1 of the Abolition of Forced Labour Convention of 1957 (No. 105), and Paragraphs 4, 6 and 7 of the Voluntary Conciliation and Arbitration Recommendation of 1951 (No. 92) mention strike action. The International Labour Conference, regional conferences, and industrial committees have also often referred to the right to strike in a way that has well-established its legitimacy in practice.[524]

According to the ILO Expert Committee on Application of Conventions (later: Committee of Experts) and to the Committee on Freedom of Association (later: CFA), the right to strike is considered a fundamental right, but not an end in itself. When strikes occur, they are seen as a failure in the process of determining working conditions through collective bargaining, which should remain the ultimate objective. Both Committees also stress that maintaining the employment relationship is a normal legal consequence of recognizing the right to strike.[525]

Since no express provision on the right to strike exists in the basic texts, the ILO supervisory bodies have had to determine the exact scope and meaning of the Conventions on this issue on secondary grounds. In 1952, the CFA confirmed the principle of the right to strike, stating that it is an "essential (element) of trade union rights". Shortly afterwards, the Committee stated that in most countries strikes are recognized as a legitimate measure by trade unions in promoting their members' interests. Although the Committee has subsequently specified the content of the right to strike in a large number of cases, it has never abandoned this position of principle. The CFA has held that these principles can be derived from provisions approved by the Conference and embodied in ILO Conventions on freedom of association.[526]

---

[524] See, for example, General Survey. Freedom of Association and Collective Bargaining, para. 142.

[525] See ibid., para. 151 and Freedom of Association. Digest of decisions and principles of the Freedom of Association Committee of the Governing Body of the ILO, para. 473.

[526] Freedom of Association. Digest of decisions and principles of the Freedom of Association Committee of the Governing Body of the ILO, p. 2.

In its General Survey in 1959, the Committee of Experts expressed the view that the prohibition of strikes of workers other than public officials acting in the name of the public powers "... may sometimes constitute a considerable restriction of the potential activities of trade unions..."[527] This position was afterwards reiterated and reinforced: "a general prohibition of strikes constitutes a considerable restriction of the opportunities opened to trade unions for furthering and defending the interests of their members (Article 10 of Convention No. 87) and of the right of trade unions to organize their activities".[528]

According to the Committee, the right to strike is one of the essential means available to workers and their organisations for promoting and protecting their economic and social interests. These interests not only have to do with better working conditions and pursuing collective occupational demands, but also with solutions to economic and social policy questions that are of direct concern to the workers.[529] Thus, the Committee's reasoning is based on the recognized right of worker and employer organisations to organize and formulate their activities in order to promote the interests of their members.

In a traditional economic relationship, one means of pressure available to workers is to suspend their services by temporarily withholding their labour by various methods, thus inflicting a cost on the employer in order to receive concessions. This economic logic cannot be applied as such to the public sector, although there, too, suspension of labour services is the last resort available to workers.[530] Hence, it comes as no surprise that in ILO jurisprudence the public sector has played a prominent role as the limits of the right to strike have been defined.

By virtue of Article 3(1) of Convention No. 87, the right to "organize activities and to formulate programmes" is recognized for worker and employer organisations. In the view of the Committee of

---

527 General Survey. Freedom of Association and Collective Bargaining, para. 147.

528 Ibid.

529 Ibid.

530 Ibid., para. 148.

Experts, strike action is part of these activities under the provisions of Article 3; it is, thus, a collective right exercised by a group of workers who decide not to work in order to achieve their demands. Therefore, right to strike is considered to be an activity of worker organisations within the meaning of Article 3. In spite of these basic principles, the practice followed in ILO Member States as to conditions and restrictions of the right to strike varies significantly. However, the principle of the strike as a means of action by organisations is widely recognized in ILO Member States.[531]

The Committee of Experts has specifically confirmed that the right to strike is an intrinsic corollary of the right to organize, protected by ILO Convention No. 87. However, the Committee has also underscored that the right to strike cannot be considered to be an absolute right: it may be subject to a general prohibition in exceptional circumstances, and it may also be governed by provisions setting up conditions for, or restrictions on, its exercise as a fundamental right.[532] As an exception to the general principle of the right to strike, the CFA has established that tasks in the essential services may constitute a legitimate reason for prohibiting strike action. However, in CFA practice this exception has been defined restrictively: essential services are only those whose interruption would endanger the life, personal safety, or health of all or part of the population.[533]

This restrictive approach is reflected in the case law of the CFA.[534] For example, when it comes to general prohibitions of the right to strike – adopted by certain countries under emergency or exceptional powers – the CFA has considered that such measures can only be justified in a situation of acute national crisis. Even then, they are permitted only for a limited period and to the extent necessary. This has been interpreted to mean genuine crises, such as those arising

---

531 Ibid. paras. 149–150.

532 Ibid., para. 151.

533 Freedom of Association. Digest of decisions and principles of the Freedom of Association Committee of the Governing Body of the ILO, paras. 540–545. See also Case Federation of Offshore Workers' Trade Unions and Others v. Norway, 38190/97 (27 June 2002).

534 See General Survey. Freedom of Association and Collective Bargaining, paras. 159–160.

as a result of a serious conflict, insurrection, or natural disaster in which the normal conditions for the functioning of society are absent.[535]

A less general but still severe prohibition may also result from the cumulative effect of provisions relating to collective labour disputes under which a conciliation process has to be commenced, at the request of one of the parties or at the discretion of the public authorities. If disputes must be referred to a compulsory arbitration procedure leading to a final award that binds the parties concerned, ILO supervisory bodies have established that a prohibition as such seriously limits the means available to trade unions to further and defend the interests of their members as it is not compatible with Article 3 of the Convention No. 87. Other similar restrictions also relate to strike objectives or methods, or the obligation to give advance notice (for example, clauses imposing a waiting period). Depending on the extent of restrictions, these may also contradict the right to strike.[536]

In many countries, legislation also contains a number of more specific, occupational restrictions on the exercise of the right to strike. Such restrictions vary in extent. Most often they concern certain categories of workers because of their status (public service), the functions they perform (essential services, role in the industrial relations system), their hierarchical status (managerial staff) or any combination of these.[537] Reflecting the principles it has accepted, the CFA has not accepted general limitations on the right to strike only on these formal or nominal grounds.

Thus, the CFA has upheld that the criterion on essentiality depends not so much on the formal public or private nature of functions as on the nature of the actual tasks carried out. It follows that ILO practice allows for situations where workers in the private or semi-private sectors perform duties that have been considered essential services. On the other hand, very broad categories exist of other workers who, although belonging to the public service, have not been regarded

[535] See ibid., para. 160.
[536] See ibid., paras. 153–155.
[537] Ibid., para. 154.

as groups for which prohibition or restriction of the right to strike would be justified on 'essential services' criteria.[538]

The Committee of Experts has somewhat widened this CFA perspective. The Committee has upheld that account must be taken of the special circumstances existing in the various ILO Member States, since interrupting certain services could prove disastrous and rapidly lead to conditions that might endanger the life, personal safety, or health of the population. For example, a strike in port or maritime transport services might more rapidly cause serious disruption to a country that for geographical reasons depends heavily on these services to provide basic supplies to its population. Along the same lines of reasoning, a non-essential service in the strict sense of the term may also become essential if the strike affecting it exceeds a certain duration. Furthermore, the Committee of Experts has considered that sanctions for strike action should be possible only where the prohibitions in question conform to the principles of freedom of association.[539]

12 Challenges posed by the Rosella Case

In the *Rosella* case, which the Court of Appeal of England and Wales referred to the ECJ in November 2005, the ECJ was asked to decide the relationship between rules on free movement of services and freedom of establishment, as protected in the EC Treaty, and fundamental rights of workers to take collective action, including industrial action.

The case is about Viking Line (later: Viking), which is a Finnish passenger shipping company that owns and operates a ferry called the *Rosella*. The *Rosella* sails under the Finnish flag between Estonia and Finland and employs a predominantly Finnish crew whose terms of employment are provided by a Finnish collective agreement negotiated by the Finnish Seamen's Union (later: FSU). Legal proceedings started when Viking decided it wanted to register the *Rosella* as an Estonian ship. Re-flagging would have allowed

538 Ibid., para. 158.
539 Ibid., para. 160.

Viking to replace the crew with Estonian seafarers. Furthermore, cheaper terms and conditions of employment would have been enabled.

In 2004, Viking commenced an application in the Commercial Court for England and Wales, for an order to prohibit the International Transport Workers' Federation (later: ITF) and the FSU from taking industrial action against Viking for the purpose of safeguarding employment and wage conditions of its members and to prevent a possible re-flagging of the *Rosella.* Viking could start proceedings in England because the ITF headquarters is based in London.[540]

In November 2003, Viking had already commenced proceedings in the Finnish District Court seeking an urgent interim injunction restraining the FSU from initiating threatened industrial action against the *Rosella* plus a fine of EUR 500,000 against the FSU. The grounds asserted for such relief included the allegation that the proposed industrial action was unlawful under Finnish law, based on the argument that the manning agreement was still in effect, and, secondly, that the threatened strike was a breach of EC law. The latter assertion had been made specifically with reference to the right of free provision of shipping services under EC Regulation 4055/86[541] and to the right of freedom of establishment under Article 43 EC Treaty. These claims were all denied by the FSU.

Viking argued in the Commercial Court for England and Wales that by preventing the re-flagging, the ITF and the FSU were infringing Viking's right to establish in Estonia or, alternatively, to provide services between Estonia and Finland. In the *Albany* case the issue had been whether the competition rules in the EC Treaty applied to a

540 The ITF is a global federation of transport workers' unions with its Secretariat based in London. The FSU is an autonomous Finnish trade union representing seamen having about 10,000 members. It is a member of the Central Organisation of Finnish Trade Unions (Suomen Ammattiliittojen Keskusjärjestö).

541 Council Regulation (EEC) No 4055/86 applying the principle of freedom to provide services to maritime transport between Member States and between Member States and third countries.

collective agreement.[542] The ECJ held in the *Albany* case that the collective agreement was, 'by reason of its nature and purpose', outside the scope of Article 85(1) EC Treaty.[543] In the *Rosella* case, the ITF and the FSU argued that collective action is simply not intended to be subject to the free movement Articles of the EC Treaty. The Commercial Court in London decided that Viking Line's claim was justified in view of Article 43 EC Treaty.

The case was next brought before the appeal court, which referred a series of questions to the ECJ. Among other things, the Court asked whether such collective action which is in question falls outside the scope of Article 43 EC Treaty and/or the Regulation 4055/86 by virtue of the EC's social policy including, *inter alia*, Title XI EC Treaty and, in particular, by analogy with the Court's reasoning in the *Albany* case.[544]

13 Emergence of a Specific Conflicts Rule on Industrial Action

So far we have been dealing with the existing rules and two cases pending in the ECJ. Before discussing the conflict between fundamental rights and EU economic freedoms in more detail, it is useful to look at unification work concerning conflicts rules on non-contractual obligations, since this work has come to have a linkage on the issue.

In April 2006, the Council reached political agreement on the Rome II Regulation, which is at present handled by the European Parliament.[545] As we have seen, enacting common conflicts rules on non-contractual obligations has been regarded as the natural extension of unifying the conflicts rules in the Community. However, the

---

542 Case C-67/96, Albany International BV v. Stichting Bedrijfspensioenfonds Textielindustrie, [1999] I-5751.

543 See ibid., para. 64.

544 In 2005, Viking decided not to re-flag Rosella, but the court proceedings continue.

545 See JUSTCIV 118, 9143/06, Proposal for a Regulation of the European Parliament and the Council on the law applicable to non-contractual obligations (Rome II).

outcome of the April Council did not fully satisfy all Member States, and Estonia and Latvia entered reservations. Presumably, the reason for this was that the Council added a separate conflicts rule on industrial action to the Rome II Proposal.

Since the preparation work in the Committee on Civil Law Matters of the Council was intensive at the same time as the *Laval* and *Rosella* cases came under the spotlight in the Scandinavian countries, it is not difficult to see a linkage between them and the new conflicts rule in the Rome II Proposal. One could assume that Sweden saw in Rome II an opportunity to seek to safeguard maintaining the Scandinavian industrial action model by means of private international law as well.[546] During the preparation of the Rome II in the Committee on Civil Law Matters, Sweden came up with a proposal about adding to the proposed Regulation a new conflicts rule on industrial action.[547]

The proposed rule reads as follows:

> Without prejudice to Article 3(2), the law applicable to a non-contractual obligation in respect of the liability of a person in the capacity of a worker or an employer or the organizations representing their professional interests for damages caused by an industrial action, pending or carried out, shall be the law of the country where the action is to be or has been taken.

It is noteworthy that this proposed Article 8a refers to industrial action carried out either by an employee or an employer or their organisations. However, interpretation of the Article is hampered by the fact that clarification is lacking in the Rome II Proposal about the

546 As far as the present author knows, Sweden found strongest support for its proposal from Finland.

547 Additionally, the European Parliament's legislative resolution contained an amendment which would have meant adding a specific rule on industrial action to Rome II. According to this Article 6a, "the law applicable to a non-contractual obligation arising out of industrial action, pending or carried out, shall be the law of the country in which the action is to be taken or has been taken". See Outcome of the European Parliament's first reading, Strasbourg, 4 to 7 July 2005.

relationship between Article 8a and the basic conflicts rule set out in Article 3(1). According to Article 3(1), the law applicable to a tort or delict would be the law of the country in which the damage occurs, irrespective of the country in which the event giving rise to the damage occurred and irrespective of the country or countries in which the indirect consequences of that event occur. One might think that this basic rule would already have safeguarded the outcome now sought by a specific rule by way of Article 8a. However, the new Article would ensure that when industrial action is taken in one Member State with effects in another, the law applicable to the damages caused by this action is the law of the State where the action was taken. In other respects, the added value of this specific rule appears unclear.

Although two amendments were made to the Preamble of the proposed Regulation in order to clarify the role of Article 8a, no light was shed on the relationship between Articles 3(1) and 8a. The term 'industrial action' has not been clarified in the text of Article 8a but Recital 14a of the proposed Directive clarifies that it would govern, for example, strikes and lock-outs. Moreover, Recital 14a states that the exact concept of industrial action, such as strike action or lock-out, varies from Member State to Member State and is governed by each Member State's internal rules. Therefore, the proposed Regulation takes as a general principle that the law of the country where the industrial action was taken should apply in aiming to protect the rights and obligations of workers and employers. It is noteworthy that although Recital 14a deals with the nature of the right to industrial action, it says nothing about the fundamental nature of this right. When dealing with fundamental rights, EC instruments often point this feature out.

According to Recital 14b of the proposed Directive, the special rule on industrial action in Article 8a is without prejudice to the conditions relating to the exercise of such action in accordance with national law. Moreover, the rule of Article 8a would be without prejudice to the legal status of the representative organisations of workers or trade unions as foreseen in Member State domestic law. The question as to what kind of damages the law applicable to an industrial action governs has not been dealt with in the Proposal. It could have been explicitly set out in the Proposal if the idea was to only cover remedy and compensation for the damage caused by industrial action.

Latvia and Estonia provided a common declaration to be included in the minutes of the April 2006 Council meeting. According to this declaration, these countries recognise that industrial action is one of the "essential" rights of a worker, an employer, or the organisations representing their professional interests. The principle provided in Article 8a should apply only to cases that arise directly from exercise of those essential rights. Moreover, Latvia and Estonia stress that application of Article 8a should not constitute any further restrictions on freedom to provide services within the Community.

A third Member State that explicitly expressed its concern about Article 8a was Greece. Accordingly, it provided a statement to be included in the minutes of the Council meeting. The Greek delegation wanted to point out that "application of Article 8a of the Regulation would probably cause problems for shipping, given that vessels would be exposed to rules which varied according to the laws of the Member States of their ports of call, irrespective of whether those vessels were in full conformity with the laws of the flag State". The declaration and statement above again reveal the tensions within the EU as regards appropriate means of protecting the right to industrial action when EU economic freedoms are at stake.

14 Need for a New Fundamental Rights Approach in the EU

From the standpoint of fundamental rights, both the *Laval* and the *Rosella* cases have the potentiality to be of landmark importance in defining relations between Articles 43 and 49 EC Treaty on the one hand and the right of freedom of association and the right to strike as derived from that fundamental right, on the other.[548] Against the background of the ILO core Conventions on Freedom of Association and the whole construction of collective rights based on that, the significance of the forthcoming ECJ decisions could be of universal

[548] See also Eklund, "The Laval Case", p. 208.

nature. In essence, these two cases can be claimed to illustrate how a highly developed regional legislative approach might suddenly contradict fundamental rights.

According to Article 6(2) of the Treaty on European Union, the Union respects fundamental rights, as guaranteed by the ECHR. The ECJ, which has been paying increasing attention to protection of fundamental rights, has consistently held that fundamental rights form an integral part of the general principles of law, the observance of which it ensures.[549] For that purpose, the Court draws inspiration from the common constitutional traditions of the Member States and from the guidelines supplied by international treaties for protection of human rights. In the *ERT* case, the Court stated that the ECHR has special significance in that respect.[550]

With regard to the role of the right to industrial action under EC law, it should be emphasised that although the Posted Workers Directive does not regulate industrial action rights or their application, these rights are protected in EC law as fundamental rights. The fundamental nature of industrial action rights has also been confirmed in Article 28 of the Charter of Fundamental Rights in the EU, according to which "workers and employers, or their respective organisations, have, in accordance with Community law and national laws and practices, the right to negotiate and conclude collective agreements at the appropriate levels and, in cases of conflicts of interest, to take collective action to defend their interests, including strike action".[551]

---

549 See, in particular, the judgments in Case C-4/73 Nold v. Commission, [1974] ECR 491, para. 13 and Case C-260/89, Elliniki Radiophonia Tiléorassi AE and Panellinia Omospondia Syllogon Prossopikou v. Dimotiki Etairia Pliroforissis and Sotirios Kouvelas and Nicolaos Avdellas and others, [1991] ECR I-1295, para. 41. It should also be noted that the European Constitution would significantly affect fundamental rights protection in the EU.

550 Case C-260/89, Elliniki Radiophonia Tiléorassi AE and Panellinia Omospondia Syllogon Prossopikou v. Dimotiki Etairia Pliroforissis and Sotirios Kouvelas and Nicolaos Avdellas and others, [1991] ECR I-1295, para. 41.

551 The Charter would be an integral part of the Constitutional Treaty.

The EC Treaty confirms the fundamental nature of EU economic rights. In addition to the fundamental economic rights of free movement guaranteed by the EC Treaty, fundamental labour rights, such as industrial action rights, are protected by EC law. The significance of the ECHR and the European Social Charter should here be emphasised. Moreover, the right to engage in industrial action is protected by several human rights conventions and strengthened by well-established ILO practice, discussed above. In addition, the significance of industrial action rights is confirmed by the fact that they enjoy protection by constitutions of many Member States, while, according to the ECJ, the common constitutional traditions of the Member States form part of EC law.

From the perspective of EC law, the fundamental problem in the *Laval* case is, in fact, how to reconcile protection of industrial action rights and the freedom of movement of services. Following the current approach of the ECJ, the solution could be sought by looking at the principles that the Court presented in the *Schmidberger* case. The Court stated that protection of fundamental rights recognised in EC law is a legitimate interest that justifies restriction of obligations set in EC law, such as the obligation to guarantee the fundamental right of free movement. Additionally, the *Omega* case, which has been said to confirm the centrality of human rights in the EC legal order, follows this reasoning.[552] Accordingly, the Court could state in the *Laval* and *Rosella* cases that the right to industrial action is a fundamental right that justifies restricting an obligation provided by EC law.

We have seen that the right to industrial action enjoys protection deriving from many international human rights documents. From the perspective of the principal objective of human rights protection, and of recognition of the right of industrial action as an inviolable labour right, one might question the above approach adopted by the ECJ.[553] It is useful to pause at this point and consider whether the existing approach in EC law provides the only option for

---

552 See Chu, "'Playing at Killing' Freedom of Movement", p. 94.

553 See also Hepple, Labour Laws and Global Trade, p. 240, where he criticises the ECJ's 'offensive use' of fundamental rights, i.e. elevating EU economic freedoms to the status of fundamental rights.

the Court to resolve the issue. Giving priority to EU economic freedoms and regarding fundamental rights as 'justified restrictions' is open to the criticism that fundamental rights cannot be set on the same plane as economic rights. Nor, too, can they be set on a lower plane than economic rights by regarding them merely as 'justified restrictions' on EU economic freedoms.

Hence, it can be asked whether fundamental rights that clearly enjoy status as human rights, should be basically regarded as being independent from EU economic freedoms. If this can be achieved, then these rights might be considered to constitute independent grounds for preventing application of EC law on economic freedoms as far as it contradicts those fundamental rights. Otherwise, if the present regional approach in EC law is followed, the outcome might turn out to be less suitable from the standpoint of true fundamental rights protection: one could claim that, in the final analysis, European integration means subordinating fundamental rights to EU economic freedoms on certain conditions. Even if this basic approach were modified by adding emphasis to fundamental rights protection, it seems to be less satisfactory from the standpoint of that very fundamental rights protection. The basic reasoning so far adopted by the ECJ, as it is, might easily prompt serious concerns on a downgrading of fundamental rights.

Finally, it should be emphasised that adopting a new approach towards fundamental rights protection in the EU would not mean rejecting justified restrictions on the right to industrial action, exemplified by ILO legal practice discussed above. Thus, a need to balance EU economic freedoms against fundamental labour rights can, and probably should, be taken into account without using the existing approach, which seems to be leading to undervaluing the status of fundamental rights.

Chapter VI Future Prospects

1 Introduction

Originally, private international law was meant to be a 'localisation method' for ascertaining the legal order with which an international legal relationship had the strongest connection.[554] The strongest connection still plays an important role, although the material result of choice of law has gained increasing importance in determining the applicable law. Increasing materialisation of choice of law rules in Europe is not unproblematic because of the contradictions between the new kind of choice of law legislation and the fundamental principles of private international law. On some occasions, these problems concern the way in which the new choice of law legislation prioritises the forum law instead of the application of the foreign law being determined as the *lex causae*.

In terms of the predictability of choice of law, there is a limit as to how far the materialisation development can be taken. In order to control this development, the private international law dimension of protective legislation should be taken into consideration when such legislation is being prepared.[555] The EC legislator should pay more attention to how the special choice of law rules of secondary EC legislation relate to the whole choice of law-related legislation. For example, in the ongoing preparation of the Rome I Regulation, the role of consumer law directives containing conflicts rules needs to be addressed. As stated in chapter II, if the possibility of choosing the applicable law no longer exists, the role of mandatory provisions that affect choice of law needs to be resolved.

The EU is, of course, an organisation of regional integration. From the standpoint of economic integration, the internal market is an economic area, so conflicts rules on contractual obligations should

---

554 See Jänterä-Jareborg, "Efterlevande make, intern skyddslagstiftning och IP", p. 301.

555 See ibid., pp. 301–302.

also serve its functioning. However, from the standpoint of the protective framework of consumers and labour known as ‘Citizens’ Europe’ or ‘Social Europe’, vital policy concerns exist that cannot be directly linked to the aims of deeper economic integration. Rather, these concerns might often be understood as a kind of counter force to economic considerations. What should also be noted is that some of these concerns are global by nature while others are regional.

2 Private International Law in Transition

Globally, efforts to unify private international law have been mainly carried out at the Hague Conference on Private International Law, which has been much more successful in the field of international family law than in the field of international contract law. The problems involved with Hague Conference cooperation arise from the heterogeneity of the Conference Member States. This also results in negotiations being concluded with neither a guarantee of the success of the project nor the international implementation of the convention. This was exemplified by the Hague Sales Conventions discussed in chapter II.

The Conventions as such do not guarantee that they will be harmoniously regulated and implemented in the Member States. The sanction system based on international law could be applied to breaches of the Conventions but this has never been done.[556] In many respects, it is worth expecting that the forthcoming membership of the EC in the Hague Conference will begin a new era.[557] It might restrain regionalisation of conflicts law in issues where international conflicts rules already exist. Since the required amendments of the Statute of the Conference have been formulated in a neutral way, this also enables other international organisations to join.

---

[556] See Leinonen, “Alueellisesta yhteistyöstä maailmanlaajuiseen ja takaisin – lakiyhteistyöstä kansainvälisen yksityisoikeuden alalla”, p. 650.

[557] See Liukkunen, “Perspectives on the Unification of Private International Law in Europe”. See also Proposal for a Council Decision on the accession of the European Community to the Hague Conference on Private International Law. COM(2005) 639 final.

In Europe, private international law is in transition. The core areas of conflicts law affecting cross-border service provision are no longer in national hands. European integration has taken two different paths in a direction that strengthens the position of private international law and to a large extent makes the conflicts rules statutory. One of the two European paths is marked by the Hague Programme, whereas the other is more 'shadowy'. It has been sketched in this study through analysis of various internal market directives that contain specific conflicts rules.

Consideration of the outcome of choice of law has played a distinct role when conflicts rules have been drafted for secondary EC law. The materialisation of conflicts rules has made them more flexible. This has been based on an effort to find the fairest solution for individual cases, but the materialisation has happened largely at the expense of the predictability and legal certainty of choice of law. In this respect, serious problems are involved in the materialisation of private international law. In terms of legal certainty, specific conflicts rules of EC law are particularly problematic because they are used in directives. In certain cases, the complexity of the regulatory approach has led to notable variation in the manner the conflicts rules have been transposed by EU Member States. One example is the transposition of the E-Commerce Directive.

The proposed use of the principle of mutual recognition in the two EC legislative initiatives discussed in this study contradicts the existing conflicts law rules of the Rome Convention. With the Rome Convention, both consumers and employees have already received special status in choice of law. This special status should also be respected when developing internal market law further. Now the Rome I Proposal seeks to establish a new model for consumer protection. Adopting this model would mean that the conflicts approach in consumer and employee protection would diverge from each other in the future. Party autonomy would no longer be permitted in consumer contracts, whereas in employment contracts the parties would be permitted to select the applicable law. What still needs to be resolved is the question of the scope of the extension of party autonomy proposed in Article 3(2) of the Rome I Proposal. The extension has been considered an improvement for business parties, but its impact on the weaker party contracts has been so far ignored. This study has found the suggested extension of party autonomy in the case of employment contracts unjustified.

3 Human and Fundamental Rights in Conflicts Law

The break with neutral conflicts rules has meant that various objectives of substantive law are now being considered in private international law. It is also increasingly typical for European private international law to consider the objectives of integration, something which may occasionally lead to conflicts in the relationship between human and fundamental rights and the EU economic freedoms. However, essentially linked to the progress of integration is the fact that the approach that emphasises human and fundamental rights obligations has gained more momentum with the EU Charter of Fundamental Rights. Since, in terms of global governance, private international law has become an increasingly important field of law, it is interesting to look at the role of human and fundamental rights from the viewpoint of some of its central principles.

One of the core principles of private international law is the classic *ordre public* principle. It enables the provisions of the law of a foreign state to be rejected if they are contrary to the foundations of the legal order of the forum state. *Ordre public* can be defined as an inviolable part of the legal order of the forum state. The point of departure is that states decide the content of the fundamental principles of their legal order. The only case in which a court can refuse to apply the provisions of a foreign state is when their application in an individual case would lead to an outcome contrary to the foundations of the legal order of the forum state. Whether the *ordre public* principle is applied or not may depend on how closely the case is connected with the forum state. In the German legal literature, emphasis can be found which observes that the more important the fundamental right, the lower the threshold for applying the principle.[558]

---

558 See, for example, Junker, Internationales Privatrecht, p. 249.

Although it has to be stressed that resorting to the *ordre public* principle should be rare and its scope of application limited, it is basically undeniable that Member States can freely determine what they consider to be the foundations of their legal order. The scope of application of the principle has become more extensive with the increased significance of human and fundamental rights. The application of the principle in cases where the law of a foreign state conflicts with the human and fundamental rights rules of the forum law can be based on the fundamental social views of the state and seen as part of the national legal effects of human rights obligations.

The *ordre public* principle has a strong foothold in international procedural law. The status of the principle can be viewed in light of the enforcement of a foreign ruling in two international cases. *Pellegrini v. Italy* was about enforcing a foreign ruling on the annulment of a marriage.[559] According to the ecclesiastical courts of the Vatican, the marriage of Mrs. Pellegrini was annulled on the ground of consanguinity. Mrs. Pellegrini was of the opinion that her defence rights had been infringed in the ecclesiastical courts. She had not been given a proper opportunity to appear as a defendant in the courts that handled the case. She had been summoned to appear in a court but she had not been informed in detail of her ex-husband's application, i.e. the grounds for the case, nor of the fact that she would have had the right to the assistance of a lawyer.

The Italian courts ruled that the judgement given in the Vatican was enforceable, and the European Court of Human Rights was to decide whether enforcement of the foreign judgement should be disallowed by virtue of the ECHR. As the Vatican is not a signatory to the Convention, only the obligations of Italy were under scrutiny. The Court decided that a breach had occurred of the requirements for a fair trial as laid down in Article 6(1) of the ECHR. Enforcement of a foreign law could be rejected solely on the basis that the ruling violated Article 6(1). As the European Court ruled that a breach of the Convention alone could be a basis for rejecting enforcement of a judgment, there was no need to resort to the *ordre public* principle. The logic behind the ruling was that the violation of human rights

559 See Case Pellegrini v. Italy, 30882/96, [2001] ECHR 480 (20 July 2001).

obligations, without the support of the rules of international procedural law, can in itself constitute a basis for rejecting enforcement of a judgment. Thus, human rights obligations were considered an independent ground for rejecting enforcement.

However, the ECJ has adopted a different position. In *Krombach* the Court ruled that a clear violation of the ECHR provided grounds for applying the *ordre public* provision of the Brussels Convention, predecessor of the Brussels I Regulation.[560] Thus, the Court did not use a provision of the ECHR as an independent ground for rejecting enforcement of the judgment but instead applied the Brussels Convention provision that included the *ordre public* principle. *Michael Bogdan* writes that, although a conflict between a foreign ruling and a human rights convention can be resolved by means of the *ordre public* principle, it would be more appropriate to use violation of human rights obligations as an independent ground for denying enforcement. He bases his approach on the view that violating a human rights convention can be considered more serious than violating a convention on the recognition and enforcement of judgments.[561]

It must be stressed that these cases involved a regional human rights document and were applied by two strong regional institutions. However, both cases demonstrate that human rights have gained increasing importance in decision-making concerning the enforcement of foreign judgments. This is a matter of ensuring procedural justice as part of human rights protection. Human rights protection and the status of the *ordre public* principle can also be analysed from the standpoint of the application of conflicts rules. Additionally, in choice of law this principle protects core values of legal order. Thus, we could say that the principle is an ultimate protective human rights norm in private international law.

It is important to note that in addition to the *ordre public* principle, internationally mandatory rules may gain increasing importance, for example in protecting the fundamental rights of the

---

560 See Case C-7/98 Dieter Krombach v. André Bamberski, [2000] ECR I-1935.

561 Bogdan, "Erkännande och verkställighet av med den europeiska människorättskonventionen oförenlig utländsk dom", pp. 28–29.

weaker contracting party. As we have seen, the Rome Convention has established the principle on internationally mandatory rules in European private international law, and internationally mandatory rules have acquired growing importance in Europe. These rules are commonly considered to be of a stronger public interest or have, for example, the character of a strong socially protective norm. Courts have quite considerable discretionary power in the application of these rules because legislation rarely states clearly which substantive provisions are internationally mandatory. While identifying and applying these provisions, courts must observe human and fundamental rights.

Clearly, human rights are more protected by the *ordre public* principle than by internationally mandatory rules. When a foreign law applicable to a contract does not respect a human right, the *ordre public* principle can be used to reject the application of the law in question and to protect the human right concerned. The principle covers all situations where the outcome of applying a foreign law would be contrary to the foundations of the legal order of the forum state. The criteria for applying internationally mandatory rules are not as strict. Moreover, the content of internationally mandatory rules is generally more extensive than that of the provisions covered by the *ordre public* principle.

However, the principle does not determine which country's law should be applied if the law of a foreign state is inapplicable because it conflicts with the foundations of the law of the forum. It is often thought that the law of the forum state would then become applicable. It should be noted that the *ordre public* principle and internationally mandatory rules operate 'in different directions'. The *ordre public* principle is used to reject application of the law of a foreign state, whereas internationally mandatory rules are used to apply some other law than the *lex causae*. In any case, these rules may have a complementary protective effect, for example when the *lex causae* or special conflicts rules that should protect the weaker contracting party do not do so.

The possibility was discussed earlier of directly applying international human rights conventions in international procedural law, and now the same question should be examined from the standpoint of choice of law. *Bogdan* has represented a view according to which applying the law of a foreign state should not be possible if it would violate human rights enshrined in the ECHR. By virtue of, for example, the Swedish Constitution, the provisions of the Convention can be considered to belong to the foundations of the country's legal order and thus their violation would automatically be against the legal order. According to *Bogdan*, the most natural approach would be to view the provisions of the ECHR as independent grounds for rejecting the application of the law of a foreign state. He also points out that this is not merely a theoretical question because, normally, in order for the *ordre public* principle to be applied, application of the foreign law would have to be in obvious conflict with the foundations of the legal order.[562] Being able to refer to the ECHR in choice of law instead of the *ordre public* principle is significant for the strengthening of human rights protection.

It might also be possible to use this approach in applying certain other core international human rights documents. In practice, this would mean, for example, that a court would not have to resort to the *ordre public* rule of Article 16 of the Rome Convention in cases where it must be decided whether the law of a foreign state can be ignored because it violates human rights. A similar approach could be applied when considering whether a foreign judgment should be recognized and implemented.

4 Challenges posed by Globalisation

Globalisation prompts consideration of the need to redefine the objectives of conflicts law. This need arises both from normative and from societal developments. Globalisation broadens the perspective of traditional international law and private international law, and brings them together increasingly often.[563] Nowadays, research on global law

---

562 See ibid. and Bogdan, Svensk internationell privat- och processrätt, p. 79.

563 According to *Berman*, for example, it is now being understood that, because of globalisation, international law needs a wider framework than ever before, a framework that sets the development of transnational norms in the intersec-

typically raises questions on, for example, the protection of human rights in conflicts law cases. As we have seen, protection of human rights should also be considered in the light of the principles of private international law. Moreover, the materialisation of private international law is a significant trend in terms of human rights protection. Generally speaking, for example in Europe, the significance of positive and negative *ordre public* principles in promoting fundamental rights has been increasing. Under certain conditions, courts may set aside these principles in choice of law and apply human rights documents directly.

From a systematic standpoint, global law is becoming its own field of law, but the norm production on which it is based is fragmented. According to *Fischer-Lescano* and *Teubner*, the fragmentation of global law is more fundamental than any one limited standpoint can reveal. However, the fragmentation of law is only a manifestation of the fundamental and manifold fragmentation of global society. The authors suggest that aiming at uniform global law is useless and that the fragments of global law can, at best, be made vaguely compatible.[564]

It should be emphasised that in cross-border service provision, the use of *soft law* is not a novelty. International commercial law has long been characterised by *soft law* elements and one can claim that for the most part their use has been balanced. Yet, globalisation has led to a development where more *soft law* means more fragmentation.

Fischer-Lescano and *Teubner* have emphasised the growth in the importance of different conflicts rules. The increase in the use of private international law in EC law is obvious. However, the fragmentary development of EC legislation emphasised in this study has not been in the spotlight. Examples of hidden conflicts rules used in this study are, *inter alia*, those EC provisions that use choice of law rules to combine company and labour law norms to complement each

---

tion of private international law and procedural law, comparative legal science, cultural analysis of law, and traditional international law. See Berman, "From International Law to Law and Globalisation", p. 489.

564 See Fischer-Lescano – Teubner, "Regime-Collisions: The Vain Search for Legal Unity in the Fragmentation of Global Law", p. 1004.

other. In the EU, private international law has become an increasingly important field of law for transnational interaction, although its use has often been based on situation-specific argumentation by the legislator.

In terms of research, the pursuit of coherence in global law involves redefining the criteria of systematisation, for example, by emphasising human and fundamental rights in the classification of various norm sources.[565] If the tendency to use choice of law rules in EC legislation grows, changes must also be considered to the systematisation criteria of choice of law rules, in which case the materialisation trend of private international law could be taken into consideration.

This study has shown that at a normative system level, the EC legislator is very slowly beginning to recognize serious problems of coherence in the current European conflicts approach. The question of coherence concerns not only efficiency but also fairness and justice. In this sense, Europe could also learn something from the American experience of fragmentation that has been put critically in the limelight in the ongoing US conflicts discussion examined in this study. The same applies *vice versa*.

5 Challenges to Fundamental Rights in the EU

This study has looked at the regulatory competition in company law, first and foremost, from the standpoint of the possibility of cross-border transfers of registered offices. As long as these cross-border transfers in the EU are possible only for an SE and an SCE, we cannot really speak of regulatory competition of company law in the full sense of the term, at least not as far as private international law is concerned. A directive proposal on cross-border transfers of registered offices, which is currently being drawn up, is highly interesting in this respect. The related Directive on cross-border mergers supports the view adopted in this study on the EC regulatory approach to employee

565 See Pöyhönen, Uusi varallisuusoikeus, p. 69.

rights of participation in cases of cross-border changes of registered office or company form.

At present, a central factor boosting regulatory competition between Member States is being able to register a company in a Member State only when the legislation of that state is more favourable than that of the state in which the company *de facto* operates. If, in addition to EC legislation, ECJ case law which strengthens freedom of establishment is considered, it can be observed that during the present decade, international company law has become significantly more European, particularly as regards cross-border restructuring.

In order to secure employee involvement rights in cross-border corporate restructuring and minimum terms of contract for posted employees in service trades, the EC legislator has created particular choice of law rules for secondary law. The application of legal rules on employee involvement rights is complicated because the directives that contain provisions on these rights combine rules from both company and labour law. In cross-border service trade, on the other hand, the rules of commercial law have been combined with labour law rules on employee protection. This has led to tensions at the intersections of company and labour law, and trade and labour law. The tensions stem, for instance, from how the four freedoms of the EU relate to mandatory social protection regulation and internationally recognized fundamental labour rights.

In recent years, legal development has created new tensions between the EU economic freedoms and the labour laws of the Member States. These tensions have taken different shapes. Some tensions relate to extending freedom of establishment. The recent strengthening of freedom of establishment has raised the question as to whether it should be possible to restrict companies' freedom of establishment in order to protect employee involvement rights. This question becomes immediate in cases where the maintenance of employee participation in company administration is not protected by EC legislation. Another illustration of the tensions is how exceptionally difficult has been the question of cross-border application of the Directive on the Transfer of Undertakings. In legal literature, opinions differ particularly on the extent to which employees' terms of employment should be retained in cross-border restructuring.

The *Laval* and *Rosella* cases pending in the ECJ pose the question of how far freedom of service provision and establishment should be limited in order to protect fundamental rights, and specifically in these cases, industrial action rights. In recent years, for example, the Charter of Fundamental Rights of the EU has advanced the strengthening of the status of fundamental rights in the Union. Moreover, recent ECJ case law indicates that acceptable grounds for restricting the four EU economic freedoms have specific connections with protecting fundamental rights. In this respect, the right to industrial action, which is protected by the law of the Member States and international human rights documents, enjoys stronger status than, for example, the right to employee involvement.

According to ECJ case law, the accepted grounds for restricting EU economic freedoms include employee protection. Thus, protection of employee involvement rights should also be considered an acceptable ground for restricting freedom of establishment. In some Member States, employee involvement rights are also protected by the constitution. From ECJ case law, one can conclude that it is possible to set more extensive restrictions on EU economic freedoms by appealing to fundamental rights than by referring to other justified grounds. Even when the grounds for restriction are acceptable and pass the three-part test established by the ECJ (acceptable, necessary and proportionate, non-discriminatory), it must still be determined whether a balance in the case exists between grounds for restriction, such as the protection of fundamental labour rights, and the requirements of the fundamental economic freedoms of the EU.

This study has raised the question whether the EC law paradigm – setting fundamental rights to the status of 'justified restrictions' in relation to EU economic freedoms – is, in the final analysis, appropriate. It is important not just to look at the question from the standpoint of a European, that is to say, a regional, approach, but also from that maintained by several human rights documents at the international level. It could be argued that the ECJ should seek to establish a new approach towards fundamental rights for situations where they might conflict with EU economic freedoms.[566] Because of its fundamental rights status, the Court could regard protection of the right to industrial action as independent from the paradigm of EU economic freedoms. Considerable doubt can be thrown on whether the current approach is the best available from the standpoint of not downgrading human rights protection. It should be emphasised that the approach to fundamental labour rights of the ECJ has a bearing on the entire European social model.

6 The Many Futures of the European Conflicts Rules

Peter Hay writes that justice in conflicts law has many faces.[567] To some extent, it might be an oversimplification use the division of 'conflicts justice' and 'material justice'. One is tempted to say that conflicts law in the EU has many futures, so that the prevailing one is just on the horizon. The two separate directions of conflicts law should be assessed together in order to provide a more balanced approach in the future. Depending on the orientation chosen, the European approach could provide a remarkably more coherent legal framework. Ultimately, the decision-making on the orientation rests in the hands of the EU Member States.

This study has analysed the increasing fragmentation of conflicts rules in EC law from the standpoint of the general principles of private international law. For example, the status of private international law in the border zone between company and labour law is problematic because the special choice of law rules of secondary law have often been created case-specifically, following the approaches and general doctrines of company and labour law rather than those of private international law. Conflicts rules of this kind are prepared in the EU within the framework of sector-specific policies

566 On the possibility of fundamental rights as 'a grand legal narrative' in the framework of the European unification of private law, see Wilhelmsson, "The Ethical Pluralism of Late Modern Europe and Codification of European Contract Law", pp. 141–146.

567 Hay, "Flexibility versus Predictability and Uniformity in Choice of Law. Reflections on Current European and United States Conflicts Law", p. 399.

and not as part of justice and home affairs. Those preparing these rules have in fact often ignored certain fundamental questions of private international law, while the relationship between the specific rules and general choice of law rules has remained unclarified. This is detrimental to the coherence of private international law.

However, the present trend in Europe is in favour of unifying law by using the conflicts law approach in practice in every field of private law. Given the materialisation of the conflict of laws in Europe, it is to be expected that specific conflicts rules used in EC law will serve the particular objectives of European economic integration also in the future. Yet, private international law should not be used for the purposes of integration at the cost of legal certainty. A European conflicts approach can be developed to take better account of the needs of both companies and individuals only if fragmentation does not proceed further.

The way private international law has been affected by European integration can be considered from the viewpoint of the extent to which European choice of law legislation is universal or regional in its scope of application. Regulatory projects on choice of law belonging to the field of Title IV EC Treaty are typically universal. In this respect, they differ from the specific choice of law legislation of internal market law, which is typically restricted to the EU area. As in the Rome Convention, the Rome I and Rome II Proposals are also based on the idea that the applicable law should be applied even if it is the law of a non-Member State. Moreover, conflicts rules contained in these two Proposals do not require the cases to be connected with a Member State. One of the grounds for the universality of the Rome I and Rome II Proposals has been that the provisions of the Brussels I Regulation are also universal in the sense that the Regulation concerns both intra-community cases and cases that have connections with non-Member States.

The conflicts rules of secondary EC law, whose scope of application is regional, have been built mainly for the internal needs of the EC. However, these conflicts rules do not always directly indicate their regional scope of application. The regionality of a choice of law rule may emerge from a requirement that, in order to be applied, the case must be connected with a Member State. Nevertheless, directives do not always stipulate clearly enough the kind of borderline cases that are connected with both the Community and non-Member States. Sometimes conflicts rules of EC directives are applied to these cases as well.

It has been said that the heritage of *von Savigny* can be seen in contemporary European conflicts rules: they are multilateral, and a connecting factor is used to determine the applicable law regardless of whether the law is that of the forum or any other country.[568] However, rules on jurisdiction and choice of law form an entity. Multilateral conflicts rules as such do not prevent forum shopping and they do not ensure that the same substantive rules will be applied regardless of the place of the proceedings.[569] For decisional harmony, it is not enough that countries adopt identical conflicts rules. There is a need, also, to ensure that such rules are applied in a similar manner.[570]

7 Fragmentation of Conflicts Rules in EC law

There is wide debate in Europe on the fragmentation of harmonised contract law. Arguments have been made for the creation of a common frame of reference for European contract law. In this study, special attention has been paid to the increase in the amount of unified conflicts rules and the fragmentation problem in private international law. The study has shown that the problem of the fragmentation of conflicts rules is not just the problem of some limited field of EC law. There are two sides to the problem: firstly, there is a large number of fragmented conflicts rules, and secondly, there are increasingly many quality problems in private international law. It is difficult to establish the full extent of the fragmentation problem because of sectoral

568 Kronke, "Capital Markets and Conflict of Laws", p. 271.

569 See Juenger, "The Problem with Private International Law", p. 294.

570 *Jänterä-Jareborg* has paid much attention to the existing problems of the application of foreign law in Europe. She calls for approximation of rules and practices in EU Member States that concern ascertaining the content of foreign law. Unless this is done, the outcome of the application of foreign law remains unpredictable. See Jänterä-Jareborg, "Foreign Law in National Courts – A Comparative Perspective", p. 321.

differentiation of the law-drafting. Yet, it is obvious that the problem has either been given little attention or brought up only as a special problem of some particular field, such as consumer law or insurance law.

In the following, the discussion of the problem of fragmentation is summarised by means of five examples. The aim is to create a basis for evaluating how the fragmentation manifests itself at EC law level. The fragmentation is also discussed in light of the Jack-in-the-Box Theory of EC law by *Thomas Wilhelmsson*. According to the theory, the participation of EC law in the decision-making radically increases legal uncertainty at national level. EC law sometimes 'bounces up' like a Jack-in-the-Box in unexpected situations.[571] Finally, I propose ways to avoid fragmentation.

7.1 Hidden Conflicts Rules

As demonstrated above, the EC legislation that affects choice of law can remain completely silent about its private international law dimension. In such cases, it is left to the ECJ to decide whether such a dimension exists. Therefore, it cannot be considered clear that a directive which does not contain express provisions on how it should be applied in private international law cases would not have such an effect. For example, the *Ingmar* case shows that some provisions of a directive can be internationally mandatory even if the text of the directive does not state their internationally mandatory nature. The ECJ stated that certain provisions of the Directive in question had to be observed despite the fact that the agency contract contained a choice of law clause. The Court interpreted the Directive as if it had originally contained hidden conflicts rules.

In this particular case, the private international law dimension of EC legislation came as a surprise to many. Critics of the Court's decision have pointed out, for example, that such legislation does not leave the contracting parties with much influence on the nature of their contractual relationship. The Directive on the Transfer of

---

[571] See Wilhelmsson, "Jack-in-the-Box Theory of European Community Law".

Undertakings is an example of a directive which is significant with regard to changes in cross-border business operations but whose provisions state nothing about its application in conflicts cases. Article 1 of the Directive hints towards its applicability to cross-border operations but it has been considered uncertain how the Directive should be interpreted. The ECJ could take the same approach as in the *Ingmar* case and rule that certain provisions of this Directive could be considered internationally mandatory.

Sometimes the conflicts rules of EC law have been placed in the same EC statute as material harmonisation rules in such a complicated way that they are almost impossible for the Member States to locate and understand. For example, conflicts rules on employee involvement rights have been explicitly recorded in the relevant directives, but it has proven to be too difficult for many Member States to recognize them all. This seems to be one reason why some Member States have failed to transpose the central conflicts rules of the EWC Directive.

Article 3(6) of the EWC Directive concerns the choice of the applicable law in determining the controlling undertaking in a group of companies. The undertaking is determined in accordance with the applicable Member State law. Therefore, if for example in Finland it must be determined whether the Finnish, German or Dutch company belonging to a group is the controlling undertaking, conflicts rules of international company law must be resorted to. On many occasions, the conflicts law dimensions of Article 3(6) of the Directive have remained unnoticed. As in the above example, the application of the Article requires first, that the law applicable to the company, the *lex societatis,* is defined. However, the law of a non-Member State cannot be applied.[572] Because the criteria for defining the controlling undertaking are different in each Member State, a special rule has been included in Article 3(2) of the Directive which dictates when an undertaking belonging to a group of undertakings can be considered as the controlling one.

The conflicts rules of the EWC Directive combine company and labour law by means of private international law. The conflicts rules

[572] See in more detail Article 3 of the EWC Directive.

have, however, been to a certain extent untransposed, and this problem has not been addressed in the reports from the Commission on the transposition of the Directive. Conflicts rules have, thus, become hidden, even though they have been explicitly recorded in the Directive.

A third example is provided by EC law instruments with certain conflicts issues that should have been solved beforehand. After the instruments have been issued, it has been common knowledge that not all conflicts issues had been solved that would have been relevant in terms of the application of the instruments. As a result, the Member States now interpret the existing legal status in different ways. Some of the Member States interpret the new legislation to potentially include hidden conflicts rules, whereas others leave the question for the ECJ to solve. For example, in EC company law the Regulation on SE is unclear in not stating how the transfer of an SE's registered office affects the company statute. The answer to the question whether the Regulation obligates the company to adjust to the company legislation of its new home state cannot be considered clear.

The fourth example is to some degree related to the third. Here I refer to that EC legislation which is unclear whether it concerns choice of law, i.e. whether it contains conflicts rules or not. Some Member States have interpreted the country of origin principle used in the E-Commerce Directive to contain conflicts rules, whereas some have not. The diversity of interpretations is partly explained by the as yet unestablished content of the country of origin principle in internal market law.

A fifth example is provided by the impact of the EC legislation on the freedom of establishment on the international company law of the Member States. The supersession of real seat theory by incorporation theory is based on ECJ case law regarding freedom of establishment. The States that previously applied real seat theory have had to modify their rules of international company law to be compatible with freedom of establishment. Yet, for example, the Regulation on SE seems to be based on real seat theory as well as on incorporation theory. Similarly in labour law, the EWC Directive serves as an example that there remains room for real seat theory in the application of secondary legislation. There is yet another significant observation which is that, whereas this reversion to real seat theory has occurred at the level of secondary EC legislation, the conflicts rules of the company law of the Member States are mainly unwritten.

The above-described fragmentation of conflicts rules extends to different fields of law and illustrates the regulatory system's incoherency, caused by the conflicting value base behind the legislation. It is largely explained by the structure of the decision-making system of the EC; new statutes are accepted in sectoral ministerial councils operating independently of each other within the authority granted to them by the EC Treaty.

Wilhelmsson's Jack-in-the-Box theory illustrates the difficulties EC law creates at the national level. When opening the boxes of the national legal system, we are never sure what the EC has hidden in them. The fragmentation of conflicts rules discussed in this study shows that in private international law, the Jack-in-the-Box theory can be extended to the EC law level: we are never certain which box of secondary legislation the Jack-in-the-Box is hiding in this time. Thus, it is not just a problem of national legislation but also a problem of EC legislation.[573] Knowledge of EC law is not sufficient to solve these problems, because the application of conflicts rules also requires competence in private international law.

7.2 Towards improved Coherence

On the basis of the special features of EC law analysed above, it could be argued that legal fragmentation exists because the EC legislator has begun to 'improvise' in the use of conflicts rules when trying to adjust private international law to serve the objectives of integration. The problem of fragmented conflicts rules lies less in that they cause rifts in the EC legal order, but more in that they breach the quite carefully

573 See, for example, Smits, "Diversity of Contract Law and the European Internal Market", pp. 163–165. The author observes that EC law suffers from inconsistencies and contains conflicting rules. As this study has shown, one of the problems of EC law is the existence of 'conflicting conflicts rules'.

built fundamental framework of European private international law that originates in the Brussels Convention and the Rome Convention. It is on the basis of this well-established framework that the ongoing communitarisation of private international law as part of the 'freedom, security and justice' of the Hague Programme is largely built.[574]

The fragmentation of private international law examined in this study is mainly the problem of secondary EC legislation. How, then, should sectoral conflicts rules be used? First of all, it should be noted that there are some limits to be considered when using conflicts rules to meet the growing needs of the development of the internal market.[575] Private international law is an established field of law with a long history, and it is based on certain principles, the bearing of which is accepted beyond the boundaries of national legal orders. How well the sectoral conflicts rules used in EC law function depends on how firmly and consistently they are rooted in the foundations of private international law. Private international law cannot be built on a single material legal order, not even the legal order of the EC.

Flexible management and solving problems arising from a lack of material harmonisation has become a typical function particularly of the EC legislation on choice of law. Also the reconciliation of the material legislation of different fields of law by means of conflicts rules has come to serve the same goal. It can be maintained that new conflicts rules have not always been created just because of the needs of conflicts law concerning the particular object of the legislation, but also because of the promotion of the internal market. This causes problematic situations where boundaries have to be drawn with regard

---

574 See Liukkunen, "Perspectives on the Unification of Private International Law in Europe".

575 Similar problems of the fragmentation of private law rules in EC law are commonly debated in Europe. As *Zimmermann* critically observes in "Savigny's Legacy. Legal History, Comparative Law and the Emergence of a European Legal Science", on pp. 581–582, "the present state of European legal unification is not at all reassuring, for we are dealing with no more than fragments of – more or less – uniform law, inserted rather unorganically and in a somewhat higgledy-piggledy fashion into the respective national legal systems. Rather than having gained in coherence, rationality and predictability, the law has tended to become disjointed".

to the basic instruments of choice of law. The basic premise should be that conflicts rules would be included as far as possible in the basic instruments on choice of law, Rome I and Rome II. Even when the matter at hand is outside their scope private international law should be used in a coordinated manner and, above all, by taking the basic principles of the field into account.

Private international law is first and foremost a field of law which aims at providing answers to questions concerning the applicable national law in cases with connections to different countries. Although the material importance of conflicts rules has increased and in certain issues material considerations have considerable significance, it must be emphasised that conflicts rules generally regulate material legal issues only indirectly.

8 Concluding Remarks

The framework of cross-border service trade is versatile. In choice of law, we can learn much from the experiences gained from the failure of the Hague Sales Conventions. Similarly, we should also consider the benefits that could arise from creating a set of norms for European contract law on the basis of the widely accepted CISG.

In the field of private international law, the objective of uniform solutions regardless of the states where they are made has long been the guideline of legal policy. With regard to this objective, the regionalisation of conflicts rules creates certain tension, which cannot be controlled without special care and consideration from the regional legislators. There is a need to seek a balance between regional and other international legislation. One of Europe's most central challenges is to untangle the skein of special conflicts rules and in this respect return to managed and coordinated law-making in private international law.

When discussing the cross-border service trade human and fundamental rights should also be considered. I have argued above for the application of conflicts rules which would be a move towards better human rights protection in conflicts law. The grounds I have presented are still taking shape as globalisation proceeds, but it is obvious that the doctrine of private international law has proven to be able to show the way for a 'Citizens' Europe', which is built on respect for human and fundamental rights. Likewise, this study has argued for independence for these rights in situations where they are in conflict with the four economic freedoms of the EU. Further, private international law has to determine the extent to which human and fundamental rights can be evaluated on terms dictated by the freedoms of the internal market.

This study has shown that, generally speaking, European private international law is clearly not facing similar pressures to change as those of its US counterpart. Although the Rome I Proposal can be argued to contain certain excesses related to the pursuit of legal certainty at the expense of the flexibility required in cross-border interaction, the European unification of conflicts rules can be seen to constitute quite a useful method of private international law. Even with certain deficiencies, the Rome Convention is a manifestation of a system shaped by a long development process and also legitimised by a certain conceptual clarity and simplicity.

However, throughout this study I have highlighted the complexity of the legal framework of cross-border services within the EU. In the conflict of laws, two separate rule-oriented development trends are at work within the Union. They both deserve attention in order to develop EC law further by improving the coherence and coherency of the rules.

From a global standpoint, an isolated consideration of conflicts rules within one single region is insufficient. Indeed, some of the observations made in this study seek to point up the problems of the limitation imposed by focusing attention only on the EU. We have also seen that for the sake of true human and fundamental rights protection, a wider framework is required. Enacting too many regional conflicts rules has its problems. It has been suggested that the legal policy objective of the Community should be to maximise the amount of universal choice of law legislation and to use regional conflicts rules only in special circumstances.[576] This objective involves observing the contracting activities of the Hague Conference on Private International Law and ensuring that it has enough coherency.

To conclude, globalisation of the legal environment provides a particular challenge for conflicts law. The central status of private international law is strengthened by the tendency of late modern law to extend beyond individual fields of law, as illustrated by the intertwining of international company and labour law. Additionally, in public international law the role of private international law comes up increasingly often in the intersection of different fields of law. All this might give us a glimpse of private international law as a cosmopolitan seeking to grasp the global challenges of cross-border interaction, such as the possibility of developing 'intercontinental' conflicts rules on contractual obligations.

[576] See, for example, Kreuzer, "Zu Stand und Perspektiven des Europäischen Internationalen Privatrechts – Wie europäisch soll das Europäische Internationale Privatrecht sein?", especially p. 78 ja 86.

Bibliography

Aarnio, Aulis: “Oikeussäädöksiä tulkitsemassa – Interpreting Statutes. A Comparative Study”, in Korkein oikeus 75 vuotta. Helsinki: Lakimiesliiton kustannus 1993, pp. 253–274.

Ahlberg, Kerstin – Bruun, Niklas: “Sweden: Transition through collective bargaining”. (http://arbetsratt.arbetslivsinstitutet.se/filer/pdf/kerstin%20ahlberg/transition%20through%20collective%20bargaining.pdf, last visited 12/09/2006)

Armstrong, Kenneth A.– Bulmer, Simon J.: The Governance of the Single European Market. Manchester – New York: Manchester University Press, 1998.

Basedow, Jürgen: “The Gradual Emergence of European Private Law”, in Einhorn, Talia – Siehr, Kurt (eds.): Intercontinental Cooperation Through Private International Law. Essays in Memory of Peter E. Nygh. The Hague: T.M.C. Asser Press 2004, pp. 1–18.

Basedow, Jürgen: “Consumer Contracts and Insurance Contracts in a Future Rome I-Regulation”, in Johan Meeusen – Marta Pertegás – Gert Straetmans (eds.): Enforcement of International Contracts in the European Union. Convergence and Divergence between Brussels I and Rome I. Antwerp – Oxford – New York: Intersentia 2004, pp. 269–294.

Berger, Klaus P.: “The Principles of European Contract Law and the Concept of ‘Creeping Codification’ of Law”, in European Review of Private Law, 2001, pp. 21–34.

Berman, Paul Schiff: “From International Law to Law and Globalisation”, in Columbia Journal of Transnational Law, 2005, pp. 485–556.

Bernstein, Herbert – Lookofsky, Joseph: Understanding the CISG in Europe. Second Edition. The Hague – London – New York: Kluwer Law International 2003.

Biagi, Marco: "Guest Editorial. Fortune Smiles on the Italian EU Presidency: Talking Half-Seriously About the Posted Workers and Parental Leave Directives", in IntJCompLLIR, 1996, pp. 97–109.

Blanpain, Roger – Colucci, Michele: The Globalization of Labour Standards. The Soft Law Track. The Hague: Kluwer Law International 2004.

de Boer TH. M.: "Forty Years On: The Evolution of Postwar Private International Law in Europe", in de Boer, TH. M. (ed.): Forty Years On: The Evolution of Postwar Private International Law in Europe. Deventer: Kluwer 1990, pp. 1–14.

de Boer, TH. M.: "The EEC Contracts Convention and the Dutch Courts", in RabelsZ, 1990, pp. 24–62.

de Boer, TH. M.: "Forum Preferences in Contemporary European Conflicts Law: The Myth of a 'Neutral Choice'", in Mansel, Heinz-Peter – Pfeiffer; Thomas – Kronke, Herbert – Kohler, Christian – Hausmann, Rainer (eds.): Festschrift für Erik Jayme. Band I. München: Sellier. European Law Publishers 2004, pp. 39–55.

Bogdan, Michael: "Ordre public, internationellt tvingande rättsregler och kringgåendeläran i EG-domstolens praxis rörande internationell privaträtt", in SvJT, 2001, pp. 329–346.

Bogdan, Michael: "Erkännande och verkställighet av med den europeiska människorättskonventionen oförenlig utländsk dom", in SvJT, 2003, pp. 18–29.

Bogdan, Michael: Svensk internationell privat- och processrätt. Sixth Edition. Stockholm: Norstedts juridik 2004.

Bonell, M.J.: The UNIDROIT Principles of International Commercial Contracts and CISG – Alternatives or Complementary Instruments? (http://www.cisg.law.pace.edu/cisg/biblio/ulr96.html, last visited 12/09/2006)

Bruun, Niklas: Posting of Workers: Do the EU Rules work? A Nordic Perspective. European Parliament, Mini-Hearing, Thursday, 20 April 2006, Brussels.

Cheatman, Elliot, E. – Reese, Willis, L. M.: "Choice of the Applicable Law", in Colum. L. Rev., 1952, pp. 959–980.

Chu, Gary: "'Playing at Killing' Freedom of Movement. Case C-36/02, Omega Spielhallen- und Automatenaufstellungs-GmbH v. Oberbürgermeisterin der Bundesstadt Bonn, judgement of the European Court of Justice, 14 October 2004, nyr.", in Legal Issues of Economic Integration, 33(1), 2006, pp. 85–94. ('Playing at Killing' Freedom of Movement)

de Cruz, Peter: Comparative Law in a Changing World. Second Edition. London: Cavendish Pub. 1999.

Dammann, Jens C.: "The future of codetermination after Centros: Will the German corporate law move closer to the U.S. model?", in Fordham Journal of Corporate & Financial Law, Vol. 8, 2003.

Dammann, Jens C.: "Freedom of Choice in European Corporate Law", in The Yale Journal of International Law, 2004, pp. 477–544.

Davies, Paul: "Posted Workers: Single Market or Protection of National Labour Law System?", in CMLR, 1997, pp. 571–602.

Ebke, Werner F.: "Centros – Some Realities and Some Mysteries", in American Journal of Comparative Law, 2000, pp. 623–660.

Ebke, Werner F.: "Überseering: 'Die wahre Liberalität ist Anerkennung'", in JZ, 2003, pp. 927–933.

Eklund, Ronnie: "Utstationering av arbetstagare", in SvJT, 2000, pp. 260–269.

Eklund, Ronnie: "The Laval Case", in Industrial Law Journal, 2006, pp. 202–208.

Evju, Stein – Holo, Lars: "Labour Law and the Labour Market in Norway", in Neal, Alan C. (ed.): European Social Policy and the Nordic Countries. Papers presented at a seminar in Brussels, 15 and 16 May, 1995. Dartmouth: Ashgate 2000, pp. 133–144.

Fawcett, James J. – Harris, Jonathan M. – Bridge, Michael: International Sale of Goods in the Conflict of Laws. Oxford: University Press 2005.

Fentiman, Richard G.: "English Private International Law at the End of the 20th Century: Progress or Regress?", in Symeonides, Symeon C. (ed): Private International Law at the End of the 20th Century: Progress or Regress? XVth International Congress of Comparative Law. The Hague – London – Boston: Kluwer Law International 2000, pp. 165–190.

Finland's Trade Policy Programme 2005.

Fischer-Lescano, Andreas – Teubner, Gunther: "Regime-Collisions: The Vain Search for Legal Unity in the Fragmentation of Global Law", in Michigan Journal of International Law, 2004, pp. 999–1045.

Forslag til Lov om udstationering af lønmodtagere. Lovforslag nr. L 47. Folketinget 1999–2000. Denmark (Lovforslag nr. L 47, Folketinget 1999–2000)

Forte, Angelo: The United Nations Convention on Contracts for the International Sale of Goods: Reason or Unreason in the United Kingdom.

(http://www.cisg.law.pace.edu/cisg/biblio/forte.html, last visited 12/09/2006)

Frankenberg, Günter: "Critical Comparisons: Re-thinking Comparative Law", in Harvard International Law Journal, 1985, pp. 411–455.

Franzen, Martin: "Niederlassungsfreiheit, internationales Gesellschaftsrecht und Unternehmensmitbestimmung", in Recht der Arbeit, 2004, pp. 257–320.

Freedom of Association. Digest of decisions and principles of the Freedom of Association Committee of the Governing Body of the ILO. Fourth (revised) Edition, Geneva: ILO 1996.

Gekiere, Wouter: "The Proposal of the European Commission for a Directive on Services in the Internal Market: An Overview of its Main Features and Critical Reflections", in Blanpain, Roger (ed.): Freedom of Services in the European Union. Labour and Social Security Law: The Bolkestein Initiative, The Hague: Kluwer Law International 2006, pp. 3–18.

General Survey. Freedom of Association and Collective Bargaining. ILO 1994. (http://www.ilo.org/ilolex/english/surveyq.htm, last visited 12/09/2006)

Graham, Ronnie: "Mutual Recognition and Country of Origin in the Case Law of the European Court of Justice", in Blanpain, Roger (ed.): Freedom of Services in the European Union. Labour and Social Security Law: The Bolkestein Initiative, The Hague: Kluwer Law International 2006, pp. 37–49.

Halbach, Günter – Paland, Norbert – Schwedes, Rolf – Wlotzke, Otfried: Übersicht über das Arbeitsrecht. 8. Rev. Ed. Bonn: Bundesministerium für Arbeit und Sozialordnung 2000.

Hartley, T.C.: "Pleading and Proof of Foreign Law: The Major European Systems Compared", in ICLQ, 1996, pp. 271–292.

Hartley, T.C.: "The European Union and the Systematic Dismantling of the Common Law of Conflict of Laws", in ICLQ, 2005, pp. 813–828.

Hay, Peter – Lando, Ole – Rotunda, Ronald D.: "Conflict of Laws as a Technique for Legal Integration", in Cappelletti, Mauro – Seccombe, Monica – Weiler, Joseph (eds.): Integration through law: Europe and the American federal experience. Vol. 1. Methods, tools and institutions. Book 2. Political organs, integration techniques and judicial process. Berlin – New York: Walter de Gruyter 1985, pp. 161–258.

Hay, Peter: "Flexibility versus Predictability and Uniformity in Choice of Law. Reflections on Current European and United States Conflicts Law", in Rec. des Cours, Vol. 226, 1992, pp. 215–412.

Hay, Peter – Weintraub, Russel J. – Borchers, Patrick J.: Conflict of Laws. Cases and Materials. Twelfth Edition. New York: Thomson – West 2004.

Held, David – McGrew, Anthony – Goldblatt, David – Perraton, Jonathan: Global Transformations. Politics, Economics and Culture. Oxford: Polite 1999.

Held, David – McGrew, Anthony: Globalization / Anti-Globalization. Cambridge: Polity 2002.

Hellner, Michael: "The E-Commerce Directive and Private International Law", in Andrea Schulz (ed.): Legal Aspects of an E-Commerce Transaction. International Conference in The Hague 26 and 27 October 2004. München: Sellier. European law publishers. 2006, pp. 107–121.

Hepple, Bob: The Legal Consequences of Cross Border Transfers of Undertakings within the European Union. A Report for the European Commission DG-V. May 1998.

Hepple, Bob: Labour Laws and Global Trade. Oxford – Portland, Oregon: Hart Publishing 2005.

Hernández-Breton, Eugenio: "An attempt to regulate the problem of 'characterization' in private international law", in Mansel, Heinz-Peter – Pfeiffer, Thomas – Kronke, Herbert - Kohler, Christian – Hausmann, Rainer (eds.): Festschrift für Erik Jayme, Band 1, München: Sellier. European Law Publishers GmbH, München, 2004, pp. 331–338.

Hill, Alfred: "For a Third Conflicts Restatement – But Stop Trying to Reinvent the Wheel", in 75 Ind. L. J., 2000, pp. 535–539.

Honnold, John: "Article 6. The Contract and the Convention". Excerpt from John O. Honnold, Uniform Law for International Sales under the 1980 United Nations Convention, 3rd ed. (1999), pp. 77–87. (http://www.cisg.law.pace.edu/cisg/biblio/ho6.html, last visited 12/09/2006)

Hoppe, Jeannine: Die Entsendung von Arbeitnehmern ins Ausland. Kollisionsrechtliche Probleme und internationale Zuständigkeit. Eine Untersuchung anhand praktischer Vertragsgestaltungen. Berlin: Duncker & Humblot, 1999. (Die Entsendung von Arbeitnehmern ins Ausland)

Hopt, Klaus J.: "European Company Law and Corporate Governance: Where does the Action Plan of the European Commission Lead?" ECGI - Law Working Paper No. 52/2005.

Husa, Jaakko: "Melodies on Comparative Law", in Nordic Journal of International Law, 2005, pp. 161–173.

Husa, Jaakko: "Emancipation or Deprivation for the European Legal Mind? The Contribution of Legal Traditions Approach", in Maastricht Journal of European and Comparative Law, 2006, pp. 81–107.

ILC, 30th Session, 1947, Report VII, Freedom of Association and Industrial Relations. ILO.

Jakhelln, Henning: "The Rights of Seafarers", in Sailors, 2001, pp. 1–38.

Jakhelln, Henning: Oversikt over arbeidsretten. Third Edition. Oslo: N.W Damm & Søn 2004.

Jayme, Erik: Article 1, in Bianca-Bonell Commentary on the International Sales Law. (http://www.cisg.law.pace.edu/cisg/biblio/jayme-bb1.html, last visited 12/09/2006)

Jayme, Erik: "The American Conflicts Revolution and its Impact on European Private International Law", in de Boer, TH.M. (ed.): Forty Years On: The Evolution of Postwar Private International Law in Europe. Deventer: Kluwer 1990, pp. 15–27.

Jayme, Erik: "Internationales Privatrecht und postmoderne Kultur", in ZfRV, 1997, pp. 230–236.

Jayme, Erik: Multicultural Society and Private Law. German Experiences. Rome: Centro di studi e ricerche di diritto comparato e straniero, 1999, Saggi, conferenze e seminari, 33.

Joerges, Christian: On the Legitimacy of Europeanising Europe's Private Law: Considerations on a Law of Justi(ce)-fication (*justum facere*) for the EU-Multi-Level System. EUI Working Paper Law No. 2003/3.

Jokela, Heikki: Irtaimen kaupasta kansainvälisen yksityisoikeuden kannalta. Helsinki: Suomalainen Lakimiesyhdistys 1960.

Juenger, Friedrich K.: "The Problem with Private International Law", in Basedow, Jürgen – Meier, Isaak – Schnyder, Anton K. – Einhorn, Talia – Girsberger, Daniel (eds.): Private Law in the International

Arena. From National Conflict Rules Towards Harmonisation and Unification – Liber Amicorum Kurt Siehr, The Hague, The Netherlands: T.M.C. Asser Press 2000, pp. 289–309.

Juenger, Friedrich Karl: "The Recognition of Money Judgments", in Juenger, Friedrich Karl (ed.): Selected Essays on the Conflict of Laws. New York: Ardsley 2000, pp. 281–320.

Junker, Abbo: Internationales Arbeitsrecht im Konzern. Tübingen: Mohr 1992.

Junker, Abbo: Internationales Privatrecht. München: Beck 1998.

Junker, Abbo: "Empfiehlt es sich, Art. 7 EVÜ zu revidieren oder aufgrund der bisherigen Erfahrungen zu präzisieren?", in IPRax, 2000, pp. 65–73.

Junker, Abbo: "Betriebsverfassung im europäischen Vergleich", in ZfA, 2001, pp. 225–243.

Junker, Abbo: Grundkurs Arbeitsrecht. Fifth Rev. Edition. München: Verlag C. H. Beck 2006.

Jänterä-Jareborg, Maarit: "Efterlevande make, intern skyddslagstiftning och IP", in Håstad, Torgny – Lindblom, Per Henrik – Saldeen, Åke (eds.): Festskrift till Anders Agell. Uppsala: Iustus förlag 1994, pp. 285–302.

Jänterä-Jareborg, Maarit: "När är harmoniserade gemenskapsregler internationellt tvingande?", in Europarättslig Tidskrift, 2001, pp. 403–412.

Jänterä-Jareborg, Maarit: "Foreign Law in National Courts – A Comparative Perspective", in Rec. des Cours, Vol. 304, 2004, pp. 181–385.

Kahn-Freund, Otto: General problems of private international law. Leyden: A. W. Sijthoff 1976.

Kay, Herma Hill: "A Defense of Currie's Governmental Interest Analysis", in Rec. des Cours, Vol. 215, 1989, pp. 9–204.

Kennedy, David: "The Methods and Politics of Comparative Law", in Bussani, Mauro – Mattei, Ugo (eds.): The Common Core of European Private Law, The Hague: Kluwer Law International 2002, pp. 131–207.

Kersting, Christian – Schindler, Clemens Philipp: "The ECJ's Inspire Art Decision of 30 September and its Effects on Practice", in German Law Journal, 2003, pp. 1277–1291.

Kieninger, Eva-Maria: "The Legal Framework of Regulatory Competition Based on Company Mobility: EU and US compared", in German Law Journal, 2004, pp. 741–770.

Kindler, Peter: "'Inspire Art' – Aus Luxemburg nichts Neues zum internationalen Gesellschaftsrecht", in NZG, 2003, pp. 1086–1090.

Kozyris, P. John: "Interest Analysis Facing its Critics – And, Incidentally, What Should Be Done About Choice of Law for Pro-ducts Liability", in Ohio St. L. J., 1985, pp. 569–593.

Kristiansen, Jens: Arbejdsretlig lærebog. Copenhagen: Forlaget Thomson A/S 1999.

Kreuzer, Karl: "Zu Stand und Perspektiven des Europäischen Internationalen Privatrechts – Wie europäisch soll das Europäische Internationale Privatrecht sein?", in RabelsZ, 2006, pp. 1–88.

Kronke, Herbert: "Capital Markets and the Conflict of Laws", in Rec. des Cours, Vol. 286, 2000, pp. 245–385.

Lando, Ole: "The 1985 Hague Convention on the Law Applicable to Sales", in RabelsZ, 1987, pp. 60–85.

Lando, Ole: "The 1955 and 1985 Hague Conventions on the Law Applicable to the International Sale of Goods", in RabelsZ, 1993, pp. 155–174.

Lando, Ole: "The Principles of European Contract Law and the lex mercatoria", in Basedow, Jürgen – Meier, Isaak – Schnyder, Anton K. – Einhorn, Talia – Girsberger, Daniel (eds.): Private Law in the International Arena. From National Conflict Rules Towards Harmonisation and Unification. Liber Amicorum Kurt Siehr. The Hague: T.M.C. Asser Press 2000, pp. 391–404.

Lando, Ole: "Optional or Mandatory Europeanisation of Contract Law", in European Review of Private Law, 2000, pp. 59–69.

Lando, "Some Features of the Law of Contract in the Third Millenium". (http://frontpage.cbs.dk/law/commission_on_european_contract_law/literature/lando01.htm, last visited 12/09/2006)

Lando, Ole: "The European Principles in an Integrated World", in European Review of Contract Law, 2005, pp. 3–18.

Lando, Ole: "The EEC Convention on the Law Applicable to Contractual Obligations", in CMLR, 1987, pp. 159-214.

Lando, Ole: "Liberal, Social and 'Ethical' Justice in European Contract Law", in CMLR, 2006, pp. 817–833.

Legrand, Pierre: "European Legal Systems are not Converging", in ICLQ, 1996, pp. 52–81.

Legrand, Pierre: "Uniformity, Legal Traditions and Law's Limits", in JT, 1996–1997, pp. 306–322.

Legrand, Pierre: "The Impossibility of 'Legal Transplants'", in MJ, 1997, pp. 111–124.

Leinonen, Antti T.: “Alueellisesta yhteistyöstä maailmanlaajuiseen ja takaisin – lakiyhteistyöstä kansainvälisen yksityisoikeuden alalla”, in DL, 2001, pp. 645–660.

Liukkunen, Ulla: “Yleissitovien työehtosopimusten soveltamisesta kansainvälisiin työsopimuksiin Suomessa”, in DL, 2001, pp. 871–878.

Liukkunen, Ulla: Lainvalinta kansainvälisissä työsopimuksissa – erityisesti lähetettyjen työntekijöiden kannalta. Second, Rev. Edition. Helsinki: Kauppakaari, Lakimiesliiton Kustannus 2002.

Liukkunen, Ulla: The Role of Mandatory Rules in International Labour Law – A Comparative Study in the Conflict of Laws. Helsinki: Talentum 2004.

Liukkunen, Ulla: Globalisaatio, EU ja henkilöstön osallistuminen. Tutkimus globalisaatiojuridiikasta ja eurooppaoikeudesta erityisesti rajat ylittävissä yritysjärjestelyissä. Helsinki: Edita 2005.

Liukkunen, Ulla: “Norwegian International Labour Law and the European Integration – Some Observations”, in Arbeidsrett, 2005, pp. 211–217.

Liukkunen, Ulla: “Kansainvälinen yksityisoikeus ja Euroopan integraatio”, in LM, 2006, pp. 339–362.

Liukkunen, Ulla: “Perspectives on the Unification of Private International Law in Europe” in Frände, Dan – Liukkunen, Ulla – Sankari, Suvi – Storskrubb, Eva: In the Footsteps of Tampere. Justice in the European Union. Helsinki: Faculty of Law 2006, pp. 51–72.

Liukkunen, Ulla: “The Method of Understanding and Internal Viewpoint – on the Interface between Comparative Law and Private International Law”, (forthcoming in ZVglRW 2/2007).

Lookofsky, Joseph: “Alive and Well in Scandinavia: CISG Part II.”

(http://www.cisg.law.pace.edu/cisg/biblio/lookofsky1.html, last visited 12/09/2006)

Lookofsky, Joseph: "The 1980 United Nations Convention on Contracts for the International Sale of Goods". (http://www.cisg.law.pace.edu/cisg/biblio/lookofsky.html, last visited 12/09/2006)

Lookofsky, Joseph: Understanding the CISG in Scandinavia. Second Edition. Copenhagen: DJØF 2002.

Lookofsky, Joseph: "In dubio pro conventione? Some thoughts about opt-outs, computer programs and preemption under the 1980 Vienna Sales Convention (CISG)", in Duke J. of Comp. & Int'l L., 2003. (http://www.law.duke.edu/journals/djcil/articles/djcil13p0263.htm, last visited 12/09/2006)

López Rodríguez, Ana: Lex Mercatoria and Harmonisation of Contract Law in the EU. Copenhagen: DJØF 2003.

Lurger, Brigitta – Vallant, Sonja: "Grenzüberschreitender Wettbewerb im Internet – die Umsetzung des Herkunfts-landprinzips der E-Commerce-Richtlinie in Deutschland und Österreich", in RIW, 2002, pp. 188–202.

MacCormick, D. Neil – Summers, Robert S.: Interpreting Statutes. A Comparative Study. Aldershot – Brookfield USA – Hong Kong – Singapore – Sydney: Dartmouth Publishing 1991.

Magnus, Ulrich: "EGBGB 30", in Magnus, Ulrich (ed.): J. von Staudingers Kommentar zum Bürgerlichen Gesetzbuch mit Einführungsgesetz und Nebengesetzen. IPR Einleitung zu Art 27 ff EGBGB [u.a.].13. Edition. Berlin: Sellier de Gruyter 2002. (Magnus in Staudingers Kommentar)

Magnus, Ulrich: "Action Plan for a European Contract Law. European Contract Law and CISG".

(http://europa.eu.int/comm/consumers/cons_int/safe_shop/fair_bus_pract/cont_law/stakeholders/5-35.pdf, last visited 12/09/2006)

Magnus, Ulrich: UN-Kaufrecht, in Julius von Staudingers Kommentar zum Bürgerlichen Gesetzbuch mit Einführungsgesetz und Nebengesetzen. Wiener UN-Kaufrecht (CISG). Neubearbeitung 2005. Berlin: Sellier – de Gruyter 2005. (Wiener UN-Kaufrecht (CISG))

Magnus, Ulrich: "25 Jahre UN-Kaufrecht", in ZeUP, 2006, pp. 96–123.

Malmberg, Jonas: "Collective Agreements and Competition Law in Sweden", in Bruun, Niklas – Hellsten, Jari (eds.): Collective Agreements and Competition Law in the EU. The Report of the COLCOM-project. Helsinki: Kauppakaari Oyj 2001, pp. 187–208.

Malmberg, Jonas: "The Collective Agreement as an Instrument for Regulation of Wages and Employment Conditions", in Stability and Change in Nordic Labour Law, Scandinavian Studies in Law, Vol. 43, Stockholm: Almqvist & Wiksell 2002, pp. 189–213.

Malmberg, Jonas: "Arbetstagarens ställning vid gränsöverskridande företagsövergångar", in SvJT, 2004, pp. 792–808.

Mankowski, Peter: "Herkunftslandsprinzip und deutsches Umsetzungsgesetz zur e-commerce-Richtlinie", in IPRax, 2002, pp. 257–266.

Mankowski, Peter: "Wieder ein Herkunftslandprinzip für Dienstleistungen im Binnenmarkt", in IPRax, 2004, pp. 385–395.

Markesinis, Basil S.: "The Destructive and Constructive Role of the Comparative Lawyer", in RabelsZ, 1993, pp. 438–448.

Mattila, Heikki E. S.: Vertaileva oikeuslingvistiikka. Helsinki: Lakimiesliiton Kustannus 2002.

Max Planck Institute for Comparative and International Private Law: Comments on the European Commission's Proposal for a Regulation of the European Parliament and the Council on the Law Applicable to Contractual Obligations (Rome I), 2006. (Max Planck Institute's Comments 2006)

Max Planck Institute for Foreign Private and Private International Law: Comments on the European Commission's Green Paper on the Conversion of the Rome Convention of 1980 on the Law Applicable to Contractual Obligations into a Community Instrument and its Modernization, 2003. (Max Planck Institute's Comments 2003)

von Mehren, Arthur T.: Explanatory Report on the 1986 Hague Sales Convention. The Hague: HCCH Publications 1987.

Meeusen, Johan: "Directive 94/45 concernant les comités d'entreprise européens: aspects de droit international privé", in Rigaux, Marc – Dorssemont, Filip (eds.): Comités d'entreprise européens. Examen juridique du comité d'entreprise européen: vers un amendement de la directive CE 94/45. Antwerpen – Groningen: Intersentia Rechtswetenschappen 1999, pp. 237–273.

Meeusen, Johan: "Fifteen Theses on Brussels I, Rome I and the European Union's Institutional Framework", in Meeusen, Johan –Pertegás, Marta –Straetmans, Gert (eds.): Enforcement of International Contracts in the European Union. Convergence and Divergence between Brussels I and Rome I. Antwerp – Oxford – New York: Intersentia 2004, pp. 43–76.

Micheler, Eva: "Current Developments. Private International Law", in ICLQ, 2003, pp. 521–534.

Mitbestimmung modernisieren. Bericht der Kommission Mitbestimmung. 2004.

Morse, C. G. J.: "Making English Private International Law", in Fawcett, James (ed.): Reform and Development of Private International

Law. Essays in Honour of Sir Peter North. Oxford: Oxford University Press 2002, pp. 273–302.

Neville, Mette – Winther-Sørensen, Niels – Engsig Sørensen, Karsten: "Free Movement of Companies under Company Law, Tax Law and EU Law", in Neville, Mette – Engsig Sørensen, Karsten (eds.): The Internationalisation of Companies and Company Laws. Copenhagen: Djøf 2001, pp. 181–228.

Nordic Group for Private International Law (NGPIL): Proposal for Amendments to the Convention on the Law Applicable to Contractual Obligations, 2003. (NGPIL Proposal 2003)

North, Peter: "Is European Harmonisation of Private International Law a Myth or a Reality? A British Perspective", in de Boer, Th. M.: Forty years on: The Evolution of Postwar Private International Law in Europe. Deventer: Kluwer 1990, pp. 29–48.

Notat om problemstillinger i forbindelse med gennemførelsen af udstationeringsdirektivet. Arbejdsministeriet, 27. juli. Denmark 1999.

O'Hara, Erin A. – Ribstein, Larry E.: "From Politics to Efficiency in Choice of Law", in U. Chi. L. Rev, 2000, pp. 1151–1232.

Oliver, Covey, T.: "Standardization of Choice-of-Law Rules for International Contracts: Should there be a New Beginning?", in The American Journal of International Law, 1959, pp. 385–392.

Peters, Anne – Schwenke, Heiner: "Comparative Law beyond Post-Modernism", in ICLQ, 2000, pp. 800–834.

Peterson, Courtland H.: "American Private International Law at the End of the 20th Century: Progress or Regress?", in Symeonides, Symeon C. (ed): Private International Law at the End of the 20th Century: Progress or Regress? XVth International Congress of Comparative Law. The Hague – London – Boston: Kluwer Law International 2000, pp. 413–444.

Plender, Richard – Wilderspin, Michael: The European Contracts Convention. The Rome Convention on the Choice of Law for Contracts. Second Edition. London: Sweet & Maxwell 2001.

Position of the European Group for Private International Law on the draft directive of the European Parliament and the Council on services in the internal market, 23 November 2004.

Prop. 1990/91:162 om viss fredspliktsregler. (Prop. 1990/91:162)

Prop. 1998/99:90. Utstationering av arbetstagare. (Prop. 1998/99:90)

Pöyhönen, Juha: Uusi varallisuusoikeus. Helsinki: Talentum Media 2003.

Ramberg, Jan: International Commercial Transactions. Stockholm: ICC – Kluwer Law International – Norstedts Juridik AB 1998.

Rammeloo, Stephan: Corporations in Private International Law: A European Perspective. Oxford: University Press 2001.

Rehm, Gebhard M.: "Vom Außenseiter zum Liebling? Liechtensteinische Gesellschaften mit deutschem Verwaltungssitz als unternehmerische Gestaltungsoption. Zugleich eine Besprechung des BGH-Urteils vom 19.9.2005, II ZR 372/03", in Der Konzern, 2006, pp. 166–197.

Reimann, Mathias: "A New Restatement – For the International Age", in Indiana Law Journal, 2000, pp. 575–589.

Report of the High Level Group of Company Law Experts on a Modern Regulatory Framework for Company Law in Europe. Brussels, 4 November 2002.

Restatement of the Law of Conflict of Laws, Saint Paul: American Law Institute Publishers 1934.

Restatement of the Law, Second, Conflict of Laws, 2d., Vol. 1, Saint Paul, Minn.: American Law Institute Publishers 1971. (Second Restatement)

Rinze, Jens: "The Scope of Party Autonomy under the 1980 Rome Convention on the Law Applicable to Contractual Obligations", in Journal of Business Law, 1994, pp. 412–430.

Roth, Wulf-Henning: "Case law. Court of Justice, Case C-212/97, Centros Ltd v. Erhvervs- og Selskabsstyrelsen, Judgment of 9 March 1999, Full Court", in CMLR, 2000, pp. 147–155.

Roth, Wulf-Henning: "From Centros to Überseering: Free Movement of Companies, Private International Law, and Community Law", in ICLQ, 2003, pp. 180–186.

Schall, Alexander: "European Framework for the Mobility of Companies", in Van Hulle, Karl – Gesell, Harald (eds): European Corporate Law. Baden-Baden: Nomos 2006, pp. 3–24.

Schlechtriem, Peter: Internationales UN-Kaufrecht. Third Revised Edition. Tübingen: Mohr Siebeck 2005.

Schön, Wolfgang: "Playing different games? Regulatory competition in tax and company law compared", in CMLR, 2005, pp. 331–365.

Scoles, Eugene F. – Hay, Peter – Borchers, Patrick J. – Symeonides, Symeon J.: Conflict of Laws. Fourth Edition. St. Paul, MN: Thomson West 2004.

Sigeman, Tore: Arbetsrätten. En översikt av svensk rätt med europarätt. Göteborg: Fritzes Förlag AB 1995.

Sigeman, Tore: "Nordic Labour Law. A Brief Presentation from a Comparative Perspective", in JT, 2002-03, pp. 497–503.

Sigeman, Tore: “Fri rörlighet för tjänster och nationell arbetsrätt”, in Europarättslig Tidskrift, 2005, pp. 465–495.

Smits, Jan M.: “Diversity of Contract Law and the European Internal Market”, in Smits, Jan (ed.): The Need for a European Contract Law. Empirical and Legal Perspectives. Groningen: Europa Law Publishing 2005, pp. 155–186.

Straetmans, Gert: “The Consumer Concept in EC law”, in Meeusen, Johan –Pertegás, Marta –Straetmans, Gert (eds.): Enforcement of International Contracts in the European Union. Convergence and Divergence between Brussels I and Rome I. Antwerp – Oxford – New York: Intersentia 2004, pp. 295–322.

Symeonides, Symeon C.: “The Need for a Third Conflicts Restatement (And a Proposal for Tort Conflicts)”, in Ind. L. J., 2000, pp. 438–474.

Symeonides, Symeon C.: “The American Choice-of-Law Revolution in the Courts: Today and Tomorrow”, in Rec. des Cours, Vol. 298, 2003, pp. 9–448.

Symeonides, Symeon C.: “Codifying Choice of Law for Contracts: The Oregon Experience”, in RabelsZ, 2003, pp. 726–747.

Symeonides, Symeon C. – Perdue, Wendy Collins – von Mehren, Arthur T.: Conflict of Laws: American, Comparative, International. Cases and Materials. Second Edition. St. Paul, MN: Thomson West 2003.

Tetley, William: “A Canadian looks at American Conflict of Law Theory and Practice, Especially in the Light of the American Legal and Social Systems (Corrective vs Distributive Justice)”, in Columbia Journal of Transnational Law, 1999, pp. 299–373.

Teubner, Gunther: "Legal Irritants: Good Faith in British Law or How Unifying Law Ends Up In New Divergences", in Modern Law Review, 1998, pp. 11–32.

Thue, Helge J.: "Irma-Mignon-Formelen. En konfliktskapende regel", in TfR, 1965, pp. 578–610.

United Nations Conference on Contracts for the International Sale of Goods, Vienna 10 March – 11 April 1980, Official Records UN Doc. A/Conf. 97/19.

Utstationering av arbetstagare. Betänkande av Utredningen om genomförandet av EG:s direktiv om utstationering av arbetstagare. Statens offentliga utredningar 1998:52. Arbetsmarknadsdepartementet. Stockholm 1998. (SOU 1998:52)

Van Hulle, Karel: "Introduction – European Corporate Law: United in Diversity", in Van Hulle, Karel – Gesell, Harald (eds.): European Corporate Law. Baden-Baden: Nomos 2006, pp. 1–2.

Veasey, E. Norman: The Role of Judiciary in Corporate Law, Corporate Governance and Economic Goals. Company Law Reform in OECD Countries. A Comparative Outlook of Current Trends. Stockholm, Sweden. 7–8 December 2000.

Verhagen, H. L. E.: "The Tension Between Party Autonomy and European Union Law: Some Observations on Ingmar GB Ltd v Eaton Leonard Technologies Inc.", in ICLQ, 2002, pp. 135–154.

de Vries, Sybe A.: Tensions within the Internal Market. The Functioning of the Internal Market and the Development of Horizontal and Flanking Policies. Groningen: Europa Law Publishing 2006.

Väyrynen, Raimo: "Globalisaation voimat ja vastavoimat", in Economic Trends, 6/2003, pp. 26–29.

Weiss, Manfred: "The Future of Workers' Participation in the EU", in Barnard, Catharine – Deakin, Simon – Morris, Gillian S. (eds): The Future of Labour Law: Liber Amicorum Sir Bob Hepple QC. Oxford: Hart Publishing 2004, pp. 229–251.

Weiss, Manfred: "Recent Developments in German and European Labour Law", in Müller-Jentsch, Walter – Weitbrecht, Hansjörg (eds.): The Changing Contours of German Industrial Relations München: Rainer Hampp Verlag 2003, pp. 157–173.

Werlauff, Erik: EU-Company Law. Common Business Law of 28 States. 2nd edition. Copenhagen: DJØF 2003.

Werlauff, Erik: SE – the law of the European Company. Copenhagen: DJØF 2003.

Wilhelmsson, Thomas: "Jack-in-the-Box Theory of European Community Law", in Krämer, Ludwig –Micklitz, Hans-Wolfgang – Tonner, Klaus (eds.): Law and Diffuse Interests in the European Legal Order, Liber amicorum Norbert Reich. Baden-Baden: Nomos 1997, pp. 177–194.

Wilhelmsson, Thomas: "Vastuu ja yksityisoikeuden systeemi", in LM, 1997, pp. 1180–1205.

Wilhelmsson, Thomas: "Sopimusoikeuden eurooppalaistuminen ja oikeudellisten toimijoiden roolit – useampi kokki keittää paremman sopan", in LM, 2003, pp. 1098–1118.

Wilhelmsson, Thomas: "The Ethical Pluralism of Late Modern Europe and Codification of European Contract Law", in Smits, Jan (ed.): The Need for a European Contract Law. Empirical and Legal Perspectives. Groningen: Europa Law Publishing 2005, pp. 123–152.

Winship, Peter: "Private International Law and the U.N. Sales Convention", in Cornell Int'l L.J., 1988, pp. 487–533.

Wymeersch, Eddy: "Centros: A landmark decision in European Company Law", in Baums, Theodor – Hopt, Klaus J. – Horn, Norbert (eds.): Corporations, Capital Markets and Business in the Law. Liber Amicorum Richard M. Buxbaum. The Hague: Kluwer Law International 2000, pp. 629–654.

Wymeersch, Eddy: "Company Law in Europe and European Company Law", in 1st European Jurists Forum. Nürnberg: Nomos Verlagsgesellschaft, 2001, pp. 85–163.

Wymeersch, Eddy: "The transfer of the company's seat in European company law", in CMLR, 2003, pp. 661–695.

Zimmermann, Reinhard: "Savigny's Legacy. Legal History, Comparative Law, and the Emergence of a European Legal Science", in LQR, 1996, pp. 576–605.

Örücü, Esin: The Enigma of Comparative Law. Variations on a Theme for the Twenty-First Century. Leiden – Boston: Martinus Nijhoff Publishers 2004.

European Community Documents

Amended proposal for a Council Directive on harmonisation of the legislation of Member States on the safeguarding of employees' rights and advantages in the case of mergers, takeovers and amalgamations. COM(75) 429.

Amended proposal for a Directive of the European Parliament and of the Council on credit agreements for consumers amending Council Directive 93/13/EC. COM(2005) 483 final/2.

Amended proposal for a Directive of the European Parliament and of the Council on services in the internal market. COM(2006) 160 final.

Commission Services Working Document. Memorandum on rights of workers in cases of transfers of undertakings. Undated document.

Common position adopted by the Council on 24 July 2006 with a view to the adoption of a Directive of the European Parliament and of the Council on services in the internal market. Brussels, 24 July 2006, 10003/4/06, REV 4.

Communication from the Commission to the Council and the European Parliament: An Internal Market Strategy for Services. COM(2000) 888 final.

Communication from the Commission to the Council and the European Parliament on European Contract Law. COM(2001) 398 final.

Communication from the Commission to the European Parliament and the Council: A more coherent European contract law. An action plan. COM(2003) 68 final.

Communication from the Commission to the Council, the European Parliament, the European Economic and Social Committee and the

Committee of the Regions: Report on the implementation of the Internal Market Strategy (2003–2006). COM(2004) 22 final.

Communication from the Commission to the European Parliament and the Council: European Contract Law and the revision of the *acquis*: the way forward. COM(2004) 651 final.

Communication from the Commission to the Council, the European Parliament, the European Economic and Social committee and the Committee of the Regions: Second Implementation Report of the Internal Market Strategy (2003–2006). COM(2005) 11 final.

Communication from the Commission: Guidance on the Posting of Workers in the Framework of the Provision of Services. COM(2006) 159 final.

Council Draft programme of measures for implementation of the principle of mutual recognition of decisions in civil and commercial matters. OJ C 12, 15.1.2001, p.1.

European Council Tampere 15–16.10.1999: Conclusions of the Presidency.

Green Paper on the conversion of the Rome Convention of 1980 on the law applicable to contractual obligations into a Community instrument and its modernization. COM(2002) 654 final.

Implementing the Community Lisbon programme: Proposal for a Directive of the European Parliament and of the Council on payment services in the internal market and amending Directives 97/7/EC, 2000/12/EC and 2002/65/EC. COM(2005) 603 final.

JUSTCIV 118, 9143/06, Proposal for a Regulation of the European Parliament and the Council on the law applicable to non-contractual obligations (Rome II).

Note from the Praesidium. Draft Charter of Fundamental Rights of the European Union. Text of the explanations relating to the complete text of the Charter as set out in CHARTE 4487/00 CONVENT 50. Brussels, 11 October 2000

Mario Giuliano, Paul Lagarde, Report on the Convention on the law applicable to contractual obligations. OJ C 282, 1980, 31.10.1980. (Giuliano – Lagarde Report)

Outcome of the European Parliament's first reading, Strasbourg, 4 to 7 July 2005.

Proposal for a Council Decision on the accession of the European Community to the Hague Conference on Private International Law. COM(2005) 639 final.

Proposal for a Directive of the Council on harmonisation of the legislation of Member States on the retention of the rights and advantages of employees in the case of mergers, takeovers and amalgamations. COM(74) 351 final/2.

Proposal for a Council Directive concerning the posting of workers in the framework of the provision of services. COM(91) 230 final.

Proposal for a Directive of the European Parliament and of the Council on financial collateral arrangements. COM(2001) 168 final.

Proposal for a Directive of the European Parliament and of the Council on services in the internal market. COM(2004) 2 final/3.

Proposal for a Regulation of the European Parliament and the Council on the law applicable to non-contractual obligations (Rome II). COM(2003) 427 final.

Proposal for a Regulation of the European Parliament and the Council on the law applicable to contractual obligations (Rome I). COM(2005) 650 final.

Report of the Working Party on the Transposal of the Directive concerning the Posting of Workers. Results of the Meetings. European Commission, Directorate-General for Employment, Industrial Relations and Social Affairs, Unit V/D/2, 1999. (Report of the Working Party on the Transposal of the Directive concerning the Posting of Workers)

Report from the Commission to the Council and the European Parliament on the State of Internal Market for Services presented under the first stage of the Internal Market Strategy for Services. COM(2002) 441 final.

Report from the Commission Services on the Implementation of Directive 96/71/EC of the European Parliament and of the Council concerning the Posting of Workers in the Framework of the Provision of Services. European Commission, Directorate-General for Employment, Industrial Relations and Social Affairs, Unit D.3, 2003. (Report on the Implementation of Directive 96/71/EC)

Report from the Commission to the European Parliament, the Council and the European Economic and Social Committee – First Report on the application of Directive 2000/31/EC of the European Parliament and of the Council of 8 June 2000 on certain legal aspects of information society services, in particular electronic commerce, in the Internal Market (Directive on electronic commerce). COM(2003) 702 final.

The Hague Programme: strengthening freedom, security and justice in the European Union, OJ C 53, 3.3.2005, p.1.

INTERNATIONALRECHTLICHE STUDIEN
Beiträge zum Internationalen Privatrecht, zum Einheitsrecht und zur Rechtsvergleichung

Herausgegeben von Ulrich Magnus

Band 1 Birgit Reimers-Zocher: Beweislastfragen im Haager und Wiener Kaufrecht. 1995.

Band 2 Lenja Vespermann: Schadensersatz bei Beeinträchtigung rechts- oder sittenwidriger Interessen im deutschen und französischen Recht. 1996.

Band 3 Peter Cypra: Die Rechtsbehelfe im Verfahren der Vollstreckbarerklärung nach dem EuGVÜ unter besonderer Berücksichtigung der Ausgestaltung in Deutschland und Frankreich. 1996.

Band 4 Brigitta Lurger: Regulierung und Deregulierung im europäischen Privatrecht. 1997.

Band 5 Uta Gutknecht: Das Nacherfüllungsrecht des Verkäufers bei Kauf- und Werklieferungsverträgen. Rechtsvergleichende Untersuchung zum CISG, zum US-amerikanischen Uniform Commercial Code, zum deutschen Recht und zu dem Vorschlag der Kommission zur Überarbeitung des deutschen Schuldrechts. 1996.

Band 6 Stefan Abel: Die Qualifikation der Schenkung. Zur Methode der Qualifikation im Internationalen Schuldvertragsrecht. 1997.

Band 7 Daniel Kötz: Verkäuferpflichten und Rechtsbehelfe des Käufers im neuen norwegischen Kaufrecht vom 13. Mai 1988 Nr. 27 im Vergleich zum UN-Kaufrecht vom 11. April 1980 (CISG). 1997.

Band 8 Olaf Beier: Grundsätze eines europäischen transportmittelübergreifenden Schadensrechts für den Gütertransport. Eine rechtsvergleichende Untersuchung unter besonderer Berücksichtigung der CMR, der ER/CIM 1990, des WA/HP und der HVR. 1999.

Band 9 Ulrich Krüger: Modifizierte Erfolgshaftung im UN-Kaufrecht. Die Haftungsbefreiung bei Lieferung vertragswidriger Ware gemäß Art. 79 CISG. 1999.

Band 10 Wolf-Henning Hammer: Das Zurückhaltungsrecht gemäß Art. 71 CISG im Vergleich zu den Kaufgesetzen der nordischen Staaten unter Einbeziehung transportrechtlicher Aspekte. Eine rechtsvergleichende Studie. 1999.

Band 11 Ulrich Quay: Der Consulting-Vertrag im Internationalen Privatrecht. 2000.

Band 12 Axel Halfmeier: Die Veröffentlichung privater Tatsachen als unerlaubte Handlung. Eine rechtsvergleichende Untersuchung. 2000.

Band 13 Stephanie Scholz: Lohngleichheit durch Verfahren. Eine Studie zur Förderung der Lohngleichheit durch verfahrensrechtliche Ansätze. 2000.

Band 14 Tarık Cebecioglu: Stellung des Ausländers im Zivilprozeß. Eine rechtsvergleichende Untersuchung des türkischen und deutschen Rechts. 2000.

Band 15 Gunnar Straube: Sozialrechtliche Eingriffsnormen im Internationalen Privatrecht. 2001.

Band 16 Daniela de Lukowicz: Divergenzen in der Rechtsprechung zum CISG. Auf dem Weg zu einer einheitlichen Auslegung und Anwendung? 2001.

Band 17 Mohamed Hassan Fadlalla Ali: Das islamische Ehe- und Kindschaftsrecht im Sudan. Mit Hinweisen zu den Lehren der Islamischen Rechtsschule, der anwendbaren Familienrechtsvorschriften für Nichtmuslime im Sudan und im deutschen Familienrecht. 2001.

Band 18 Ole Lando / Ulrich Magnus / Monika Novak-Stief (Hrsg./eds.): Angleichung des materiellen und des internationalen Privatrechts in der EU. Harmonisation of Substantive and International Private Law. 2003.

Band 19 Florian Schulz: Der Ersatzlieferungs- und Nachbesserungsanspruch des Käufers im internen deutschen Recht, im UCC und im CISG. Eine rechtsvergleichende Untersuchung unter Berücksichtigung der Schuldrechtskommission, der EG-Richtlinie 1999/44/EG und des Diskussionsentwurfs eines Schuldrechtsmodernisierungsgesetzes. 2002.

Band 20 Ingo Janert: Die Aufrechnung im internationalen Vertragsrecht. 2002.

Band 21 Armin Jentsch: Die Erhaltungspflichten des Verkäufers und des Käufers im UN-Kaufrecht im Vergleich zum US-amerikanischen Uniform Commercial Code und zum deutschen Recht. 2002.

Band 22 Martin Taschner: Arbeitsvertragsstatut und zwingende Bestimmungen nach dem Europäischen Schuldvertragsübereinkommen. Einheitliche Auslegung. 2003.

Band 23 Klaus Bitterich: Die Neuregelung des Internationalen Verbrauchervertragsrechts in Art. 29a EGBGB. 2003.

Band 24 Sascha J. Morgenroth: Umsetzung der Verbrauchsgüterkaufrichtlinie in Spanien und Deutschland. Umsetzung der Richtlinie 1999/44/EG des Europäischen Parlaments und des Rates vom 25. Mai 1999 zu bestimmten Aspekten des Verbrauchsgüterkaufs und der Garantien für Verbrauchsgüter in Spanien und Deutschland. 2003.

Band 25 Markus Renfert: Über die Europäisierung der ordre public Klausel. 2003.

Band 26 Henning Mordhorst: Die Behandlung vertraglicher Mobiliarsicherheiten im US-amerikanischen und deutschen Insolvenzrecht. 2003.

Band 27 Hans Markus Wulf: UN-Kaufrecht und eCommerce. Problembereiche bei der Anwendung des Wiener Übereinkommens auf Internet-Verträge. 2003.

Band 28 Julia Kaiser: Freiheit oder Schutz? Die Scheidungsfolgenvereinbarung im deutschen und im englischen Recht. 2003.

Band 29 Astrid Hillebrenner: Die private Zustimmung zu Rechtsgeschäften Dritter im englischen, dänischen und deutschen Recht. 2004.

Band 30 Irene von der Heyde: Das deutsche und italienische internationale Kindschaftsrecht im Rechtsvergleich. Favor filii oder favor filiationis? 2004.

Band 31 Sven-Michael Werner: Recht im Systemwandel. *Ein Land, zwei Systeme* und das Kontinuitätsproblem in Hongkong. 2004.

Band 32 Holger Ellenberger: Wirtschaftsrelevante Kollisionsnormen im japanischen internationalen Privatrecht. 2004.

Band 33 Sebastian Kaufmann: Parol Evidence Rule und Merger Clauses im internationalen Einheitsrecht. 2004.

Band 34 Britta Christina Weber: Eigentumsübertragung und gutgläubiger Erwerb beim Kauf von beweglichen Sachen im vietnamesischen Zivilgesetzbuch von 1995. Eine rechtsvergleichende Analyse unter Berücksichtigung des Eigentumsbegriffs im vietnamesischen Recht. 2004.

Band 35 Alexander von Saucken: Die Reform des österreichischen Schiedsverfahrensrechts auf der Basis des UNCITRAL-Modellgesetzes über die internationale Handelsschiedsgerichtsbarkeit. Ein Diskussionsbeitrag. 2004.

Band 36 Jasnica Garašić: Anerkennung ausländischer Insolvenzverfahren. Teil 1 und Teil 2. Ein Vergleich des kroatischen, des deutschen und des schweizerischen Rechts sowie der Europäischen Verordnung über Insolvenzverfahren, des Istanbuler Übereinkommens und des UNCITRAL-Modellgesetzes. 2005.

Band 37 Eugenia Kurzynsky-Singer: Anknüpfung und Reichweite des Vollmachtsstatuts. 2005.

Band 38 Timo Utermark: Rechtsgeschichte und Rechtsvergleichung bei Ernst Rabel. 2005.

Band 39 Mohamed Lakmes: Die IPR-Anknüpfung der Schuldverträge. Ein Vergleich zwischen dem deutschen und dem syrischen Recht. 2005.

Band 40 Christian Haas: Vertragsstrukturen privatfinanzierter Infrastrukturprojekte. Nationale und internationale Perspektiven. 2005.

Band 41 Tanja Herzog-Engels: Gesellschaftsrechtliche Formvorschriften und Internationales Privatrecht. 2005.

Band 42 Hassan Siahpoosh: Das Familien- und Erbrecht im Iran. 2006.

Band 43 Carola Reifenrath: Das Vertragsrecht Hongkongs und dessen zukünftige Entwicklung. Unter besonderer Berücksichtigung des englischen Common Law. 2006.

Band 44 Arkadiusz Wudarski: Der Pfandbrief und sein Treuhänder. Eine rechtsvergleichende Untersuchung zum polnischen und deutschen Recht. 2006.

Band 45 Ulla Liukkunen: Cross-Border Services and Choice of Law. A Comparative Study of the European Approach. 2006.

Band 46 Claire Anna Reifner: Die Umsetzung der Verbrauchsgüterkaufrichtlinie in Italien und Deutschland. 2007.

www.peterlang.de

Ole Lando / Ulrich Magnus / Monika Novak-Stief (Hrsg./eds.)

Angleichung des materiellen und des internationalen Privatrechts in der EU
Harmonisation of Substantive and International Private Law

Frankfurt am Main, Berlin, Bern, Bruxelles, New York, Oxford, Wien, 2003.
XV, 228 S.
Internationalrechtliche Studien. Herausgegeben von Ulrich Magnus. Bd. 18
ISBN 3-631-37121-7 · br. € 39.80*

Im letzten Jahrzehnt hat der Gemeinschaftsgesetzgeber zahlreiche Richtlinien im Bereich des Verbraucherschutzes erlassen und wichtige Staatsverträge zum internationalen Privat- und Prozessrecht in Verordnungen überführt. Dadurch ist eine Lage entstanden, die weniger durch Einheitlichkeit des Rechts, sondern eher durch eine neue Unübersichtlichkeit gekennzeichnet ist. Sowohl die einzelnen IPR-Vorschriften als auch die materiellrechtlichen Inhalte der Richtlinien und Verordnungen stehen in einem wenig klaren Spannungsverhältnis. Europa bedarf auf materiellrechtlicher und auf kollisionsrechtlicher Ebene dringend systematischerer, breitflächigerer Koordinations- und Angleichungsmaßnahmen. Dieser Band geht diesen Fragen nach. Er vereinigt die auf einer Tagung der Europäischen Rechtsakademie gehaltenen Beiträge.

Aus dem Inhalt: Privatrechtsangleichung durch die EG im Schnittfeld von Sachrecht und Kollisionsrecht *(Müller-Graf)* · The Rome Convention – on the Law Applicable to Contractual Obligations *(Plender)* · Aktuelle Probleme im Schnittbereich von Verbraucherschutz und Internationalem Privatrecht *(Staudenmayer)* · Tragweite des EVÜ für Bankgeschäfte *(Welter)* · Mandatory Rules and ordre public *(Lando)* · The Rome Convention: Experience to date before the courts of Contracting States *(Wilderspin)* · uvm.